Performance Excellence

Stories of Success from the Real World of Sport and Exercise Psychology

Edited by
Michael L. Sachs
Lauren S. Tashman
Selen Razon

ROWMAN & LITTLEFIELD
Lanham • Boulder • New York • London

Acquisitions Editor: Christen Karniski
Assistant Editor: Erinn Slanina
Production Editor: Lara Hahn
Cover Designer: Kathi Ha

Credits and acknowledgments of sources for material or information used with permission appear on the appropriate page within the text.

Published by Rowman & Littlefield
An imprint of The Rowman & Littlefield Publishing Group, Inc.
4501 Forbes Boulevard, Suite 200, Lanham, Maryland 20706
www.rowman.com

6 Tinworth Street, London, SE11 5AL, United Kingdom

Copyright © 2020 by The Rowman & Littlefield Publishing Group, Inc.

All figures courtesy of Getty Images unless otherwise noted.

All rights reserved. No part of this book may be reproduced in any form or by any electronic or mechanical means, including information storage and retrieval systems, without written permission from the publisher, except by a reviewer who may quote passages in a review.

British Library Cataloguing in Publication Information Available

Library of Congress Cataloging-in-Publication Data

Names: Sachs, Michael L., editor. | Tashman, Lauren S. (Lauren Saenz), 1980– editor. | Razon, Selen, editor.
Title: Performance excellence : stories of success from the real world of sport and exercise psychology / edited by Michael L. Sachs, Lauren S. Tashman, Selen Razon.
Description: Lanham, Maryland : Rowman & Littlefield, 2020. | Includes bibliographical references and index. | Summary: "Performance Excellence provides concise and effective lessons on a variety of psychological skills and broader concepts within the domains of exercise, sport, and performance psychology. Each lesson includes a short educational piece that centers on the select concept followed by examples that highlight how the concept works in real life."—Provided by publisher.
Identifiers: LCCN 2019046476 (print) | LCCN 2019046477 (ebook) | ISBN 9781538128886 (cloth) | ISBN 9781538128893 (paperback) | ISBN 9781538128909 (epub)
Subjects: LCSH: Sports—Psychological aspects. | Exercise—Psychological aspects. | Performance—Psychological aspects.
Classification: LCC GV706.4 .P4725 2020 (print) | LCC GV706.4 (ebook) | DDC 796.01/9—dc23
LC record available at https://lccn.loc.gov/2019046476
LC ebook record available at https://lccn.loc.gov/2019046477

Contents

Introduction		vii
1	**Teams: Cohesion, Dynamics and Culture, and Leadership**	**1**
	Is a "C" Really Necessary?—*Matthieu M. Boisvert and Todd M. Loughead*	2
	Never Satisfied—*Bernadette Compton*	6
	A Team Culture of Developing the Whole Person: UCLA Gymnastics—*Deborah Munch*	10
	On Being and Becoming Fearless Female Athletes—*Ellen J. Staurowsky*	13
	Culture Eats Teambuilding for Breakfast—*Lauren S. Tashman*	17
2	**Pursuit of Goals: Motivation, Goal Setting, and Adherence**	**23**
	Journey toward Becoming an Everyday Exerciser—*Bradley J. Cardinal*	24
	The Gruppo Ciclistico—*Jeffrey Cherubini*	28
	Perfect Pitch—*John Heil*	31
	Star-Spangled Sport—*John Heil*	34
	Ask the Kids—*Rick Howard*	37
	One Hour at a Time—*Michael L. Sachs*	41
	Uh-Oh, We Have a Ringer . . .—*Michael L. Sachs*	44
	Valuing Physical Activity/Exercise—*Michael L. Sachs*	47
3	**Identity and Transitions: Exercise Identity, Athletic Identity, Transitions, and Self-Awareness**	**51**
	Embracing Change—*Bassey Akpan*	53
	How My Athletic Role Affected My Identity—*Arna Erega*	55
	Who Am I after Everything Is Said and Done?—*Shaya Schaedler*	59

Life beyond Sport—*Alexandra Szarabajko* 62
Hello Life: This Is ~~Swimming~~ Joann, It's Nice to Meet You—
   Joann Wakefield 65
The Split Dodge—*Diana Wildermuth* 68
The Value of a Sport Transition—*Taylor Wise* 72
Leaving Sport with a Spinal Cord Injury—*Derek Zike and
   Monna Arvinen-Barrow* 75

**4 Mental Training: Imagery, Attentional Focus and Control,
Self-Talk, Arousal Control and Energy Management, and
Emotion Regulation**   **79**
Trying to Take It One Pitch at a Time—*William Brown* 81
Act It 'Til You In-act It—*Kevin Burke* 84
"It's Not a Typo"—*Mark Cheney* 88
Hurdle by Hurdle—*Michael Clark* 92
Controlling a Racing Mind While Racing the Mile—*Emily Galvin* 95
Imagining Success and Staying Positive: One Lap at a
   Time—*Alan S. Kornspan* 98
See It to Be It! How Squash Player Lenard Puski Helped
   St. Lawrence University End a Long Losing Streak against
   Trinity College—*Dora Kurimay* 101
Learning to Read Your Physiological Stress Gauge—
   William Land 105
Up and Down the Ladder: The Ebbs and Flows of a Champion
   Jockey—*Karen Lo* 108
Ride It Out: Stress and Anxiety Management Strategies on
   the Slopes—*Michelle M. McAlarnen* 111
A Tennis Journey—*Nikola Milinkovic* 115
"Be the Best" versus "Be the Best Carley"—*Deborah Munch* 119
The Background Noise of the Overachieving Helicopter
   Parent—*Kate Nolt* 122
These Are the Moments We Live for—*Maximilian Pollack* 125
Make No Mistake: Your Thoughts Build Your Game—
   Meghan Ramick and Selen Razon 129
Be the Ball—*Michael L. Sachs* 132
Imagining the Power—*Joann Wakefield* 134
Pool of Tears: In the Water They Can't See You
   Cry—*Joann Wakefield* 137
Ranger Up—*Cedric Williams and Matthew D. Powless* 141

5 Mind-set: Confidence, Emotion, Mental Toughness, Anxiety/Stress/Pressure, and Staleness/Burnout — 145

Pidä hauskaa—Have Fun!—*Monna Arvinen-Barrow, Amanda Visek, and Amie Barrow* — 146

The Big Three—*Arna Erega* — 150

The Extreme Stupor/крайний ступор—*John Heil and Paul Soter* — 153

To DNF or Not to DNF, That Is the Question . . .—*Anna-Marie Jaeschke, Michael L. Sachs, Dolores Christensen, and Lauren Tashman* — 158

Down but Not Out—*Lindsey C. Keenan* — 165

You Get to Choose—*Jen Schumacher* — 169

Confidence: A Mind-set, Not a Feeling—*Lauren S. Tashman* — 173

Teeing Up for Success by Exploring and Shifting Mindset—*Lauren S. Tashman* — 177

6 Facing and Overcoming Challenges: Mental Toughness, Anxiety/Stress/Pressure, Staleness/Burnout, Resilience, and Rehabilitation from Injury — 181

More Than That, I Was Never Just . . .—*Megan Buning and Tiffany M. Kasdorf* — 183

Coping with Injury: Deep Breathing and Praying—*Damien Clement and Monna Arvinen-Barrow* — 187

Grit at 335 Miles Per Hour: A Drag Racing Story of Guts, Resilience, Initiative, and Tenacity—*Tami Eggleston* — 190

Failing Forward—*Kerry Guest* — 194

Being There—*John Heil* — 198

Psyche of the Injured Athlete—*Laura Miele* — 201

Running to Cope or Running Away—How Much Is Too Much?—*Kate L. Nolt* — 204

Defying the Odds—*Selen Razon* — 208

Do Not Quit!—*Selen Razon and Meghan Ramick* — 211

Coming Back from Injury—*Shaya Schaedler* — 214

Life Changes for Athletic Excellence—*Tshepang Tshube, Karin Jeffery, and Stephanie Hanrahan* — 217

Unconventional Success through Injury—*Taylor Wise* — 220

Resilience and Recovery after Bike Collision—*Anna Weltman* — 223

The Dormouse: Recollections of a Lightweight Rower with Overtraining Syndrome—*Lindsay Woodford* — 228

Conclusion — 233

Appendix: Recommendations for Utilizing This Book in
the Classroom   235

Bibliography   239

Index   245

About the Editors and Contributors   249

Introduction

Welcome to *Performance Excellence: Stories of Success from the Real World of Sport and Exercise Psychology*. Why have we put together this book? We have found, through our years of teaching and applied work, that stories are very powerful. The personalized experiences and messages from those in the field and the individuals and teams with whom they have worked are extremely compelling. Jim Loehr's book *The Power of Story* (2007) highlights this nicely. Accordingly, we got the idea of soliciting contributions for this book and compiling them into the volume you are now reading.

The six chapters in this book, each dealing with a different theme, contain a variety of stories exploring various topics. Some are stories of very personal journeys individuals have taken through sport and education. Others are poignant experiences working with individuals and teams, and the successes (or lack thereof) found in these experiences. Decisions about which chapters to include and which topics are included in each chapter were somewhat arbitrary. As becomes apparent when applying sport and exercise psychology in the real world, many of these topics are interrelated, and a particular individual's or team's story may relate to multiple topics that span several themes. Our attempt at categorizing them into chapters was for the sake of presentation rather than labeling. Please feel free to find uses for stories in one chapter that may also apply to topics from other chapters.

The chapters are:

Chapter 1: Teams—Covers topics such as team cohesion, team dynamics and culture, and leadership

Chapter 2: Pursuit of Goals—Explores motivation, goal setting, and adherence

Chapter 3: Identity and Transitions—Includes stories related to exercise identity, athletic identity, transitions, and self-awareness

Chapter 4: Mental Training—Includes stories that cover a variety of mental skills topics, such as imagery, attentional focus/control, self-talk, arousal control/energy management, and emotion regulation

Chapter 5: Mind-set—Explores mind-set as a broad concept as well as various facets of mind-set, such as confidence, emotion, mental toughness, anxiety/stress/pressure, and staleness/burnout

Chapter 6: Facing and Overcoming Challenges—Includes stories that explore the role of mental toughness, anxiety/stress/pressure, staleness/burnout, resilience, and facing and overcoming various challenges including rehabilitation from injury

Each story in the book demonstrates the notions of *research to practice* and *evidence-based practice* with the inclusion of references to literature and research in order to encourage you to explore the foundations of the topics further and to provide additional resources for your teaching/applied work. Each story also includes a few "Take-Home Points" to highlight the important aspects of the story and facilitate use in the classroom and with your clients.

USING THESE STORIES

How can these stories be best used? In a broad sense, we can think of three ways in which they can be most helpful. The first is simply for intrinsic value (i.e., enjoyment, knowledge)—along the lines of the Chicken Soup for the Soul series; these stories provide short-and-sweet tales of interest and many poignant experiences. Similarly, biographies and autobiographies, such as *Let Me Tell you a Story: A Lifetime in the Game* by Red Auerbach and John Feinstein (2004), include compelling and fascinating/interesting stories. Stories provide a means for us to see ideas in action and as a way to relate through others' experiences.

The second is as a teaching tool. Many of us teach, either for a living as academicians in colleges and universities or as adjuncts for a variety of courses in various settings. These stories can bring the theory and research we present more strikingly by exhibiting real-world applications and experiences of these concepts. Consistent with the educational best practices of active learning (Bonwell & Eison, 1991) and situated learning (Brown, Collins, & Duguid, 1989), incorporating stories in the classroom helps students engage in higher forms of learning (e.g., synthesis, application) and puts their learning in context. Further explanation about how to put these stories to use in the classroom is provided in the appendix at the end of the book.

The third is as a tool in your applied work. When we work with individuals and teams we want to make a connection with our clients, to ensure that the points we are making and the topics on which we are working are brought home to our clients as powerfully as possible. Stories—especially ones our clients can relate to by virtue of sport, age, gender, and so on—can have exceptional impact on your clients, but also on your own professional development. Applied sport and exercise psychology requires adaptive rather than routine expertise (Hatano & Inagaki, 1986); thus, reading stories and cases of real-world experiences in sport and exercise psychology (i.e., worked examples; Atkinson, Derry, Renkl, & Wortham, 2000) can help both neophyte and more seasoned practitioners continue to advance knowledge, skills, and abilities (Mayo, 2002; Williams, 1992).

MAKING A DIFFERENCE

You are in positions to make a difference in people's lives through your teaching and applied work. We hope that the stories in this book can help you make that difference all the more powerfully.

REFERENCES

Atkinson, R. K., Derry, S. J., Renkl, A., & Wortham, D. (2000). Learning from examples: Instructional principles from the worked examples research. *Review of Educational Research, 70,* 181–214.

Auerbach, R., & Feinstein, J. (2004). *Let me tell you a story: A lifetime in the game.* New York, NY: Little, Brown.

Bonwell, C. C., & Eison, J. A. (1991). *Active learning: Creating excitement in the classroom.* ASH#-ERIC Higher Education Report No. 1, Washington, DC: George Washington University, School of Education and Human Development.

Brown, J. S., Collins, A., & Duguid, P. (1989). Situated cognition and the culture of learning. *Educational Researcher, 18,* 32–41.

Hatano, G., & Inagaki, K. (1986). Two courses of expertise. In H. A. H. Stevenson & K. Hakuta (Eds.), *Child development and education in Japan* (pp. 262–72). New York: Freeman.

Loehr, J. (2007). *The power of story: Rewrite your destiny in business and in life.* New York, NY: Free Press.

Mayo, J. A. (2002). Case-based instruction: A technique for increasing conceptual application in introductory psychology. *Journal of Constructivist Psychology, 15,* 65–74.

Williams, S. M. (1992). Putting case-based instruction into context: Examples from legal and medical education. *Journal of the Learning Sciences, 2,* 367–427.

Chapter One

Teams

Cohesion, Dynamics, Culture, and Leadership

Sport is ultimately comprised of individual efforts that need to be aligned to produce successful team performances. Whether a sport necessitates the coordination of those efforts in traditionally understood ways (e.g., football, soccer, hockey) or more covert ways (e.g., collegiate golf team, rowing, synergy between a runner and his or her performance team, exercise group), the dynamics, cohesiveness, and culture of the team will play a role in the performance of both the individuals separately and the team collectively. Aiding teams in optimizing their performance can involve education and consultation focused on the dynamics of the team, social and/or task cohesion, culture and influence of the environment, leadership, and communication. Myriad factors needs to be considered, such as diversity of the team (e.g., gender, ethnicity, class, age, etc.), level of competition, dynamics and culture of the sport, and so on.

The essays in this chapter touch on different elements of teams. Matthieu M. Boisvert and Todd M. Loughead discuss the concept of shared leadership and the role of being a captain in the National Hockey League. Bernadette Compton addresses building and maintaining team culture and leadership in a women's basketball team. Deborah Munch reviews the amazing story of UCLA women's gymnastics and their superb team culture. Ellen J. Staurowsky discusses the critical importance of women in sport becoming fearless female athletes. Lauren S. Tashman talks about her experiences working with a team for the first time, with an emphasis on team culture.

IS A "C" REALLY NECESSARY?
Matthieu M. Boisvert and Todd M. Loughead, University of Windsor

Leadership in sport is viewed as important by coaches, athletes, fans, and the media alike. Typically, the coach has been seen as the primary source of leadership on sports teams. However, another source of leadership emanating from the athletes has emerged, known as athlete leadership. Athlete leadership can come from two sources: Formal athlete leaders are those who occupy a leadership role based on their role within the team in the form of captain or assistant captain, while informal athlete leaders emerge as leaders on their teams through their interactions and communications with teammates (Loughead, 2017). Taken together, athlete leadership is a dynamic process where leadership responsibilities within the team can be assumed by multiple athletes (Crozier, Loughead, & Munroe-Chandler, 2017).

When leadership is viewed in this manner, all team members have the opportunity to provide leadership to their team. Therefore, athlete leadership can be viewed as a form of shared leadership among team members. In other words, reliance on officially designated leaders is losing its place within sport teams. What this ultimately means is that it is unrealistic for a captain to be able to fulfill all of the leadership responsibilities for his or her team. A good example of a team's embracing the concept of sharing leadership responsibilities among athletes is the 2019 National Basketball Association (NBA) Champion Toronto Raptors. In discussing the team's leadership, head coach Nick Nurse characterized point guard Kyle Lowry's leadership style as something that can't be measured on a stats sheet: "His natural instincts are to be a leader out there, and he shows it. He does it with his [basketball] IQ and his great knowledge of the game. He shows it with tremendous toughness as well. That's his other natural characteristic. He's blocking out guys twice his size. He's taking charges every game. He's just going to fight to win" (Schuhmann, 2019). As for small forward Kawhi Leonard, his leadership style is characterized by his consistently calm behavior regardless of the situation. Following the Raptors' win in game 3 of the NBA Finals, teammate Pascal Siakam described Leonard's leadership style: "He's always been that guy who you can look at when something goes bad. He just has that calm demeanor. It gives you that peace, knowing that everything is going to be OK" (Madu, 2019). Additionally, shooting guard Danny Green, when asked what he brings to the table from a leadership perspective, said, "Just staying really locked in, being disciplined, being professional. Fighting out certain game situations and sticking together, not complaining to referees, not criticizing each other. Positive criticism, constructive criticism is okay, but we're fighting these battles together and not to worry about things we can't control" (Grange, 2018). When asked about what a veteran player like Green adds to the Raptors, Nurse stated, "He's like the ultimate teammate, right? He does everything with a little bit of positivity and a little bit of a smile on his face 'come-on-let's-go type of attitude.' Those guys go a long way. They're fun to be around" (Grange, 2018). Based on the example above, we can see how each one of these players brought something different to the leadership of the team. These features of the Raptors' leadership are echoed by Fransen, Vanbeselaere, De Cupyer, Vande Broek, and Boen (2014), who found that team captains were not able to fulfill all of the leadership responsibilities within their respective teams. Instead, these responsibilities were accomplished by several team leaders.

If several athletes are serving in a leadership role within their team, the question then becomes: "How many athletes should fulfill a leadership role?" The answer to this question is: A lot! Crozier, Loughead, and Munroe-Chandler (2013) showed that approximately 85 percent of a team's roster should be comprised of athlete leaders, with 19 percent occupying a formal leadership role and the remaining 66 percent occupying an informal leadership role. This demonstrates that the leadership within teams is very much shared among most team members. To further support the idea that leadership ought to be shared by various team members, research has found that the team captain (formal leader) was selected only 1 percent of the time by fellow athletes as the best leader on the team (Fransen et al., 2014). Instead, the majority of participants selected a combination of both formal and informal leaders as best suited to fulfill the leadership needs of the team.

This trend toward shared athlete leadership has recently garnered mainstream media attention, with outlets such the *Washington Post* and the Associated Press calling into question the utility of a designated team captain in the modern-day National Hockey League (NHL). In early 2019, six NHL teams found themselves without a formally designated captain, that player who wears the "C" on his jersey: the Detroit Red Wings, Ottawa Senators, Toronto Maple Leafs, Vegas Golden Knights, New York Rangers, and Vancouver Canucks. For instance, after the retirement of eight-year captain Henrik Sedin, Canucks general manager Jim Benning chose not to name a new captain, believing his team wasn't ready for someone to fill Sedin's role. Beinning instead opted to name four players as alternate captains to allow players to share in the leadership responsibilities of the team (Khurshudyan, 2018).

Perhaps the most interesting case of an NHL team choosing not to name a captain is the Vegas Golden Knights, who elected to leave the captaincy vacant for their inaugural season so as not to put that pressure on one player. Instead, the team's management adopted the philosophy of having twenty-three captains—that is, the team's entire roster. This strategy proved fruitful: The Golden Knights reached the Stanley Cup Finals in their first season. Speaking to the Associated Press about the benefits of having every player share leadership responsibilities, Golden Knights goaltender Marc-André Fleury stated, "Everyone chipped in. I think we had a good group of veterans who played a lot of games. I think all together we kind of took charge of helping try to lead the team" (Whyno, 2018). Following the success of their inaugural season, the Golden Knights decided to keep the captaincy vacant for their second season and continue their philosophy of "twenty-three captains." Forward Reilly Smith shed light on this decision in an interview with Khurshudyan (2018): "Last year we needed 23 different leaders to be able to come together and build as a team. I think we kind of just roll that over into this year and try to work in a similar attitude and a similar mind-set where it takes all of us." With research showing the benefits of shared leadership, it will be interesting to see whether more teams elect to get away from captains and move toward allowing all team members to take part in the leadership process.

Take-Home Points

1. Not one athlete can fulfill all leadership responsibilities.
2. Shared leadership allows all players to develop their leadership abilities.

References

Crozier, A. J., Loughead, T. M., & Munroe-Chandler, K. J. (2013). Examining the benefits of athlete leadership in sport. *Journal of Sport Behavior, 34*, 346–64.

Crozier, A. J., Loughead, T. M., & Munroe-Chandler, K. J. (2017). Top-down or shared leadership? Examining differences in athlete leadership behaviours based on leadership status in sport. *Fizička kultura, 71*(2), 86–98.

Fransen, K., Vanbeselaere, N., De Cuyper, B., Vande Broek, G., & Boen, F. (2014). The myth of the team captain as principal leader: Extending the athlete leadership classification within sport teams. *Journal of Sports Sciences, 32*(14), 1389–97.

Grange, M. (2018, September 26). "Ultimate teammate" Green boosts Raptors' leadership, experience. Sportsnet. Retrieved from https://www.sportsnet.ca/basketball/nba/ultimate-teammate-green-boosts-raptors-leadership-experience/

Khurshudyan, I. (2018, November 27). No captain, my captain: Tradition-rich NHL teams are no longer giving players the "C." *Washington Post*. Retrieved from https://www.washingtonpost.com/sports/2018/11/27/no-captain-my-captain-tradition-rich-nhl-teams-are-no-longer-giving-players-c/?utm_term=.ce253418c397

Loughead, T. M. (2017). Athlete leadership: A review of the theoretical, measurement, and empirical literature. *Current Opinion in Psychology, 16*, 58–61.

Madu, Z. (2019, June 8). Kawhi Leonard is the perfect leader for the Raptors. *SBNation*. Retrieved from https://www.sbnation.com/2019/6/8/18657581/kawhi-leonard-raptors-warriors-nba-finals-leadership

Schuhmann, J. (2019, May 26). Lowry's leadership lifts Raptors to first Finals appearance. NBA.com. Retrieved from http://www.nba.com/article/2019/05/26/toronto-raptors-nba-finals-kyle-lowry-game-6

Whyno, S. (2018, September 18). Nothing to "C" here: Importance of NHL captains is changing. Associated Press. Retrieved from https://apnews.com/ccb-7900d318c42028f2be779e79f4a66

NEVER SATISFIED
Bernadette Compton

Overtime of the women's basketball conference final between the Fighting Eagles and the Mighty Lions. The score is tied at 70 with only seconds to play. As the star point guard for the Lions drives the ball up the court, the whistle blows. "Blocking foul, number four . . . white ball out of bounce," says the referee. The time on the clock: 1.1 seconds. The teams prepare for the final play of the overtime period with just 1.1 seconds between a champion or a second overtime period. One second. Just one second is all it takes. Time seems to pause as everyone watches the basketball sail in the air and toward the basket. With no time left on the clock, the ball falls through the net and the game is over. Just like that, with a loss in the conference championship, the season is over for the Eagles collegiate basketball team.

Ask any player or coach and they will be able to replay the closing moments vividly: the heartbreak, the numbness of being so close to proving the sporting world wrong. We all envisioned the potential of this team due to the leadership of the coaching staff, but failing to achieve the ultimate goal left a hunger inside everyone. The Eagles program had turned around within the year, from barely winning six games to playing in the conference championship. But a fire was ignited within each of the players and staff, a fire that was a product of the shift in culture. *We are never satisfied.*

The Eagles basketball team provides a wonderful and uplifting story about building and maintaining team culture and leadership—one where the athletes took responsibility and owned into their roles on the team. The use of own-in works to empower athletes and allows them to be more authentic and involved in the program instead of just being tolerant or doing something because it is expected of them. Owning-in is a process, which involves engagement *with* athletes instead of *for* athletes. The Eagles wanted a culture that was lifted off the walls of the locker room and lived in their daily behaviors on and off the field. During the offseason, the team set out to build a culture of inclusive excellence.

Inclusive excellence is framed in the context of sports goals, where excellence is dependent upon the inclusion of diverse individuals (Kauer & Krane, 2010). The key to building inclusive excellence is the development of team norms or ways of doing within the team. For example, one norm the team established is respect for all humans, regardless of gender, sexuality, religion, ethnicity, race, and nationality. The following exercises stem from a larger program on LGBTQ+ inclusion implemented to develop respect for all humans:

- *Identity Discussion:* Athletes were allowed the opportunity to discuss their social and cultural identities and how these identities impacted their sporting performance. The sport psychology consultant often provided prompts for the team to discuss or brought in recent events within the sport world.
- *If You Really Knew Me:* Athletes were provided the opportunity to think about their own lives. They were provided the following prompt and asked to provide either a low-risk (e.g., "I love to do puzzles") or a high-risk (e.g., "I am gay") response: "My name is _____ and I am from _____. One thing you cannot tell just by looking at me is _____. This is important for me to tell you because _____."

Built within the inclusive excellence framework was the goal of developing a championship mind-set. Leaders of the team expressed their concerns about past experiences with building culture. They felt culture often lived on the walls but was never experienced in their lives. To own into the culture, the team was developing and maintaining a championship mind-set, and the team's mental coach turned to Jeff Janssen's work on leadership and championship culture. Championship culture is about building both results and relationships. Team members are held to a high standard in the pursuit of a mission or purpose, but it also focuses on relationships in which everyone is treated with respect. Team members realize their roles in the larger unit and take pride in being part of something larger than themselves (Janssen, n.d.).

DiCicco and Hacker (2003) discuss the importance of leadership from all members in their book *Catch Them Being Good*, stressing that the top leaders need support from other members and should allow others to take charge depending on the situation. On the Eagles basketball team, the athletes were encouraged to take responsibility and own into their leadership roles, regardless of class rank or time played. In other words, while we had team captains, all the athletes were encouraged to step up and be leaders.

The second piece of leadership stemmed from the Eagles' coaching staff. At the beginning of the previous season, the team had experienced a head coaching change when Emma Max took over the team. Emma showed components of a transformational leader. Transformational leadership involves the process and behaviors that empower, challenge, and encourage team members to reach their full potential (Turnnidge & Côté, 2016). Emma shared her vision with the team and how it aligned with the objectives, needs, and abilities of each athlete and coach (Callow, Smith, Hardy, Arthur, & Hardy, 2009). Throughout the offseason and into her first year as the head coach, Emma ensured the athletes had what they needed while challenging them to reach their full potential and become conference champions.

Throughout the offseason, the team worked to develop a team culture they were proud to represent and set out to live it on and off the court. Team captains focused on a team standard and asked teammates how they were working to fulfill the standard as athletes and students. These standards included respect for all humans; embracing their potential; working smarter, not harder; establishing constructive competitiveness; and finishing strong. The standards all encompassed the team's mantra: *We are never satisfied.* The goal was to take the values the team worked to develop and build them into behaviors as athletes and students in the pursuit of the outcome of excellence on the court and in the classroom. As one athlete commented, "The team is working towards something bigger than ourselves, but in a way that highlights each of our strengths and helps to build on our weaknesses."

The goals for building the team culture focused on developing inclusive excellence and championship culture, which would be owned into by all members of the team. One way the athletes took ownership of the culture and lifted it from the walls of the locker room was to teach the incoming players the culture. They sat down with each new player and discussed the team's expectations on and off the court and how athletes were to represent the team in their actions concerning the team and their teammates. They also discussed the team culture with recruits to ensure they understood what would be expected of them in the program. Building team culture does not happen overnight. The culture of the Eagles is still evolving and shifting with the different objectives of excellence and performance being placed on the team, but they still align with the values the team set in the offseason. Values of respect and effort were developed from Janssen's work on leadership and team culture. The following season, the team set multiple records—such as numerous academic achievements, conference first and second teams, numerous players of the week, and overall wins—on the court and in the classroom. They also lifted the conference championship trophy and did so with pride in their team: their Eagle family.

Take-Home Points

1. Build a culture of inclusive excellence, where all members are respected regardless of their diverse backgrounds.
2. Allow all team members a voice in the culture, regardless of their role on the team.
3. Work to develop ownership and athletes to own into the development of team culture instead of them buying into the culture.

References

Callow, N., Smith, M. J., Hardy, L., Arthur, C. A., & Hardy, J. (2009). Measurement of transformational leadership and its relationship with team cohesion and performance level. *Journal of Applied Sport Psychology, 21*(4), 395–412. doi: 10.1080/10413200903204754

DiCicco, T., & Hacker, C. (2003). *Catch them being good: Everything you need to know to successfully coach girls.* London, UK: Penguin Books.

Janssen, J. (n.d.). What kind of culture do you have? Discover the 8 kinds of culture. Janssen Sports Leadership Center. Retrieved from http://www.janssensportsleadership.com/resources/janssen-blog/what-kind-of-culture-do-you-have-discover-the-7-kinds-of-cultures/

Kauer, K. J., & Krane, V. (2010). Inclusive excellence: Embracing diverse sexual and gender identities in sport. In S. J. Hanrahan & M. B. Andersen (Eds.). *Routledge handbook of applied sport psychology: A comprehensive guide for students and practitioners* (pp. 764–79). New York, NY: Routledge.

Turnnidge, J., & Côté, J. (2016). Applying transformational leadership theory to coaching research in youth sport: A systematic literature review. *International Journal of Sport and Exercise Psychology, 16*(3), 1–16. doi: 10.1080/1612197X.2016.1189948

A TEAM CULTURE OF DEVELOPING THE WHOLE PERSON: UCLA GYMNASTICS
Deborah Munch

Coach Valorie Kondos Field waves to the crowd at the UCLA-Utah State Meet, her final meet before retirement. *AS UCLA*

Two years into Valorie Kondos Field's career as UCLA head gymnastics coach, she found herself walking through the UCLA Athletic Department parking lot thinking about how much money is spent on athletics. At the time, she knew the UCLA Athletic Department was spending tens of millions a year on its athletic teams. She thought to herself, "How many trillions of dollars are spent worldwide so people, fans, and countries can basically have bragging rights and say, 'Ha! We beat you!'?" (V. Kondos Field, personal interview, January 25, 2019).

It was also at this time that Kondos Field was struggling with why she was coaching. She received the head coach position having never been a gymnast. Her background was in ballet and dance, where performances were conducted on stage and success was defined by proper preparation and executing the process. Kondos Field recognized that winning and beating others was just not in her DNA, and there had to be more to sport than bragging rights. It was that moment that Kondos Field found her "why"—her reason to coach—and something that she could get excited about. She believed that athletes are more than their sport, that the footprint they leave in life is much greater than scoring a perfect 10 in gymnastics. Kondos Field became excited about being a steward for developing extraordinary human beings and then set about spending the remainder of her coaching career, spanning a total of twenty-nine years, crafting a team culture that would enrich and develop whole human beings.

Kondos Field spends extra time and effort to ensure this culture is understood, experienced, and embraced by the team. Values are the foundation of a team culture. The behavior, decision making, and actions of the team are all influenced by the underlying guiding principles and values (Cotterill, 2012). At the heart of the UCLA gymnastics team culture is the value of growth. Kondos Field believes that if you can grow and enrich the whole person, you're going to have a better athlete. The team culture is designed to embolden whole-person development. Kondos Field encourages athletes to get jobs not for the money, but to develop a sense of self-worth and to be able to serve others. Kondos Field has individual check-in meetings with the athletes that avoid the topic of gymnastics unless the athlete wants to talk about gymnastics. Instead they talk about school, personal life, friends, interests, and struggles.

Kondos Field has seen athletes struggle with their self-identity when the day comes that they stop competing in gymnastics, so she encourages athletes to explore their own unique interests outside of sport. Each year the team takes the Enneagram, a personality assessment test, to increase their level of self-awareness and learn about how they typically respond under stress. The night before an away meet the team can be found participating in a number of games designed to help them enhance life skills. One such game is called The Great Debate. In this game, each athlete receives a debate topic, such as why UCLA should be a nudist campus or the benefits of majoring in silence. The athletes have ninety seconds to debate their topic, then are judged and scored from 1 to 10 on elements such as staying within the time limit of the debate, making eye contact with the audience, content and persuasiveness of their argument, and meeting the requirement of using and properly conjugating an SAT word. Says Kondos Field (2018), "The fact that we can help our student-athletes learn valuable life skills through our time together as an athletic team is extremely important to me" (p. 148).

Team culture is the social and psychological environment created to maximize the team's ability to achieve success (Martens, 1987). How a team defines success is important, because this definition will guide the decisions and actions of the team. When Kondos Field recognized she did not believe in winning and losing as the sole measure of success, she went about developing success principles to guide the team. She drew on the legendary basketball coach John Wooden—her mentor, friend, and fellow UCLA Athletics Hall of Famer—for a definition of success: "Success is peace of mind, which is a direct result of self-satisfaction in knowing you did your best to become the best you are capable of becoming" (Wooden & Jamison, 1997, p. 170). The

UCLA gymnastics team focuses on how they can perform their best and get 1 percent better each day. If every day they do the best they can, have no regrets, and strive to get 1 percent better, the team can finish the season having achieved success, no matter where that lands them on the scoreboard.

For a coach and team culture that does not place winning at the forefront of their team culture, the team has accumulated many honors as a seeming byproduct of their focus on developing the whole person and performing with no regrets. UCLA women's gymnastics has seven NCAA Championships, nineteen NCAA regional titles, and fourteen conference titles. Additionally, Kondos Field was inducted into the UCLA Athletics Hall of Fame and named Pac-12 Coach of the Century, four-time National Coach of the Year, and four-time Conference Coach of the Year.

Take-Home Points

1. A coach can show what is important to team culture through words, actions, values, beliefs, and team activities.
2. A core element of team culture is defining success and how it can be achieved.
3. Kondos Field chose to create a team culture that rang true to her beliefs and value system. Take time to develop something that you believe in; don't copy other teams or leaders if it doesn't feel right to you.

References

Cotterill, S. T. (2012). *Team psychology in sports: Theory and practice.* London, UK: Routledge.

Kondos Field, V. (2018). *Life is Short, Don't Wait to Dance.* New York, NY: Hachette.

Martens, R. (1987). *Coaches guide to sport psychology.* Champaign, IL: Human Kinetics.

Wooden, J., & Jamison, S. (1997). *Wooden: A lifetime of observations and reflections on and off the court.* Chicago, IL: Contemporary Books.

ON BEING AND BECOMING FEARLESS FEMALE ATHLETES
Ellen J. Staurowsky, Drexel University

Fearless: Bold–Brave–Courageous–Intrepid–Daring–Audacious[1]

On International Women's Day in 2017, New York City tourists and people working in the financial sector on Wall Street found a thought-provoking sight. Appearing opposite the iconic statue of the Charging Bull was the Fearless Girl, defiant and unyielding.[2] Commissioned by State Street Global Advisors as part of a campaign to pressure investment firms to add more women to their corporate boards, the powerful symbol of the Fearless Girl was quickly taken up on social media. The tagline for the campaign was "She makes a difference."

Initially intended as a temporary installation across from the Charging Bull, the Fearless Girl was so popular the statue remained for more than year. When it was removed to its permanent installation site across from the New York Stock Exchange, a plaque was placed at the original location noting that the Fearless Girl was on the move and inviting those who came to see her to stand in her shoes facing down the Charging Bull (Walker, 2018).

For girls and women in sport, being fearless has been a part of the job description of what it means to be an athlete and to work in the sport industry for generations. As Ignotofsky notes in her book *Women in Sport: 50 Fearless Athletes Who Played to Win* (2017), female athletes in every era have been figures of revolution, defying social conventions that often cast women in inferior roles and taking risks that pushed the boundaries of what female athletes could achieve.

In the twenty-first century, the expressions of fearless females in sport are manifest in numerous ways. The term *fearless* framed celebrations of the female athlete honorees recognized at the Women's Sports Foundation's 39th Annual Salute to Women in Sports Awards (Carr, 2018). It provided the inspiration for a fundraiser for the Rutgers University Women's Soccer team and became a popular name for youth league girls' basketball teams (ATX Fearless Girls Basketball, 2018; Rutgers University Athletics, 2018).

And fearlessness guides the actions of female athletes working for social change. Consider Riley Morrison (Lauletta, 2018), a nine-year-old basketball player and avid Golden State Warriors fan who voiced her disappointment that shoes marketed by NBA star Steph Curry were available only on the "boys" section of the shoe company's website. Posting a letter to Curry on social media, she raised his consciousness about an exclusionary practice, eliciting a response from him to "correct the problem *now*" (Lauletta, 2018; Medina, 2018). In an age of athlete activism, female athletes have stepped out and spoken up on various social justice issues, including Rachael Denhollander, Aly Raisman, and dozens more who broke the silence around sexual assault in the sport of women's gymnastics (Martinelli, 2018).

What does it take to be a fearless female competing and working in what has historically been a male dominated enterprise? According to Carey Lohrenz (2014), a former Navy lieutenant who made US military history by becoming the first female aviator to fully qualify to fly the F-14 Tomcat, the fundamentals of fearless leadership include courage, tenacity, and integrity. Leaders guided by fearlessness have a vision for their lives or organizations, are invested in promoting a culture around them supportive of that vision, are willing to put in the work necessary to be prepared to meet the challenges that arise and perform accordingly, and draw upon inner sources of resilience and strength to deal with setbacks and adversity. They also have the capacity to get out of their comfort zone and to place themselves in circumstances that test their mental and physical strength while managing to check in and ensure that those around them are taken care of and supported.

As often as the word *fearless* is taken up and used in reference to girls and women, its use reveals the complexities of gender and how it plays out in sport and society. Some, for example, have taken issue with the Fearless Girl for promoting what they call "false feminism" by ignoring the seemingly obvious impossibilities in the message. A girl could no more stop a charging bull than a piece of paper could stop a hurricane. Does such messaging cover up the continuing inequities in power that place girls and women on the margins of power? No doubt. Women still struggle for equitable treatment in both the corporate sector and within the sport industry in terms of equal pay, overcoming double standards that undermine their authority, personal safety and security, accessing opportunities, and navigating spaces where they are often underrepresented.

And yet the "falseness" of the Fearless Girl might just as well be read as its fundamental "trueness," meaning that the Fearless Girl knows she is venturing out into a world of possibility that will be beautiful as well as challenging. It is the essence of being intrepid. Adventures are exhilarating but not easy. In order to be bold, there must be something to push against. Being brave sometimes requires putting one foot in front of the other, pushing through for "five more minutes" as Lohrenz (2014) suggests. The Fearless Girl may serve as a reminder that fearless girl athletes can grow up to be fearless women athletes who have the capacity to use sport for the social good and to make a difference in the world.

Take-Home Points

1. The fundamentals of fearless leadership include courage, tenacity, and integrity.
2. Fostering fearless leaders requires vision, creation of a culture supportive of that vision, preparation, and resilience.
3. Sport is a gendered social environment that is complex.

References

ATX Fearless Girls Basketball. (2018). The transition from rec basketball to competitive basketball can be tough for 5th & 6th grade girls: We bring the fundamentals, the fun, and the fearlessness. Retrieved from http://atxfearless.com/

Carr, K. (2018, October 17). The Women's Sports Foundation celebrates the fearless female athletes creating change at the 39th Annual Salute to Women in Sports. Press release. Retrieved from https://www.prnewswire.com/news-releases/the-womens-sports-foundation-celebrates-the-fearless-female-athletes-creating-change-at-the-39th-annual-salute-to-women-in-sports-300733375.html

Ignotofsky, R. (2017). *Women in sports: 50 fearless athletes who played to win.* New York: Crown.

Lauletta, T. (2018, November 29). A nine-year-old Warriors fan got Steph Curry and Under Armour to make the NBA star's shoes available for girls. *Business Insider.* Retrieved from https://www.businessinsider.com/stephen-curry-letter-girls-shoes-riley-2018-11

Lohrenz, C. (2014). *Fearless leadership: High performance lessons from the flight deck.* Austin, TX: Greenleaf Book Group Press.

Martinelli, M. (2018, April 18). Aly Raisman wrote a powerful tribute to the first woman who accused Larry Nassar publicly. *USA Today.* Retrieved from https://ftw.usatoday.com/2018/04/time-100-aly-raisman-rachael-denhollander-gymnastics-doctor-larry-nassar-sentence-influential-people-2018

Medina, M. (2018, December 5). Stephen Curry said 9 year old's letter about Curry 5's "opened my eyes." *Mercury News.* Retrieved from https://www.mercurynews.com/2018/12/05/stephen-curry-said-9-year-olds-letter-about-curry-5s-opened-my-eyes/

Rutgers University Athletics. (2018). Women's soccer hosts fearless girl fundraiser. Press release. Retrieved from https://scarletknights.com/news/2018/5/1/womens-soccer-hosts-fearless-girl-fundraiser.aspx

Walker, A. (2018, December 10). "Fearless Girl" permanently relocated to the New York Stock Exchange. *Curbed.* Retrieved from https://ny.curbed.com/2018/11/28/18116263/fearless-girl-statue-relocation-nyse

NOTES

1. Definition as found in the Google dictionary. Retrieved from https://www.google.com/search?source=hp&ei=fWFxXMKfC5Dk_AbbqqvACA&q=fearless&btnK=Google+Search&oq=fearless&gs_l=psy-ab.3..35i39l2j0i20i263j0i67l4j0j0i67j0.795.1955..2289...0.0..0.91.683.9......0....1..gws-wiz.....0..0i131.SRhghRPpD1w

2. The sculptor for the Fearless Girl is Kristin Visbal. The Charging Bull was created by Arturo Di Modica.

CULTURE EATS TEAMBUILDING FOR BREAKFAST
Lauren S. Tashman, PhD, CMPC

The following is not a story of failure per se, but rather an attempt at imagining a rewrite of history in which important lessons learned throughout my career thus far as well as advances in research and best practice both on and off the field could be applied. During my graduate school applied training and supervision, I had the opportunity to work with a collegiate team experiencing chemistry challenges. So, like most neophyte mental coaches (particularly those ten years ago or so), I embarked on a seasonlong effort to help them work on their team dynamics.

As a grad student it was a great experience to have, as it was the first time I had the opportunity to be very integrated with a team; I attended and observed practices and games, conducted team meetings, had individual brief contact interventions, had some discussions with the coaches, and got to travel with the team to their postseason competitions. The team meetings consisted of social cohesion (i.e., efforts to assist with their relationships and communication) and task cohesion (i.e., efforts to assist with their ability to work effectively together) activities and discussions to help assist with optimizing the dynamics (e.g., Estabrooks & Dennis, 2003; Weinberg & Gould, 2019). For example, to target social cohesion we did activities that enabled the athletes to get to know each other better as athletes and teammates and helped them learn about and work on communication skills; we also had sessions that allowed them to dig into important discussions with each other to address areas of conflict. To target task cohesion, we worked on team goals, created a team mission statement, did activities that enabled them to see the ways in which they effectively and ineffectively worked together, and allowed them to debrief cohesion in competition and strategize for optimizing cohesion in upcoming competitions. The team performed well during the season, making it to postseason competition, but did not perform well in the end. So I can look back and say the efforts to assist with team chemistry were helpful, and I wouldn't call it a failure or wrong approach at the time, given the focus in the field on team-building back then. Yet now, more than fifteen years since starting my master's degree (I can't believe it's been that long!), and with the advances we've had in understanding the role of team culture (e.g., Coyle, 2018), leadership (e.g., Haslam, Reicher, & Platow, 2011), and high-performing teams (e.g., Yaeger, 2016), if I could work with this team now, I would do it differently.

Long story short: The head coach of the team was formerly the assistant coach and prior to that was a student-athlete on the team. Both of these transitions (i.e., athlete to assistant and assistant to head coach) happened in the span of only a few years, meaning that several of the athletes on the team had experienced—let's call her Janet—as their assistant coach, and a couple of them had also played with her as a teammate. Besides the obvious challenges this brought to her and the team, it was also challenging in that she didn't have much time or any support to navigate those transitions effectively, nor did she experience or undergo any coach education that would have given her important tools to prepare her for the roles and responsibilities of coaching. The following is an example that illustrates this well: One day I showed up to practice and the athletes were nowhere in sight, which was odd given that I usually arrived shortly after practice had already begun due to my class schedule. The coaches were there engaged in what from a distance looked like a heated discussion. When I approached them, the head coach told me that she had sent the athletes home because they didn't look like they cared to be at practice. As an athlete, she had been a passionate and relentlessly dedicated player, so when she saw how the team showed up that day, she thought sending them home was a punishment because it would have been the ultimate punishment for her. Now she was even more furious because the athletes left willingly—and seemed actually happy to leave—which was obviously opposite to what she had intended. As a new coach with no mentoring or education for that role, she didn't understand that key reinforcement principles might have been at work (e.g., perception of reinforcers, competing reinforcements; Weinberg & Gould, 2019). It was a Friday and they had the weekend off, so to the athletes this wasn't a punishment, whereas to the coach taking away the opportunity to practice was one of the most severe punishments a coach could give. Further, she never had the opportunity to intentionally define and communicate her identity as a coach or the culture and environment she wanted to have on her team. Her relationships with the athletes were very problematic, and this created challenges throughout their season and ultimately became a big roadblock to the team's success.

I could give much more detail about the team (e.g., sport, gender, number of athletes on the team, past performance history, cultural factors) and the coaches, as well as the context/broader environmental factors (social ecological model; Bronfenbrenner, 1992), which are important to take into consideration when working with teams (Weinberg & Gould, 2019), but for the purposes of this story it's not completely necessary. Taking into consideration advances in our and other related fields, as well as the lessons I've learned throughout many years of working with teams, instead of focusing mostly on team dynamics I would tackle this case much differently. First and foremost, I would work with the coach on developing her coaching identity, style, and approach in order to help her create the "right" environment for the team to thrive. As Jowett and Arthur (2019) discussed, a coach's leadership and relationships with his or her athletes significantly affect his or her ability to be effective and thereby enable optimal performance for the team. Thus, we would begin this work with a values-based approach (see Copeland, 2014, for a review) where she could have identified and defined her core values, explored how to engage in committed action aligned with those values, and learned how to communicate those values to her team. In tandem, we would discuss and work on her communication skills and her ability to create meaningful, effective relationships with her athletes, since the coach-athlete relationship is a significant challenge in this situation and has been shown to play a role in team cohesion and collective efficacy (e.g., Jowett & Chaundy, 2004; Jowett & Hampson, 2014).

In order to assist the coach with creating and implementing an intentional culture for the team stemming from her values, I would utilize a strategic process for changing the current ineffective culture and then defining and implementing a new culture (see Foster & Tashman, 2019; Schroeder, 2010). A team's culture defines who they are and how they behave based upon basic assumptions, values, and observable demonstrations of these assumptions and values in action (Foster & Tashman, 2019; Schein, 1984). Team culture gets created, whether intentionally or not, and working on team culture is an essential part of the consultation with the team in a coach's first year, not necessarily for the benefit of that season but for the future of the program. Lastly, I would also suggest working with the team captains in order to help them develop their leadership skills, optimally perform their roles, and assist with developing the culture, and help them navigate the challenges of the team at their level of leadership. Like coach leadership, research has shown that athlete leadership has a significant effect on team cohesion (Vincer & Loughead, 2010). However, the team is in season and does have to work effectively together while they are working on their culture. Further, other research has shown that all athletes on a team have leadership roles to play (Fransen, Vanbeselaere, De Cuyper, Vande Broek, & Boen, 2014). Thus, I would also still do the team-building work I did actually do with this team, adding in some focus on peer leadership and roles (e.g., Duguay & Loughead, 2016).

As a professional who for many years has taught graduate applied practice and ethics courses and served as a mentor for certification, I can look back and know that at the time this may have been something of a no-win ethical situation (Moore, 2003). I was just a graduate student in training, was asked only to work with the athletes, and was brought in to work with the team several weeks into the competitive season. Thus, I'm not sure that I could go back and rewrite history as I've discussed. Would I have been prepared to assist the coach and team in this way? Does our education and training in the field prepare us to do that? Are we promoting awareness outside the field that we do more than just team-building? Is this type of situation appropriate for a graduate student in training? Did I do what was best practice in the field at that time? I don't believe this story is one of failure, but given what I know now after this many years of practice, as well as what the last several years of research and discourse in and outside the field have provided, I believe my rewrite would provide a better approach to assisting this coach and team.

Take-Home Points

1. Teambuilding efforts are useful if they are designed intentionally and effectively, but an optimal team environment stems first from culture and leadership.
2. When working with a team that has not defined their culture intentionally and/or needs to change an ineffective culture, team-building can be part of the process to assist with the dynamics and cohesion, but research into practice-based approaches to leadership and culture development should be utilized.
3. Graduate education and training should prepare practitioners for real-world applied practice.
4. Research and advances in best practice are always being updated; thus, a commitment to continued learning and professional development is essential for effective applied practice.

References

Bronfenbrenner, U. (1992). Ecological systems theory. In R. Vasta (Ed.), *Six theories of child development: Revised formulation and current issues* (pp. 187–249). London, UK: Jessica Kingsley.

Copeland, M. K. (2014). The emerging significance of values based leadership: A literature review. *International Journal of Leadership Studies, 8*(2), 105–35.

Coyle, D. (2018). *The culture code: The secrets of highly successful groups.* New York, NY: Bantam.

Duguay, A. M., & Loughead, T. M. (2016). The development, implementation, and evaluation of an athlete leadership development program with female varsity athletes. *Sport Psychologist, 30*(2), 154–66.

Estabrooks, P. A., & Dennis, P. W. (2003). The principles of team building and their applications to sport teams. In R. Lidor, & K. P. Henschen (Eds.), *The psychology of team sports* (pp. 99–113). Morgantown, WV: Fitness Information Technology.

Foster, J., & Tashman, L. S. (2019). Team culture. In J. Taylor (Ed.), *Comprehensive applied sport psychology.* London, UK: Routledge.

Fransen, K., Vanbeselaere, N., De Cuyper, B., Vande Broek, G., & Boen, F. (2014). The myth of the team captain as principal leader: Extending the athlete leadership classification within sport teams. *Journal of Sports Sciences, 32,* 1389–97.

Haslam, S. A., Reicher, S. D., & Platow, M. J. (2011). *The new psychology of leadership: Identity, influence, and power.* New York, NY: Psychology Press.

Jowett, S., & Arthur, C. (2019). Effective coaching: The links between coach leadership and coach-athlete relationship—From theory to research to practice. In M. H. Anshel, T. A. Petrie, & J. A. Steinfeldt (Eds.), *APA Handbook of Sport and Exercise Psychology, Vol. 1* (pp. 419–49). Washington, DC: American Psychological Association.

Jowett, S., & Chaundy, V. (2004). An investigation into the impact of coach leadership and coach-athlete relationship on group cohesion. *Group Dynamics: Theory, Research, and Practice, 8*(4), 302–11.

Jowett, S., & Hampson, R. (2014). Effects of coach leadership and coach-athlete relationship on collective efficacy. *Scandinavian Journal of Medicine & Science in Sports, 24*(2), 454–60.

Moore, Z. E. (2003). Ethical dilemmas in sport psychology: Discussion and recommendations for practice. *Professional Psychology: Research and Practice, 34*(6), 601–10.

Schein, E. H. (1984). Coming to a new awareness of organizational culture. *Sloan Management Review, 25*(2), 3–16.

Schroeder, P. J. (2010). Changing team culture: the perspectives of ten successful head coaches. *Journal of Sport Behavior, 33*(1), 63–88.

Vincer, D. J. E., & Loughead, T. M. (2010). The relationship among athlete leadership behaviors and cohesion in team sports. *Sport Psychologist, 24,* 448–67.

Weinberg, R. S., & Gould, D. (2019). *Foundations of sport and exercise psychology* (7th ed.). Champaign, IL: Human Kinetics.

Yaeger, D. (2016). *Great teams: 16 things high-performing organizations do differently.* Nashville, TN: W Publishing.

Chapter Two

Pursuit of Goals

Motivation, Goal Setting, and Adherence

Goal setting is at the foundation of our participation in exercise and sport. If we do not have a goal for participation, be it performance excellence or simply enjoyment of the activity or perhaps losing weight or something else, we are unlikely to be participating in the first place. These goals can set the standard for one's motivation—the why of one's participation in the activity—and commitment throughout the pursuit of one's goals. While setting goals might seem straightforward, the complexity of human motivation, goal theory, and the nature of sport and exercise mean that a variety of goals might be established, and optimizing the process for setting and pursuing goals is essential. Finally, adherence is key—if one does not persist at the activity then even the most carefully constructed goals are for naught because one is not participating.

Bradley J. Cardinal eloquently talks about his journey toward exercising every day and the motivation behind his decision to do so. Jeffrey Cherubini describes wonderfully the role of a cycling group in facilitating regular physical activity and a healthy lifestyle. John Heil talks about the importance of play in growing up and providing motivation and also talks about passion as the engine of sport. Rick Howard talks about motivation for participation in children and strategies for enhancing physical activity. Michael Sachs provides a superb example of short-, intermediate-, and long-term goal setting with John Naber of Olympic swimming fame; describes the need to be flexible with one's goals, with changing circumstances dictating a different outcome goal for the track meet; and addresses motivation for participation in physical activity/exercise encompassing the concept of values.

JOURNEY TOWARD BECOMING AN EVERYDAY EXERCISER
Bradley J. Cardinal, PhD

I am a healthy, active adult. How did that happen?

In early primary school, I participated in organized soccer, basketball, and baseball. Beginning in fourth grade, football was substituted for soccer. By the time I reached junior high school, only football remained. My coaches encouraged me to add wrestling, which I did beginning in eighth grade, and I also tried track and field in ninth grade. In high school, I played football and wrestled. During my senior year, my teammates elected me captain in both sports. I went on to play college football.

Those organized sport experiences were supplemented with a variety of recreational and leisure-time physical activities, including bike riding, canoeing, downhill skiing, hiking, swimming, water skiing, and more. Some of those activities were family and friend activities and others were through my involvement with the Boy Scouts of America, where I achieved the rank of Eagle Scout. Additionally, I began lifting weights in the sixth grade, initially to help me in sports, but I also noticed accompanying increases in my self-confidence.

After three seasons, my collegiate football career ended abruptly when I experienced a career-ending injury. That injury allowed me to redirect some of my previous efforts into new areas. I tried my hand at jogging/running, including participating in some 5K, 10K, and 12K "fun runs." I added long-distance bike riding, including participating in a few 100K recreational road races, one 100-mile event, and several biathlons (i.e., biking and running combinations). I prepared for the triathlon by adding swimming; although I never competed solo in a triathlon, I did compete as part of a team.

As life continued, though, I found other forms of satisfaction and success outside of the realm of physical activity and sports. Those activities commanded increasing amounts of my attention and, as a result, physical activity would sometimes be set aside. While I still thought of myself as being physically active on a regular basis, it was often along the lines of: "What is the least amount of physical activity I need to do to stay healthy?" As a result, I rationalized that I needed to jog three to four days per week for thirty to forty-five minutes. My intentions were to do this every other day, but external events, including bad weather, would often squeeze this. My activity pattern became irregular and seasonally sporadic. This changed in 2006.

In December 2005 I was diagnosed with colon cancer. Given my overall lifestyle up to this point, I might well be described as the poster child for someone who should *not* have colon cancer. Yet I had it. As the reality of that settled in, I turned my attention toward the very same things that helped me be successful as an athlete: controlling what I could control, being resilient in the face of adversity, and applying my work ethic to reestablish my regular activity habits (Anshel, 2016; Park & Corn, 2018). A few simple words from an uncle of mine also helped. He said, "Keep moving. If you are moving, the Grim Reaper cannot catch you." Those words stuck with me. I began moving, and I set a goal not to stop.

Earlier in life I often set various performance or outcome athletic goals for myself (e.g., gain eight to ten pounds of lean body mass during a year; improve my strength, speed, and skill); and later in life I set various behavioral goals for myself (e.g., run three days a week for at least thirty minutes each). On the basis of some of my own physical activity research (Cardinal, 1999; Cardinal & Levy, 2000), I also began working toward exercising regularly for five consecutive years. In our work, we found that five years of regular exercise involvement was a characteristic associated with long-term physical activity adherence. There were other characteristics, but this temporal milestone was important. It also made for a nice behavioral target.

As a cancer patient, I also found a new source of motivation. Instead of aiming to exercise three to four days per week, I changed my goal to a daily goal of *at least* sixty minutes of exercise. Following a few failed attempts to sustain this, I am happy to share that between October 1, 2009, and September 14, 2016, I exercised every day for *at least* sixty minutes. That is 2,541 consecutive days—16 days shy of seven full years—*without missing a day*.

No holidays off, no time off for not feeling well, no alibis. Every day, I did exactly what I set out to do. Some of my journey was chronicled in the *Oregonian* (Muldoon, 2019) and in other venues. I also received support from family and friends as well as from students in my classes.

You might be wondering: What happened on Thursday, September 15, 2016? Having somehow acquired a viral infection, I woke up that morning with a high fever, passed out, and was admitted into the emergency room at a local hospital. It took approximately twelve hours before all the diagnostic testing was complete, my fever dropped below the desired threshold, and I was released to go home. I missed exercising that day. But what happened the next day, the two days after that, and every day since is important.

The next day, Friday, September 16, 2016, I did sixty minutes on a treadmill (at a slower-than-usual pace, but I did it). On that day I decided that since I could not change what had happened, I would respond by making up the day I missed. The next two days, Saturday and Sunday, I did ninety minutes each day. Though perhaps physiologically unnecessary and seemingly psychologically obsessive, it was a genuine sense of personal investment that drove me to do this (Raedeke & Burton, 1997). That is, each day of accumulated daily exercise made it increasingly harder for me to give up or stop exercising, which is also consistent with the reinforcement paradigm (Skinner, 1938). In essence, the more the days piled up, the bigger the reason (or excuse) necessary for me to miss would have to be. As of this writing, I have not missed a single day since September 15, 2016. Counting the makeup days mentioned earlier, since October 1, 2009, I have exercised 3,555 consecutive days for at least sixty minutes as of June 24, 2019.

While that pales by comparison to Ron Hill's record streak of 19,032 days (that's fifty-two years and thirty-nine days; Bernstein, 2017), I am still proud of what I am doing. I never set out to compare myself to Hill or anybody else. I am simply doing something that has personal meaning for me. I could stop and restart if I wanted to, and someday maybe I will. In the meantime, I get up each day anticipating another opportunity to invest in my health and well-being, to align my personal values and sense of identity with one another, and to be the person I aspire to be (Anshel, 2008). It brings me a sense of control and peace of mind. It also seems to have inspired others in my life to adopt positive lifestyle behaviors and habits, which further reinforces my own efforts.

Though I do not conscientiously count the days, I do know when my journey toward becoming an everyday exerciser began as well as what has transpired since. Furthermore, as much as I look forward to achieving my ten-year anniversary on September 30, 2019, I also know that each day is a beginning in and of itself.

Take-Home Points

1. Control what you can control (e.g., set behavioral or process goals versus outcome goals).
2. Formulate a self-identity around healthy, active living.
3. We all face adversity in life. Be resilient.

References

Anshel, M. H. (2008). The disconnected values model: Intervention strategies for exercise behavior change. *Journal of Clinical Sport Psychology, 2*, 357–80.

Anshel, M. H. (2016). *In praise of failure: The value of overcoming mistakes in sports and in life*. Lanham, MD: Rowman & Littlefield.

Bernstein, L. (2017, January 30). The longest running streak ever ended Saturday at 19,032 days. *Washington Post*. Retrieved from https://www.washingtonpost.com/news/to-your-health/wp/2017/01/30/the-longest-running-streak-ever-ended-saturday-at-19032-days/?noredirect=on&utm_term=.c119fd0b7824

Cardinal, B. J. (1999). Extended stage model of physical activity behavior. *Journal of Human Movement Studies, 37*, 37–54.

Cardinal, B. J., & Levy, S. S. (2000). Are sedentary behaviors terminable? *Journal of Human Movement Studies, 38*, 137–50.

Muldoon, K. (2019, January 6). Fitness 2014: Oregon State University's Brad Cardinal doesn't miss a day of exercise; you shouldn't either. *Oregonian*. Retrieved from https://www.oregonlive.com/health/2014/01/fitness_2014_oregon_state_univ.html

Park, G. H. M., & Corn, A. A. (2018). Positive psychology. In S. Razon & M. L. Sachs (Eds.), *Applied exercise psychology. The challenging journey from motivation to adherence* (pp. 417–31). New York, NY: Routledge.

Raedeke, T. D., & Burton, D. (1997). Personal investment perspective on leisure-time physical activity participation: Role of incentives, program compatibility, and constraints. *Leisure Sciences, 19*, 209–28.

Skinner, B. F. (1938). *The behavior of organisms: An experimental analysis*. New York, NY: Appleton-Century.

THE GRUPPO CICLISTICO
Jeffrey Cherubini, Manhattan College

Mia, on her fiftieth birthday, had found herself standing outside the YMCA entrance. "Trouble with treacherous treadmills," she humorously bellowed—an inside joke she shared with her trainer and new friends in her early morning group cycling class. She reflected on how things had changed and yet came back full circle. Growing up, Mia was always active, enjoying Sunday morning rides with her grandfather and his Italian cycling club while earning accolades as a three-sport varsity letter winner and All-County Female Athlete of the Year. Coaches, teachers, family, and friends had thought an athletic scholarship was all but assured.

"Has it really been over thirty years?" she thought as she questioned how she had allowed herself to lose touch with her inner athlete. Thoughts about that rogue cyclist, the life-changing crash, the fractured vertebrae, were far less frequent than in years past, but nonetheless still there. "Why was he so reckless?" was a question she had just recently acknowledged would never be answered. Instead, on this morning, Mia found herself reminiscing about the "glory days," her "love for the game," and the fun times she had with former teammates, friends, and, most of all, her grandpa. Her senses came alive when sharing these stories: the smell of grass on her soccer jersey, the sweat in her eyes during basketball practice, the salt on her lips running the track and, of course, the burning quads pushing climbs with her grandpa—she missed it all. Nevertheless, she was back in a good place now.

"Trouble with treacherous treadmills" she continued to muse—a phrase originally coined following a visit to the cardiologist. She often wondered what was more traumatic: that infamous crash in her late teens, the long hours in rehab, the unhealthy weight gain, or the embarrassment of falling off the treadmill during that dreaded stress test. To Mia it was all tied together, with the real stress test coming from the pressures of everyday living: weight gain, chronic back pain, daily fatigue, doctor appointments, responsibilities tied to her son, taking care of her ailing mom, keeping her boss happy, racing everywhere, doing this and doing that. Some days it was all just too much, and her physical activity—or lack thereof—had taken a distant back seat.

But on this day, her fiftieth birthday, a joyous sense of well-being dominated—what her Italian grandpa called his *stare bene*, or, in English, his feel good moments. How she loved those stories, the legendary cycling on the challenging Stelvio in the Alps, the *gruppo ciclistico* (his cycling group), and his fanatical Giro escapades. With all those years of disconnect, she had finally come to realize what he weaved throughout all those magnificent stories, the things that were most important to him, were the same things so valuable to her now: health, happiness, family, and her sense of freedom. The importance of acknowledging this disconnect between values and unhealthy habits, and helping clients develop and follow through on action plans that target this disconnect, is certainly critical to long-term health behavior change (Anshel, 2013).

What helped Mia reconnect? She gives the credit to Sara, her spin instructor and certified trainer. Following the treadmill incident, Mia knew that enough was enough. With the help of her cardiologist and, most of all, Sara, Mia was able to acknowledge and identify the inconsistencies between what was really important to her and her actual actions. This started with Sara helping Mia identify her values and her perceptions of barriers to physical activity as well as the benefits of healthy and unhealthy behaviors. Mia listed all of her personal pros (benefits) and cons (barriers) to being physically active. This activity also helped Mia acknowledge and address her daily thoughts (e.g., "I can never lose the weight") and behaviors (e.g., eating poorly and lack of physical activity). From here, Sara prompted Mia to examine the consistency—or better yet, inconsistency—between her most important values (family responsibilities and health) and her most unhealthy behaviors.

Through this soul searching and her willingness to accept the past and the obvious disconnect, Mia was finally ready to start taking real action. With guidance from Mia's cardiologist, Sara provided a specific individualized action plan in line with Mia's personal values and desired goals. The plan addressed not only the frequency, intensity, time, and type of physical activity desired, but also the when, where, and how specifics of starting a new exercise program. Moving from thoughts to actions, the focus of Sara's attention turned to helping Mia maintain her renewed love for cycling and stay the course with her new exercise regimen.

Enhancing Mia's readiness for change, Sara had created an environment within her cycling studio that was focused on attracting the over-fifty crowd, with an emphasis on riders reconnecting with themselves and each other both on and off the bike. Beauchamp (2019) supports this approach, having used a self-categorization theory perspective to explain how self-identities can be targeted to promote exercise adherence through group-based programming. Furthermore, Stevens, Rees, and Polman (2019) provide evidence suggesting that strong social identities within group exercise settings increase physical activity participation, satisfaction, and overall group cohesion—all leading to greater adherence. The social identities that Mia and her new friends had formed, through Sara's focus on social connectivity, have influenced the groups' attitudes and affiliations toward each other and ultimately their enjoyment and adherence to the morning cycling class. Early morning spin class in the basement of the local YMCA may seem a far cry from the northern Italian mountains her grandpa was riding, but for Mia, she felt profoundly reconnected to an innately familiar life—one filled with daily physical activity and her own *stare bene*. With this, Mia came to realize that she was now a vital member of her own *gruppo ciclistico* and enthusiastically said to her new friends, "Perhaps later we take this ride outside!"

Take-Home Points

1. Review potential disconnects between clients' core values and their unhealthy habits.
2. Develop action plans that acknowledge and identify inconsistencies between values and habits with a focus on enhancing enjoyment, interest, and social connectivity.
3. Target social identification categories, such as age and physical activity interests, when designing group-based physical activity programs.

References

Anshel, M. (2013). A cognitive-behavioral approach for promoting exercise behavior. The Disconnected Values Model. *Journal of Sport Behavior, 36*, 107–29.

Beauchamp, M.R. (2019). Promoting exercise adherence through groups. *Exercise and Sports Sciences Reviews, 47*(1), 54–61. doi: 10.1249/JES.0000000000000177

Stevens, M., Rees, T., & Polman, R. (2019). Social identification, exercise participation, and positive exercise experiences: Evidence from parkrun. *Journal of Sports Sciences, 37*(2), 221–28. doi: 10.1080/02640414.2018.1489360

PERFECT PITCH
John Heil, PhD

The pressures of sport and the drive for success, in tandem with the immediacy and emotion of the moment, can cause perspective to be lost, with adverse consequences on performance during play and on emotion after. The ability to reframe experience, to ground oneself emotionally, and to regain perspective is a great asset, albeit an elusive one. Recovery is more doable during bad times when there is a deep personal reservoir of good times marked by the wonder of sport and a sense of connectedness with those who play it. In turn, this speaks to the function of play and the role of relationships in sports, and their enduring value across time and circumstance

Play is about discovery, intuitive learning, and the enjoyment that comes with it (Huizinga, 1938/2016). It is a foundation of the sport experience. As play morphs into sport, other factors that make sport great—such as commitment, discipline, mastery, and the pursuit of excellence—define and dominate the experience. But pressure, expectation, and the rush to success in competitive sport can cause play to be lost and the value of relationships to be overlooked.

The story told below is of a moment in my backyard. At one level, this is just about a bad play, a missed ball, an error. Why remember it decades later? Because it illuminates the function of play and the role of relationships in sports. Most importantly, it provides a window into my psyche as a seven-year-old, through which I can gaze to reexperience the magic of that moment and refresh my perspective in times of distress and disappointment. What was not so apparent then, but what I have come to appreciate more with the passage of time, is the value of relationships nurtured in the shared experience of sport.

The impetus to write this comes from and is an homage to Donald Hall's (1984) essay on fathers playing catch with sons.

>Howard's perfect pitch struck home, and still resonates within
>Whispering of magic unmasked and wonders in waiting
>This pitch was set in motion long ago when fathers first played catch with sons
>And shared with boys the wisdom of men.
>It arrived long after Howard's career with the Orioles ended
>After he had returned to Virginia to set out on the great quests of life—work and family
>My sport life dawned playing catch, first with my father Earl, then my friend George
>George was a natural pitcher and I, a willing catcher
>To the rhythm of the wind up and the beat of the mitt
>We contemplated the curve ball, our first great mystery of life
>Could an elemental force, like a speeding projectile, bend in its course?
>In the fresh light of the dawn of our lives, we strained our eyes and craned our necks
>As if the answer would be revealed to us, if we looked hard enough
>Sometimes after hours of play, in the fading light of day
>The ball did seem to dance to a different tune
>All the while, Earl listened and watched with a wry sense of pleasure
>
>Howard's and Earl's paths first crossed at the Penn-Dixie Cement Corp.
>Where they shared work, devotion to family, and a passion for sports
>The country boy from Virginia and the city boy from Philadelphia became fast friends,
>And assured that each passing was a memorable occasion
>On one of the days Howard came to town
>Earl would set in motion, with a knowing nod
>The chain of events that would reveal the mystery of the curve ball
>And of the timeless ritual of fathers playing catch with sons
>The stage was set as Howard carefully rubbed the ball and moved instinctively
>To a mounded spot in the yard (an accident of home landscaping)
>I stood in half crouch, eyes wide open, ready, waiting
>As George and Earl watched from the wings
>The pitch glided on a path to my left at the upper corner of the strike zone
>And as I reached for it . . .
>Just inches from my mitt, it stopped and turned abruptly toward me,
>Burying itself, somehow softly, in my belly
>I fell to the ground, breathless, abuzz and amazed
>As Earl and Howard rushed to my aid

Rubbing away the pain
Leaving the wonder to remain

The magic thus revealed was not less profound, but more
To know that, like the perfect pitch
The path of men's lives bends
For the love of their sons
Howard and Earl are gone now
But the game of catch goes on
The perfect pitch still rings clear and true
And catch carries the tune
Of a song that beats in the hearts of men
That echoes through time from father to son
(Recited on National Public Radio, "Morning Edition," WVTF, 2000.)

Ostensibly about baseball, this is a life lesson that has served me well as a parent and a son, as a coach and a sport psychologist, across varied venues, persons, sports, and levels of play.

As the text suggests, it is about my father, Earl Heil; his best friend, Howard Wessels; me, and the best friend of my youth, George Petrie. No doubt this experience also rings true for mothers and sons and for fathers and daughters.

Take-Home Points

1. This story is about an extraordinary moment, in what is otherwise the most ordinary of circumstances. It is about the kind of opportunity that is ubiquitously available in sport to anyone who is open to it and willing to seek it out. It reflects the value in sport that is not bound by natural talent or limited by competitive success.
2. The experience speaks to the wonder of sport and the role of relationships in enabling athletes to survive and thrive in the sometimes harsh world of competitive sport.

References

Hall, D. (1984). *Fathers playing catch with sons: Essays on sport (mostly baseball)*. New York, NY: North Point Press.

Huizinga, J. (1938/2016). *Homo ludens: A study of the play element in culture*. Kettering, OH: Angelico Press.

STAR-SPANGLED SPORT
John Heil, PhD

Colin Kaepernick takes a knee, and then . . . there are bombs bursting in air—metaphorically but nonetheless meaningfully. The intersection of sport and social politics can be provocative, and often is so by design. Historically, this has provided watershed moments, for better (like the entry of Jackie Robinson into professional baseball) or perhaps for worse (like the Los Angeles and Moscow Olympic boycotts).

There is an abundance of reasons to steer clear of politics in psychological intervention. Much of the time this is understood and accepted, but sometimes is unavoidable. The athlete may seek guidance on whether to stand up—or kneel—for a cause. Or the athlete may press the psychologist for an opinion in such a way that not responding seems disingenuous and undermines the relationship. What to do? (Etzel & Skvarla, 2017; Heil, 2016).

Within these United States of America there is nothing that raises as much emotion as "The Star-Spangled Banner," whose playing is intimately intertwined with the sport experience. It is *our* anthem, born amid chaos and conflict. It is at once a symbol of rebellion and a beacon of hope and freedom (Campisi & Willingham, n.d.; Lineberry, 2007). This recent entry of social politics into sport evokes a response much like the arrival of rain on a sunny day, drenching sport with doubt and discord. Athletes, spectators, pundits, and politicians are left grappling with the power and beauty and meaning and purpose of our anthem.

Amid all that is uncertain, it is clear that sport has captured the consciousness of the nation and that sport has the power to influence society. The bigger sport becomes, the bigger its influence, and the more important it is to get it right. At the root of our star-spangled dilemma is passion. Passion is the engine of sport—making it go higher, faster, and stronger, but also making it go meaner, darker, and harsher. When passions collide, conflict follows—creating the potential for crisis, creating the opportunity for change. Like all engines, passion needs direction. Passion stays true to its course when respect is its traveling companion.

R-E-S-P-E-C-T. Diva Aretha Franklin spelled it out as she shouted it out in what is considered one of the greatest R&B songs of all time. It was the 1960s, a period of great conflict and change. This plain and simple message, delivered with great feeling, infused values into troubled times. The word *respect* (derived from the Latin *respectus*) reaches back to the Roman Empire. It means to esteem, to show appreciation, to avoid violation or interference with. It's not about being liked or being right, but is about integrity and fair play. It is the remedy to the greed and arrogance, the self-righteousness and single-mindedness, that can lead sport astray. It mattered to the Roman general Julius Caesar on the battlefield; it mattered to football icon Vince Lombardi on the playing field, and so it should matter to everyone who has a stake in the sport enterprise (Heil, 2005).

Passion comes from within. It can't be given, but it can be cultivated. Passion lives in light and dies in darkness. It will grow and sustain itself if provided the proper environment. But unbridled passion means needless conflict, which tears at the heart of sport, damaging the game and those who play it. Disrespect is to passion as kryptonite is to Superman. Passion is sport's bright side and its dark side. But unlike money, respect can be made available in abundance. It is free to give and invariably well received. Respect is an offer we can't afford to refuse. Passion plus respect is a prescription for times both good and bad. It is a guide that transcends the moment that reaches across race and nation, across the fields of play and fields of conflict.

How to infuse passion with respect? This is the challenge faced by athletes, coaches, and all stakeholders, from the playing field to the boardroom to the living room.

I do not remember the first time or how many times I have heard "The Star-Spangled Banner." While no one has ever had to explain its importance, I feel like I am still discovering its meaning.

Take-Home Points

1. Relationship rises highest and falls most precipitously when facing controversy. As a psychologist, you can't just walk away from the tough stuff. If anyone can bring sense to confounded emotion, it should hopefully be the psychologist.
2. For athletes and coaches, and for sports organizations and spectators, social protest calls upon us to revisit fundamental values and to search for ways to make us better.

References

Campisi, J., & Willingham, A. J. (n.d.). Behind the lyrics of the "Star-Spangled Banner." Retrieved from https://www.cnn.com/interactive/2018/07/us/national-anthem-annotated/

Etzel, E. F., & Skvarla, L. A. (2017, April). Ethical considerations in sport and performance psychology. In *Oxford Research Encyclopedias*. Retrieved from http://oxfordre.com/psychology/view/10.1093/acrefore/9780190236557.001.0001/acrefore-9780190236557-e-141

Heil, J. (2005, spring). Passion+Respect: A Formula for Success. *American Fencing Magazine*, 11. Available at https://oxfordre.com/psychology/abstract

/10.1093/acrefore/9780190236557.001.0001/acrefore-9780190236557-e-141?rskey=5f3Qbo&result=2

Heil, J. (2016). Sport advocacy; Challenge, controversy, ethics and action. *Sport, Exercise, and Performance Psychology, 5*(4), 281–95. Retrieved from http://dx.doi.org/10.1037/spy0000078

Lineberry, C. (2007, March 1). The story behind the Star Spangled Banner. Retrieved from https://www.smithsonianmag.com/history/the-story-behind-the-star-spangled-banner-149220970/

ASK THE KIDS
Rick Howard, MEd, CSCS, *D

This essay illustrates how to set up a fitness program that kids will enjoy and that will increase their desire to be physically active. The kids in this story participate in a program that connects fitness to tennis as part of their after-school tennis training. Kids are assigned into groups using the current United States Tennis Association (USTA) age-matched skill competency breakdown (Cioffi, n.d.), which matches them pretty evenly for fitness level as well. It is critical for these overscheduled aspiring athletes to find balance in their lives and make fitness fun. Burnout and stress are unfortunate consequences of sports. The kids with whom I work were surveyed in school last year and revealed that academics and sports were their key stressors—they were in fifth grade!

I have found that the best way to ensure the kids are having fun is to ask them what fun means to them. The number one reason kids play sports is that it is fun, and the number one reason why they stop is that it no longer is fun (Visek et al., 2015). Our role is to provide kids the ability to solve movement problems so that they become self-determined participants in lifelong physical activity. Including them in the process is a terrific way to increase their motivation, confidence, and competence, key predictors of being active throughout the life course (Kohl & Cook, 2013).

The Story

Kids' lives are completely structured (Hofferth & Sandberg, 2001). While it is important to include structured programming of fundamental movement skills—such as running, catching, rolling, and landing that occur in all three planes of motion, using the foundational movement patterns of hinging, squatting, lunging, pushing, pulling, bracing, and rotating as the basis of their structured exercise program—it is equally important for kids to discover their own movement abilities by giving them guidelines but not specific rules (semistructured play) and opportunities to play with no guidance or rules (free play; Barreiro & Howard, 2017). Too often, we have been taught to promote skills and drills, specific exercise programs in a completely structured setting, but quite often this is the same environment that caused the stress in the first place. Movement mastery occurs from teaching, coaching, cueing, and discovering. We start with small successes and build on them.

When selecting exercises, games, and activities for kids, be sure to figure out how every child can be successful and build on that success. I always start with a game, exercise, or position (yoga tree pose, for example) that I know a child who has not had the chance to be recognized for his or her ability gets to be recognized. I open it up for him or her to select the next game, exercise, or activity, if desired. (Some kids are so unused to getting to choose that they opt to have me help them at first with a recommendation, such as giving them a choice among three activities.) This process involves taking the time to get to know the kids and what their strengths and weaknesses are, but it is very rewarding to see the proud faces of children who have been recognized for their ability. By letting kids choose, you learn what they think is fun, which helps you connect with them, identify their performance competencies, and build on past success.

Another way to ask the kids is to have them bring in games they enjoy with the others. Kids often have their favorite go-to game, which is great, but after several sessions I will ask them to change one dimension or rule of the game to make it different. The kids get very creative with modifications of the game and often alternate between the original version and a modified version. One example is dodgeball, which is not enjoyed by all kids (nor is it permissible in school). Modifications include being able to use exercise mats as shields, using balls of different sizes and textures, and allowing a teammate back in when a ball is caught. The kids figure out differentiated learning all by themselves, have each student play at their comfort level, and provide opportunities for kids to be a team and play more by eliminating elimination.

Asking the kids also means knowing when kids need to be kids. Sometimes the structure of games, exercises, and drills—as fun as they can be—are more than the kids can handle on a given day. Since incorporating free play is so important to kids' overall positive youth development, it is important for youth practitioners to be able to take cues from kids that they need a break. The cues will not always be verbal. They might include not wanting to participate when usually they are active participants. They might be disruptive, talkative at the wrong times, or withdrawn. It is incumbent upon us to be able to recognize the signs that kids need a break and give them time to be kids.

Take-Home Points

1. Make sure kids get to have fun, as they define it. Ask the kids what kinds of games, exercises, and activities they like and give the kids time to do them.
2. Include all three types of play. Kids need structure, but not all the time. Experts recommend that kids spend no more than the number of hours equal to their age at practice and playing sports each week (Jayanthi, Pinkham, Dugas, Patrick, & Labella, 2013). A ten-year-old, therefore, should have structured activity ten hours or fewer per week. That leaves lots of time for unstructured play and semistructured play.
3. Get to know your group so that you can mindfully recognize each and every one throughout the course of your program. Vary the way in which you recognize your kids; you might let them choose the next activity, game, or exercise; suggest how groups are formed for games; or lead a game, activity, or exercise of their choosing.
4. Use these take-home points with adults, too. I recently had a group of senior golfers play hot potato with a medicine ball, changing the distance apart they were, throwing position (nondominant-side rotation, for example), or the weight and texture of the medicine ball. They all had fun, got great exercise, and really let their competitive streaks show.

References

Barreiro, J., & Howard, R. (2017). Incorporating unstructured free play into organized sports. *Strength and Conditioning Journal, 38*(2), 11–19.

Cioffi, R. (n.d.). *Youth tennis progressions*. Retrieved from https://www.usta.com/en/home/play/youth-tennis/programs/southern/10-and-under-youth-tennis-progression.html

Hofferth, S., & Sandberg, J. (2001). How American children spend their time. *Journal of Marriage & Family, 63*(2), 295–308.

Jayanthi, N, Pinkham, C., Dugas, L., Patrick, B., & Labella, C. (2013). Sports specialization in young athletes: Evidence-based recommendations. *Sports Health, 5*(3), 251–57.

Kohl, H. W. III, & Cook, H. D. (2013). *Educating the student body: Physical activity and physical education: Relationship to growth, development, and health. Taking physical activity and physical education to school.* Washington, DC: Committee on Physical Activity and Physical Education in the School Environment; Food and Nutrition Board; Institute of Medicine, National Academies Press.

Visek, A. J., Achrati, S. M., Mannix, H., McDonnell, K., Harris, B. S., & DiPietro, L. (2015). The fun integration theory: toward sustaining children and adolescents sport participation. *Journal of Physical Activity and Health, 12*(3), 424–33.

ONE HOUR AT A TIME
Michael L. Sachs, PhD

John Naber is one of the greatest swimmers in US swimming history, specializing in the backstroke. He is a graduate of the University of Southern California, where he led the Trojans to four consecutive NCAA men's swimming championships. He was undefeated in backstroke in four years of NCAA competition. He is a member of numerous halls of fame and has been active in the Olympic movement, including two terms as president of the US Olympic Alumni Association (Naber, n.d.).

Naber tells a wonderful story that illustrates the epitome of short-, intermediate-, and long-term goal setting. For a quick review, short-term goals focus on today's practice/training/event, perhaps even up to this week's tasks/events. Intermediate-term goals refer to the next six months or so, and long-term goals are beyond that time frame—next year, and five, ten, or twenty years into the future. Not all such types of goals are relevant for all individuals in all parts of their lives, of course, but all matter to some extent.

In terms of purpose, short-term goals give us the direction and focus needed for our efforts to be successful today, tomorrow, and this week. That intense focus can keep motivation high and provide regular reinforcement when we achieve these goals. Intermediate-term goals set the stage for our efforts for the next few months, with a blueprint laid down that builds upon the short-term goals we are accomplishing on a regular basis. Finally, long-term goals are that beacon we are striving for and will ideally reach in the longer term. Within performance settings, ideally our short- and intermediate-term goals are challenging yet attainable, providing the motivation to continue striving on a regular basis toward our long-term goals (Roberts & Kristiansen, 2013).

Drawing upon the old Chinese saying, "A journey of a thousand miles begins with a single step," as we progress from short-term goals to long-term goals it may be helpful to use the metaphor of a staircase or a ladder (Gould, 2015). As you will see below, Naber offers a perfect example of the staircase method—4,800 steps from the bottom (59.9, but let's say 59.5 for argument's sake) to the top (55.5 and hopefully Olympic gold), with each step representing an improvement of 1/1200 of a second. Naber was watching the Summer Olympics in 1972 and focusing on the swimming events, especially his specialty stroke—backstroke. He tells this superlative story about goal setting:

> My personal best in the 100 back was 59.9. Roland Matthes, winning the same event for the second consecutive Olympics (1972), went 56.3. I extrapolated his, you know, three Olympic performances and I figured in 1976, 55.5 would have been the order of the day. That's what I figured I would have to do. So I'm four seconds off the shortest backstroke event on the Olympic program. It's the equivalent of dropping four seconds in the 440 yard dash. It's a substantial chunk. But because it's a goal, now I can decisively figure out how I can attack that. I have four years to do it in. I'm watching TV in 1972. I've got four years to train. So it's only one second a year. That's still a substantial chunk. Swimmers train ten or eleven months a year so it's about a tenth of a second a month, giving time off for missed workouts. And you figure we train six days a week so it's only about 1/300th of a second a day. We train from six to eight in the morning and four to six at night so it's really only about 1/1200th of a second every hour. Do you know how short a 1200th of a second is? Look at my hand and blink when I snap, would you please? OK, from the time when your eyelids started to close to the time they touched, five 1200th of a second elapsed. For me to stand on a pool deck and say, "During the next 60 minutes I'm going to improve that much," that's a believable dream. I can believe in myself. I can't believe that I'm going to drop four seconds by the next Olympics. But I can believe I can get that much faster. Couldn't you? Sure. So all of a sudden I'm moving. (Sport Medicine, n.d.)

Naber wound up winning gold medals in four events at the 1976 Olympics in Montreal, all in world record time. He achieved his long-term goal in the 100m by swimming 55.49, a world record that stood for seven years. He compiled a book including stories from "America's greatest Olympic motivators" (Naber, 1999) and is now a sports broadcaster and motivational speaker.

Take-Home Points

1. Use short-, intermediate-, and long-term goals as part of your goal setting process.
2. Work with a coach, teammate, friend, or sport psychologist to ensure that your goals are challenging but attainable for you at all three levels (short-, intermediate-, and long-term).
3. Review your goals regularly and revise them as needed.

References

Gould, D. (2015). Goal setting for peak performance. In J. M. Williams & V. Krane (Eds.), *Applied sport psychology: Personal growth to peak performance* (7th ed.) (pp. 188–206). New York, NY: McGraw-Hill.

Naber, J. (n.d.) John Naber website. Retrieved from http://www.johnnaber.com

Naber, J. (1999). No deposit, no return. In J. Naber (Ed.), *Awaken the Olympian within* (pp. 54–63). Torrance, CA: Griffin Publishing Group.

Roberts, G. C., & Kristiansen, E. (2013). Motivation and goal setting. In S. J. Hanrahan & M. B. Andersen (Eds.), *Routledge handbook of applied sport psychology* (pp. 490–99). London, UK: Routledge/Taylor & Francis.

Sport Medicine & Science Council of Saskatchewan. (n.d.). Goal setting. Retrieved from: http://www.smscs.dreamhosters.com/wp-content/uploads/2016/01/goalsetting.pdf

UH-OH, WE HAVE A RINGER...
Michael L. Sachs, PhD

It was a lovely Thursday evening in Tallahassee, Florida, in early August 1978. The Gulf Winds Track Club was having one of its all-comers meets, wherein anyone could come and compete in various track events, which differed each week and ranged from 100 meters to two miles. This evening featured the two-mile race.

I competed regularly, just to see how I would do on the track and check my speed (alas, never fast). I could hold about a six-minute pace for a 10,000m road race (almost all my races were on the roads or trails), and thought a nice performance goal for this evening would be a sub-six-minute average for the two miles, perhaps 11:50 or so. Looking around as we got up to start the race, however, I recognized most of the runners there, friends or acquaintances from the local running community, and realized I was about as fast (or slow) as they were. I immediately thought about an outcome goal of actually winning the race or at least placing in the top three.

Outcome goals are, of course, not in our control, and so are preferably not recommended, but performance goals are in our control, and I thought achieving my performance goal might lead to a nice outcome. Alas, just before the race was about to begin, the starter said, "Hold up a second; we have another runner." We looked around and saw, across the track, another runner indeed, striding across the field to the starting line. I saw who it was and immediately recalibrated my outcome goal. One must be flexible, especially when it comes to outcome goals (Gould, 2015; Roberts & Kristiansen, 2013).

The runner striding across the field to the starting line was Ken Misner, a former All-American runner from Florida State University (where I was pursuing my PhD). He looked like an elite runner—wiry, with just the perfect musculature for a distance runner—and was wearing only shorts, no T-shirt and no running shoes (barefoot). I immediately realized that winning the race was totally inconceivable, and the question became how many times I would be lapped in a two-mile race (pretty embarrassing). Ken's personal record for the two-mile was about 8:50, which meant I would be finishing up a mile and a half while he finished the race. I would be close to finishing lap 6 while he was finishing lap 8, so there was the potential that I would be lapped three times. I recalibrated my outcome goal to finish in the top three, ditching the outcome goal of winning the race, but added a performance goal of not getting lapped more than twice.

I am pleased to report that Ken was thundering down the home stretch to finish the two miles as I passed the starting line finishing lap 6, so I did not get passed three times (only twice; still a humbling experience). The years have erased the memory of my finishing time and place, but not the memory of Ken's beautiful stride across the field and the elite runner lined up next to us at the starting line. That is one of the beauties of road races (and the occasional local track meet)—you can start a race with a world record holder/champion/All-American and potentially win if you are fast enough. We don't get to compete against the elite in tennis or golf or basketball, but in running we can.

In the end, the performance goals (and the process goals that get us there), are still key, but having flexibility for both performance and outcome goals is critical. If the summer rains had come and made the environmental conditions miserable, I would have had to adjust my performance goal for a slower time. But the weather was great, so I kept my performance goal intact. Just the competition changed, and so the outcome (at least as far as potentially winning the race) had to be adjusted. But in my dreams . . .

Take-Home Points

1. Use performance goals and process goals as part of your goal-setting process.
2. Use outcome goals if you need to, but be prepared to adjust them as called for in given situations.
3. Review your goals regularly and revise them as needed

References

Gould, D. (2015). Goal setting for peak performance. In J. M. Williams & V. Krane (Eds.), *Applied sport psychology: Personal growth to peak performance* (7th ed.) (pp. 188–206). New York, NY: McGraw-Hill.

Roberts, G. C., & Kristiansen, E. (2013). Motivation and goal setting. In S. J. Hanrahan & M. B. Andersen (Eds.), *Routledge handbook of applied sport psychology* (pp. 490–99). London: Routledge/Taylor & Francis.

VALUING PHYSICAL ACTIVITY/EXERCISE
Michael L. Sachs, PhD

Most individuals will say that physical activity is a good thing—it is important to be physically active to do all the things we want to do in life. However, when it comes to exercise, occasionally it is seen as a "four-letter word" (Ciaccio & Sachs, 2018). Exercise is interpreted as running a marathon or some such lofty endeavor. In reality, however, exercise is more a focused attempt at a regular program of physical activity, which is what we want people to be doing. Physical activity is great, but can be more "random," such as cleaning the house, gardening, walking the dog, and so on. What's important is getting people to be more physically active on a regular basis.

Thus, determining whether people value physical activity (and other positive health behaviors) is an essential starting point. Most will say yes. These positive health values may include eating right, not drinking (too much), not using drugs, getting enough sleep/rest, and so on. For example, I worked with Jim, a forty-four-year-old lawyer in Philadelphia who indicated these were indeed his values. However, he also noted the morbid old joke about heart attacks for lawyers—if you haven't had a heart attack by the time you are forty, you aren't working hard enough. The idea is that working so hard means not getting any exercise, not eating right, working long hours, toiling in a high stress environment, and so on.

Fortunately, Jim had failed the heart attack test, but he was overweight and very out of shape. He had found he couldn't keep up with his wife, Maria, and his two children, Lauren and Selen, without getting overly tired. This was a perfect situation to present the Disconnected Values Model, developed by Anshel (2008; Cherubini & Anshel, 2018). Anshel proposed a process that begins with identifying one's values, such as engaging in regular physical activity, eating right, and so on, and then involves examining how these values align—or, more often, do not align—with one's actual behavior. One then decides if there is a desire to have a connection between one's values and one's behaviors. If so, then behavioral strategies are implemented to do so. A decisional balance scale is helpful in this regard, weighing the pros and cons of changing the various behaviors (Berger, Weinberg, & Eklund, 2015). In the end, the aim is to prepare the client to decide that the scales be tipped toward making the changes (e.g., more physical activity, eating better, and so on).

Jim and I went through this process, and Jim decided he did want to align his values with his behavior. This was great news for Jim and his family. No more walking time bomb—hopefully. We started with a walk around the block and progressed to walking thirty minutes a day when he came home from work, before dinner, sometimes with Lauren and/or Selen accompanying him to talk about their days. Jim also wanted to do some strength training, so I made a referral to a personal trainer to evaluate Jim's strength and flexibility and work with him on developing a plan that would work for his busy schedule. The local Planet Fitness was a cost-effective fitness facility open twenty-four hours a day that fit perfectly into Jim's schedule. This was all encompassed within setting short-, medium-, and long-term goals for Jim's health and well-being (Weinberg & Gould, 2015). Starting with the short-term goal of walking around the block allowed us to progress to the medium-term goal of thirty minutes of walking and also develop a long-term goal of running some local 5K road races with Lauren and Selen.

I also referred Jim to a registered dietitian to develop a healthier eating plan, especially for those work lunches at his law firm. He was already eating fairly well at home (Maria was knowledgeable about nutrition and prepared healthy, nutritious meals at home), but we also reduced the snack items available and substituted healthier snacks at home with the support and encouragement of Maria, Lauren, and Selen.

The process was not without its ebbs and flows. As we have learned from the Transtheoretical Model of Behavior Change (Cardinal, 1997), relapse to earlier stages of behavior is not uncommon. Jim had progressed from precontemplation (not even thinking about making any changes) to contemplation (thinking about making changes once he saw he was not keeping up with

Lauren and Selen). Then came preparation: contacting me and making an appointment to talk. Jim was ready and moved to action. However, action occasionally took a hiatus (e.g., relapse), with occasional ebbs of inactivity and poor eating every so often associated with work pressures. However, after six months and additional consultations, Jim could see not only how he was sabotaging himself but also the benefits he was getting from the behavior changes in which he was engaged, and finally stuck with it (exercise adherence, as we call it). After six months of action, Jim moved on to maintenance. He was regularly exercising and was even talking about starting to run a bit and maybe participating in a local 5K race or two with Lauren and Selen, who were both excellent runners (his long-term goal). Now, two years later, Jim has continued to eat well and exercise regularly and is doing great!

Take-Home Points

1. Assessing one's values about physical activity and other healthy lifestyle factors is a useful process.
2. Deciding if these values align with one's behaviors is critical in developing self-awareness and establishing motivation for change.
3. Going through a process of evaluation and then change takes time, but can be achieved if the motivation is there.

References

Anshel, M. H. (2008). The Disconnected Values Model: Intervention strategies for health behavior change. *Journal of Clinical Sport Psychology*, 2, 357–80.

Berger, B. G., Weinberg, R. S., & Eklund, R. C. (2015). *Foundations of exercise psychology* (3rd ed.). Morgantown, WV: Fitness Information Technology.

Cardinal, B. J. (1997). Predicting exercise behavior using components of the transtheoretical model of behavior change. *Journal of Sport Behavior*, 20(3), 272–83.

Cherubini, J., & Anshel, M. H. (2018). Alternative models of health behavior change. In S. Razon & M. L. Sachs (Eds.), *Applied exercise psychology: The challenging journey from motivation to adherence* (pp. 49–65). New York: Routledge.

Ciaccio, J. B., & Sachs, M. L. (2018). A rose by any other name . . . In S. Razon & M. L. Sachs (Eds.), *Applied exercise psychology: The challenging journey from motivation to adherence* (pp. 15–19). New York: Routledge.

Weinberg, R. S., & Gould, D. (2015). *Foundations of sport and exercise psychology* (6th ed.). Champaign, IL: Human Kinetics.

Chapter Three

Identity and Transitions

Exercise Identity, Athletic Identity, Transitions, and Self-Awareness

Those who participate in exercise and sport have some element of their identity tied into athletic identity and/or exercise identity. With athletic identity, one part of one's being (in many cases, a large part) is connected with being an athlete. Similarly, those who exercise regularly have part of their identity tied into being an exerciser in general or in a specific type of exercise (e.g., a runner, a swimmer). Athletes and exercisers go through various transition periods. For example, many athletes transition from being an athlete in their mind (for example, an intercollegiate athlete or a professional one) to either a nonparticipant (unfortunately) or, hopefully, to being an exerciser. This transition from an athletic identity to an exercise identity is fraught with challenges, and not everyone navigates this journey successfully. In the realm of exercise, individuals who are striving to exercise regularly can benefit from transitioning to a strong exercise identity (e.g., "I run, so I'm a runner"). The development of self-awareness can assist in understanding one's identity as well as making transitions smoothly and effectively when needed.

Bassey Akpan wonderfully describes the transition from athletic identity to exercise identity through CrossFit. Arna Erega talks eloquently about her transition from her role as an athlete to her postathletic career. Shaya Schaedler reviews her own transition from athletic identity as a swimmer to a multidimensional identity set. Alexandra Szarabajko notes her transition from an athletic career to incorporating other identities, such as being a professional in exercise and sport psychology. Joann Wakefield talks about her transition from collegiate swimming to her postcollegiate identities. Diana Wildermuth address the lacrosse world and the transition of an elite lacrosse player to postcompetitive existence. Taylor Wise discusses Jane's transition from an athletic identity to developing and embracing multiple identities beyond those of being an athlete. Derek Zike and Monna Arvinen-Barrow poignantly discuss Zike's transition from athletic identity as a hockey player to a postathletic identity, due to a spinal cord injury, as a professional in exercise and sport psychology.

EMBRACING CHANGE
Bassey Akpan

As individuals, we engage in many roles that require us to take on numerous identities: for example, athlete, teacher, student, bank teller, and so on. But what does it mean for those whose composite is that of a student-athlete? At face value, these are students obtaining an education while simultaneously playing a varsity sport. But so much more goes into that identity. I was a student-athlete in high school, where I competed in cross country and the 800m for track and field. Brewer, Van Raalte, and Linder (1993) define athletic identity as the degree to which an athlete identifies with the athlete role. In my case, I took proud ownership of my identity as an athlete and loved to be acknowledged as such. However, as I would soon experience, the time came to address the phenomenon of retirement from competitive sport, whether involuntarily (e.g., injury) or voluntarily (e.g., graduation). Student-athletes are vulnerable to adjustment problems as well as emotional and psychological distress, all of which can impact how well they transition to life beyond competitive sports (Kissinger, Newman, Miller, & Nadler, 2011). My own athletic career required adjustments early on due to knee injuries. For the countless student-athletes in these predicaments, the question then becomes, "So what now?"

Schlossberg (1981) defines transition as "an event or non-event that results in a change in assumptions about oneself and the world and thus requires a corresponding change in one's behavior and relationships" (p. 4). Transition can be a particularly difficult process for athletes who dedicate a significant amount of time and energy to their sport. I loved to run, and involuntarily giving it up competitively due to graduation and lingering injuries was difficult. Like many athletes, my identity was still intertwined with sports. To compensate for the loss of competitive running, I began to delve into other activities that allowed me to strengthen other identities while maintaining a certain level of physicality. Gradually, my athletic identity transitioned into an exercise identity. Anderson and Cychosz (1994) define exercise identity as when an individual's self-concept includes an emphasis on previous exercise behavior and allows this self-concept to direct future exercise behavior. Much like this definition describes, I started off by going to fitness boot camps and classes at the gym. Then I discovered CrossFit and found that it provided me feelings to what I had experienced when I was part of an athletic team. There was challenge, hard work, sweat, complaints about the workout of the day (WOD), a sense of accomplishment, and, most importantly, fun! Exercising in groups through CrossFit has helped me retain one of my many salient identities. When I transitioned out of competitive sport, what I missed the most was the relationships I had cultivated from being an athlete. It was difficult for me to find that feeling of connectedness solely by going to the gym. Along with its other benefits, CrossFit provided an approachable, close-knit community of individuals who liked challenges and competing as much as I do.

Much as Schlossberg (1981) defined transition, events may invoke adaptation to a new role or behavior. Just as each race is different, each transition experience is different. Where one person may have an easier adjustment to life after competitive sport, another may struggle. One of the best pieces of advice I received when running was "Run the mile you are in," which applied not only to my races but also to life in general. It helped me to focus on my running and push through any rough patches I may have encountered during a race. I adapted through my transition from sport and was able to keep the athlete inside of me thriving with alternative forms of exercise.

Take-Home Points

1. Identity is fluid, not fixed, despite how strongly you may associate with a specific identity; discover your interests to establish how you view yourself beyond competitive sport.
2. Remember that transition can be difficult and there are people (e.g., sport psychologists, coaches, friends) who can provide support. You are not alone.
3. Run the mile you are in. Establishing an exercise identity through CrossFit was helpful for my process; however, not everyone enjoys CrossFit. Figure out what works best for you and do that.

References

Anderson, D. F., & Cychosz, C. M. (1994). Development of an exercise identity scale. *Perceptual and Motor Skills*, *78*, 747–51.

Brewer, B. W., Van Raalte, J. L., & Linder, D. E. (1993). Athletic identity: Hercules' muscles or Achilles heel? *International Journal of Sport Psychology*, *24*, 237–54.

Kissinger, D. B., Newman, R., Miller, M. T., & Nadler, D. P. (2011). Athletic identity of community college student athletes: Issues for counseling. *Community College Journal of Research and Practice*, *35*, 574–89.

Schlossberg, N. K. (1981). A model for analyzing human adaptation to transition. *Counseling Psychologist*, *9*, 2–18.

HOW MY ATHLETIC ROLE AFFECTED MY IDENTITY
Arna Erega, MA, LPC

Athletic identity forms at an early age, and, as Brewer, Van Raalte, and Linder (1993) define it, is the degree to which athletes identify with their athletic role. An identity can be reinforced when it is activated through repeated interaction with others (Menke & Germany, 2019). Often people recognize athletic talent very early in life (Heird & Steinfeldt, 2013), when they receive reinforcement for their talents and success from people surrounding them, including parents, coaches, peers, teammates, and so on (Menke & Germany, 2019). Conceptualization of athletic identity comes in the form of cognitive structure and a social role (Heird & Steinfeldt, 2013). Cognitive structure of athletic identity helps identify how an individual interprets information, copes with various situations, and supports behavior that is consistent with one's athletic role (Heird & Steinfeldt, 2013; Menke & Germany, 2019). Social role, on the other hand, involves receiving support from people around the athletes in the form of their perceptions, which continue to emphasize the athletic dimension (Heird & Steinfeldt, 2013). The more the athletic role is strengthened, the more one continues to identify with the athletic role, thus strengthening the athletic identity in his or her self-concept (Heird & Steinfeldt, 2013).

I was a Croatian hurdler who earned a full athletic scholarship at a Division I midwestern university in the United States. At the time, I was a multiple

Croatian national record holder in the 60m hurdles and 100m hurdles and ran exceptional results for my age categories, which earned me performances in four European Championships, four World Championships, and the European Youth Olympic Games. I ran the best time in the world for fourteen-year-old girls in the 100m hurdles in 2003, a record that stood for eleven years. I also contributed to winning a conference championship and made it through NCAA regionals. After graduation, I pursued my childhood dream of competing in the Olympics.

From a very young age, I was involved in sports and have been very successful. From the athletic identity standpoint, I was aware of my talents, which were reinforced by my coaches and my parents. I also enjoyed attention from the press every time I won a major race or ran an exceptional result. Peers, teammates, and other athletes always asked me questions about my training and diet and how was I able to make such great progress, which all contributed to the social role of athletic identity and further fed into my cognitive structure that was developing internally at the same time.

From the cognitive structure standpoint, I was very focused. Although hyperactive early on in life, I found track and field as an outlet for my extra energy. Growing up, I maintained my focus on making it to the Olympics one day, but also focused on earning a track scholarship at a US university. I understood that a key step to make it to the Olympics one day was to compete at the collegiate level in a Division I university in the United States. During my high school years, I maintained my hyperfocus on athletics and chose to engage only in things that would help me be a better athlete, while eschewing typical teenage activities such as socializing and recreation. I maintained a healthy diet and was very conscious of my food choices, never indulging in fast food meals, unlike my friends, who didn't care as much about what they ate and how it affected their bodies. I followed a strict training regimen, often training twice a day before and after school, which limited the time I could spend with my friends. I devoted myself to honing my skills by watching training videos and studying my craft, while my classmates and friends hung out or engaged in other fun activities. I looked at every life situation through the lens of an elite athlete and prioritized what I needed to do to maintain that status.

Later on, upon graduating college and preparing for the 2012 London Olympics, I suffered an ankle injury that resulted in surgery, forcing me to miss the trials and therefore missing the opportunity to make my first Olympic team. I was devastated and had difficulty adjusting to my new reality, suffering from depression as a result. For about six months I withdrew into myself. I questioned who I was, as I had spent my entire life focusing on track and being the best athlete I could be and neglected to develop other aspects of my self-concept while growing up. During this period, I only attended classes and did just enough work to get by. I felt sorry for myself. However, after a while I slowly talked myself back to my regular routine. I knew the time was coming to start offseason training and that next year would be a new year. I spent a few months grieving the lost opportunity and was ready to stop feeling pity for myself and get back to work, because that was what I knew how to do best. I started to implement several mental strategies. First, I would remind myself daily that getting back into racing shape is a process and I had to take it one day at a time. Second, in order to avoid getting frustrated and putting too much pressure on myself, I evaluated each practice by focusing on and jotting down what went well and what I would work on during the next practice. This approach helped me maintain a positive attitude even during the bad days. I was not ready to compete in 2013; however, I did return to the normal training schedule I had before my surgery in the summer of 2012. I was back competing in the 2014 indoor season, running the times that were not too far off of my personal best. At the end of the summer of 2015, I decided to retire from professional running and focus on advancing my professional career by pursuing graduate school full time.

Development of athletic identity starts early and is easily reinforced in children who show athletic talent (Heird & Steinfeldt, 2013). Athletes who identify strongly with their athlete role may do so at the expense of other dimensions of their self-concept, which may affect them negatively later on in life, causing them to have a more challenging time coping with issues (Heird & Steinfeldt, 2013). Developing an athletic identity is not an issue. In the face of failure, injury, or an abrupt ending to one's athletic career, we may raise concerns if one experiences psychological distress due to strong identification with the athletic role (Carter, 2009; Heird & Steinfeldt, 2013). In situations when all one wants to do is be an athlete, we must consider that even the most fruitful of careers will eventually end, necessitating the transition out of an athlete role into a different one.

Take-Home Points

1. Assess how strongly athletes identify with their athletic identity and assist them in identifying how the athletic identity may play a role in other domains of their lives.
2. Assist athletes in identifying skills they can use to help them cope as they are dealing with injury and failure.
3. When athletes are transitioning out of sport, assist them in recognizing how they can utilize their athletic skills as they begin or continue to build on dimensions of self-concept that are not directly related to athletics.

References

Brewer, B. W., Van Raalte, J., & Linder, D. E. (1993). Athletic identity: Hercules' muscles or Achilles heel? *International Journal of Sport Psychology, 24*, 237–54.

Carter, J. E. (2009). Disordered eating in college student-athletes. In E. F. Etzel, A. P. Ferrante, & J. W. Pinkey (Eds.), *Counseling college student-athletes: Issues and interventions* (2nd ed., pp. 303–22). Morgantown, WV: Fitness Information Technology.

Heird, E. B., & Steinfeldt, J. A. (2013). An interpersonal psychotherapy approach to counseling student athletes: Clinical implications of athletic identity. *Journal of College Counseling, 16*(2), 143–57. doi: 10.1002/j.2161-1882.2013.00033.x

Menke, D. J., & Germany, M. (2019). Reconstructing athletic identity: College athletes and sport retirement. *Journal of Loss and Trauma, 24*, 17–30. doi:10.1080/15325024.2018.1522475

WHO AM I AFTER EVERYTHING IS SAID AND DONE?
Shaya Schaedler, MEd

"I am a swimmer." After swimming competitively from the age of six, earning multiple All-American honors and obtaining a full-ride athletic scholarship to a Division I university in the Pac-12 Conference, "I am a swimmer" was the only thing I could say about myself. It was true until right before my senior year of swimming in college. I remember how earth shattering it felt when my coach told me he would no longer coach me moving forward. I remember feeling all of my goals slipping from my fingertips. I remember looking at the assistant athletic director, who asked me, "Who are you if you aren't a swimmer?" My only answer was, "I don't know." Since I was six years old, I had been a competitive athlete. Since I was six years old, I was told my future depended on swimming—and I believed that. Since I was six years old, I dreamed of becoming am NCAA champion. At twenty-one years old, and through no choice of my own, I realized I would never live my dreams. I was utterly lost.

As a child, adolescent, and young adult, my athletic identity enabled me to succeed. Identifying as a swimmer first and foremost allowed me to stay committed to practicing through the grueling hours and to maintain my confidence through setbacks, injuries, and self-doubt. My athletic identity kept me on task and moving forward because, despite the unpredictability of life, "I am a swimmer" *always* rang true. However, in having my athletic identity be my only identity, I felt that I had nowhere to go and nothing to offer without it. For many, athletic identity defines who we are and everything we are. On the one hand, while this identity can bring success in our sports, this same unidimensional identity can lead to difficulty in transitioning out of sport and to feelings of confusion surrounding a new role and identity in the world (Crook & Robertson, 1991).

Because of this exclusive athletic identity, many athletes fail to recognize the skills they have developed through athletics as being valuable to other settings and careers (McKnight et al., 2009). Transferrable skills are not about specifics. They are often abstract concepts. Common life skills developed through athletics include time management, adaptability, ability to meet deadlines, and perseverance, which are invaluable in most settings. Unfortunately, most athletes do not recognize these capabilities as transferrable skills (Danish, Petitpas, & Hale, 1993).

When my athletic career ended, I did not understand how much of it could be salient to other careers. As I quickly found out during my first panel interview for graduate school, I was able to draw from my athletic experience when asked how I would best overcome adversity. In that moment, I realized that moving forward was far less about the specific skills I was lacking but believed I so desperately needed to continue my education, and far more about my ability to work hard and remain resilient in the face of adversity, which my lifetime of swimming had prepared me to do easily. This seemingly small revelation opened the door for developing confidence in myself and my skills outside of the world of athletics.

Learning to move away from an athletic identity can be hard. As athletes, we are often trained to be tough, and we may internalize help-seeking behavior as a weakness. Feeling this way, combined with a potential loss of a previous support system of teammates and coaches, can lead to feelings of isolation and loneliness (McKnight et al., 2009). Identifying and recognizing support systems such as family, significant others, friends, and retired athletes can ease transitions for athletes. Furthermore, counselors and sport psychologists are trained to help with life transitions, and career-counseling services are available as a support system to athletes (McKnight et al., 2009). Counselors and psychologists have access to many resources and tools to explore potential careers while providing a safe, nonjudgmental space to process the complicated emotions that are commonly experienced with identity loss and life transitions. Using support systems is not a sign of weakness; rather, it is a sign that we are able to recognize that we need help sometimes. Seeking help provides the opportunity to continue to grow and learn from others and to develop better, healthier lives.

Transitioning out of athletics can feel devastating, like giving up everything that has brought success, confidence, and pride. But at the end of the day, athletic identity is only one aspect of ourselves. We are not one dimensional. We are all also friends, brothers, sisters, students, innovators, creators, professionals, activists, and endless other identities and roles unique to each of us. When our athletic careers are done and gone, we are not also done and gone. We simply must allow our other identities to become more salient. The athlete part of our identities does not leave us. Instead, we can adapt our athletic identity into our future work. Many of the skills and abilities we learn through our athletic careers—such as timeliness, tenacity, and the ability to perform under pressure—are invaluable to other career paths. The first steps are to bring these skills to active awareness, to recognize them as transferrable, and to allow confidence in our capabilities. Overall, developing a multidimensional identity, understanding that skills learned and applied in athletics are transferable to new areas, and using support systems can help ease the pain of transitioning out of sports. At the end of the day, when everything is said and done, you are still you and that will never change. Embrace yourself and all that you have to offer.

Take-Home Points

1. Recognize that your athletic identity is only one part of you, not all of you.
2. Identify strengths, skills, and abilities developed through athletics that are valuable to other career paths.
3. Utilize your support systems. Remember that transitioning out of athletics can be difficult for any athlete and that you are not alone. Work with a counselor or sport psychologist if you are having trouble transitioning.

References

Crook, J. M., & Robertson, S. E. (1991). Transitions out of elite sport. *International Journal of Sport Psychology, 22*(2), 128–53.

Danish, S. J., Petitpas, A. J., & Hale, B. D. (1993). Life development interventions for athletes: Life skills through sports. *Counseling Psychologist, 22*(3), 352–85.

McKnight, K. M., Bernes, K. B., Gunn, T., Chorney, D., Orr, D. T., & Bardick, A. D. (2009). Life after sport: Athletic career transitions and transferable skills. *Journal of Excellence, 13*, 63–77.

LIFE BEYOND SPORT
Alexandra Szarabajko

For fifteen years of my life, I identified myself as a student-athlete. At the age of ten, I was first introduced to track and field at a sports club in Germany. The sport brought me fun and joy, and it pushed me to my limits. The older I got, the more structured my life around track and field became. All I knew was eat, school, practice, sleep, and repeat—and I enjoyed doing it. The social, emotional, and physical sacrifices I made for my sport eventually paid off when I accepted an athletic scholarship offer from a Division I university in the United States. As an international student in the United States, I was first worried about not being able to fit in; however, my doubt was quickly removed when I met my new teammates. I was able to connect with them and other college athletes on campus due to one thing we had in common: We were all student-athletes. The companionship I experienced by being a part of this in-group on campus helped me successfully transition into being a part of the university and local community more broadly. I was not an international student exclusively, but rather an international student-athlete. There was a certain amount of pride associated with that.

That said, while in college, I slowly started thinking about my future after graduation. Knowing that I was not going to earn a fortune from sprinting and jumping and that I was not going to compete at a professional level forever, I started to discover interests beyond my sport. One of the first courses I fell in love with was psychology. A light bulb went off when I heard about the field of sport psychology. I began researching information regarding this career path, as well as using the information I was learning to help me perform better (e.g., psychological skills). My passion for something other than my sport began to grow, and experiencing success in both increased my self-confidence. By the time I graduated, I had acquired academic skills and I was determined to pursue a graduate degree related to sport psychology. Fortunately, I was offered a graduate assistant position at the same university and I felt excited about this new transition.

However, my initial excitement dissipated during my first week of graduate school. I was asked to introduce myself to my new cohort, and it felt strange not being able to call myself a student-athlete anymore. That same day, I walked past the track and watched my former teammates practicing from afar, wishing I was doing the same workouts I once had dreaded so much. Though I was not missing having to adhere to rigorous practice schedules, I did miss having a structured day and being a part of the team. Suddenly, I had too much time to spare, and this was the point where the void of not having my sport hit me—I felt as if part of my identity was lost.

The experience of identity loss in athletes after ending a career and transitioning into a new profession outside of their sport can be both disorienting and traumatic. While most athletes report a successful transition out of their sport, an estimated 20 percent of retired athletes report feelings of distress (Lavallee, Nesti, Borkoles, Cockerill, & Edge, 2000). The severity of the distress depends on one's athletic identity, which is the extent to which one's personal identity has been linked to sport. The stronger one's athletic identity and commitment to sport, the greater the risk for emotional difficulties when ending an athletic career (Brewer, Van Raalte, & Linder, 1993).

I experienced different stages of grief throughout my transition. At the beginning, I refused to accept the loss of my athletic identity and I was determined to continue to practice with my former teammates whenever my schedule would allow me to. Although my teammates supported my staying and training with them, I struggled to find meaning in doing the tough workouts without a goal. The times of trying to qualify for a conference championship were over, and practicing track for the sole purpose of feeling a sense of belonging was not entirely satisfying. Practicing with my teammates did not help me to maintain my athletic identity, and this realization in turn increased my grief. The feeling was so severe that I decided to avoid the track for months, because I had trouble coping with my emotions.

Overcoming these emotions was not an easy task. However, developing another identity as a student alongside my identity as an athlete helped me in my transition. I recognized that the skills I learned through my sport, such as determination, motivation, performing under pressure, and teamwork, were transferrable and desirable for my emerging professional interests. Thus, I devoted my time and energy to my professional development. Additionally, instead of distancing myself from sports completely, I expanded my horizon and discovered other activities that brought me joy. I joined an intramural ultimate frisbee team, played tennis and volleyball with friends, and took exercise courses at the recreation center. My love for sport turned into a love to exercise, and my curiosity about other activities grew. Being aware of the strengths that transferred into other areas and developing new exercise interests helped me in my personal transition from student-athlete to physically active graduate student.

It is important to educate athletes about sport career retirement and the potential emotional roller-coaster that might be experienced going through similar transitioning processes (Brooks, Reifsteck, Powell, & Gill, 2019). Slowly diminishing the athletic identity and supporting athletes in developing a wide range of skills and coping strategies will aid them in making a successful transition after sport.

Today I identify myself as a graduate student who is pursuing a doctoral degree in psychosocial kinesiology and a master's degree in public health. I continue to use the skills I learned from my time as a student-athlete and aspire to having a career as an educator and researcher whose goal is to motivate others to enhance their psychological and physiological health through physical activity.

Take-Home Points

1. Do not commit exclusively to your identity as an athlete: Be aware of your other roles and expand your horizons.
2. Discover interests, skills, and activities beyond your sport.
3. Be aware of the qualities you have gained through the sport and how you could transfer them into a different career.

References

Brewer, B. W., Van Raalte, J. L., & Linder, D. E. (1993). Athletic identity: Hercules' muscles or Achilles heel? *International Journal of Sport Psychology, 24,* 237–54.

Brooks, D. D., Reifsteck, E. J., Powell, S. M., & Gill, D. L. (2019). Moving beyond college sports: Participants' views of the *Moving On!* transition program. *International Journal of Kinesiology in Higher Education, 3*(1), 2–11. doi: 10.1080/24711616.2018.1489743

Lavallee D., Nesti M., Borkoles E., Cockerill I., & Edge A. (2000). Intervention strategies for athletes in transition. In D. Lavallee & P. Wylleman (Eds.), *Career transitions in sport: International perspectives* (pp. 111–30). Morgantown, WV: Fitness Information Technology.

HELLO LIFE: THIS IS ~~SWIMMING~~ JOANN, IT'S NICE TO MEET YOU
Joann Wakefield

Joann Wakefield is a former Division I swimmer who specialized in sprint freestyle and breaststroke at Eastern Illinois University during the years 2012 to 2016. While an EIU Panther, she was a member of the team-record-setting 400 freestyle relay in 2014 as well as a member of the College Swimming and Diving Coaches Association of America (CSCAA) Scholar All-American Team holding the highest DI women's swim team GPA for the 2014–2015 school year. She also cracked the EIU All-Time Top Times in the 50 freestyle, 100 breaststroke, 200 freestyle relay, and 200 medley relay.

The following story depicts how challenging transitioning out of competitive sport can be, especially if athletic identity is high. Athletic career transition is most commonly spurred by four causes: age, deselection, injury, and free choice (Taylor & Lavallee, 2010). Further, there are many factors related to quality of transition, including athletic identity, personal demographics, voluntariness of decision, injury and health, career and personal development, education, financial status, self-perception, control, the amount of time past transition, and life changes (Brown, Webb, Robinson, & Cotgreave, 2018; Park, Lavallee, & Tod, 2013). Athletic career transition can be constructive (e.g., Knights, Sherry, & Ruddock-Hudson, 2016) and less stressful with proper use of coping strategies, social support, psychosocial support, preretirement planning and research, and life skills development program involvement (Park et al., 2013; Taylor & Lavallee, 2010).

My transition was involuntary. My eligibility was exhausted and I was graduating college. Collegiate eligibility exhaustion is something all student-athletes know will come but do not always welcome. If I could have, I would have kept swimming at the college level until my body could not bear it any longer.

We arrived home around 9:00 p.m., unpacked a few essential bags, and inflated the air mattress in the room I grew up in. My very last race had been on Saturday, February 20, but it was not until this moment it hit me like a ton of bricks. Alone in the room I wept myself to sleep because I had lost someone very close to me: *myself*. I felt empty and alone. I did not know who I was or my purpose, even though I would be starting graduate school in August. Hours earlier I had walked across the stage at my college graduation, and shortly after I had moved out of my college home. I no longer had my teammates close by 24/7, races to pour all my strength and heart into, or coaches to guide and support me. Eight years of club swimming. Four years of high school swimming. Four years of collegiate swimming. Back and forth . . . blurry black lines . . . breathing patterns . . . battling the clock. As of February 2016, 76 percent of my young life had revolved around competitive swimming. I spent the entire summer leading up to graduate school in a perpetual loop of negative thoughts, tears, fear, and unhealthy coping strategies. Swimming was a way of life, swimming was *me*—or so I thought.

A few months into my graduate studies I began to notice a shift in my thought processes. I started realizing and believing I was more than Joann the swimmer; I was a daughter, sister, friend, student, mentee, instructor, role model, aspiring sport and performance psychology professional, and much more. Over the years, while passing on peer birthday parties, movie nights, and family functions for two a day practices and weekend long meets, I had lost sight of the many puzzle pieces that created Joann Wakefield. Sure, swimming occupied a large chunk of my collegiate experience, but I also participated in academic clubs; completed two minors; gained a mentor who introduced me to the world of sport psychology, undergraduate research, publication, and conference presentations; peer-led a freshman university foundations course; worked summer jobs; and completed an internship in two divisions of a collegiate athletic department.

I moved nine hundred miles away from home and a bedroom full of swimming awards to begin a graduate degree and career that melded my life's sport experience and passion with meaningful work. This event was a catalyst for my positive transition out of sport. I have been a retired athlete for three and a half years and still miss competing in the pool more days than not. If I am completely honest, I am still working on positively coping with my loss of swimming and regular training. I spent sixteen years of my life tied to a strictly regimented practice and school schedule; I do not expect everything to fall into place right now. I have had the chance to spend more time participating in hobbies I enjoy, like reading, crafting, spending time in nature, and cheering on the athletic teams I work with. One aspect I am still struggling with is regular physical activity. I miss having coach-led workouts. Finding a balance between accepting my retired athlete body and discovering my optimal motivation for regular physical activity has been a constant work in progress. I have considered becoming involved in group fitness classes, CrossFit, and/or master's level swimming. Over time, I have accepted and embraced my new journey in life. My swimming career will always affect the steps I take in life. I received my master of science in kinesiology with an emphasis in sport and exercise psychology, and now serve as a collegiate athletic academic advisor at a Division I university while pursuing sport and performance mental coaching opportunities.

Take-Home Points

1. The unknown does not need to be scary. Embrace the opportunity for limitless possibilities.
2. Find a way to meld your sport/performance passion into your career after competitive sport.
3. You are not alone. Lean on and communicate with those you hold close and connect with peers experiencing transition out of sport.

References

Brown, C. J., Webb, T. L., Robinson, M. A., & Cotgreave, R. (2018). Athletes' experiences of social support during their transition out of elite sport: An interpretive phenomenological analysis. *Psychology of Sport and Exercise, 36*, 71–80.

Knights, S., Sherry, E., & Ruddock-Hudson, M. (2016). Investigating elite end-of-athletic-career transition: A systematic review. *Journal of Applied Sport Psychology, 28*, 291–308.

Park, S., Lavallee, D., & Tod, D. (2013). Athletes' career transition out of sport: A systematic review. *International Review of Sport and Exercise Psychology, 6*(1), 22–53.

Taylor, J., & Lavallee, D. (2010). Career transition among athletes: Is there life after sports? In J. M. Williams (Ed.), *Applied sport psychology: Personal growth to peak performance* (6th ed.) (pp. 542–62). Boston, MA: McGraw-Hill Higher Education.

THE SPLIT DODGE
Diana Wildermuth, PhD, NCC, LCC

There are often two distinct sides to one's athletic identity. The first is who the athletes believe they are, and the second, perhaps more important, is how others perceive them. This is often referred to as the public self and the private self. Some researchers suggest the more one is tied to one's athletic identity, the better performer one will become (Stephan & Brewer, 2007). Others will argue, however, that the more an athlete overidentifies, the higher the likelihood of issues such as low self-esteem, high anxiety, reduced effort, and other mental health concerns (Heird & Steinfeldt, 2013). In this profile with Major League Lacrosse (MLL) player Matt Mackrides, we learn about his path to performing at the highest level of the sport and what athletic identity means to him.

Matt grew up in a family of four boys, all competitive athletes who played multiple sports during multiple seasons. The Mackrides family has a long history of producing talented athletes. His father was an athlete in college, and his grandfather, Bill Mackrides, was a quarterback for the Philadelphia Eagles. Matt was also an excellent football player, playing the sport during high school and feeling pressured to live up to the family legacy. At the same time, he was recognized as a talented lacrosse and baseball player. Upon entering high school, Matt felt he had to decide and identify what sport he would play in the spring, as baseball and lacrosse often competed for his time. He chose lacrosse. He was a member of his high school state championship lacrosse team and the USA U-19 Gold Medal lacrosse team, was recognized as All-State and All-American, and was actively recruited to play in college. He was known for his swift skills, scoring in tight spaces, creativity in making goals, and ability to use both hands. As his high school career ended, he chose to attend Penn State University for his education and an opportunity to play lacrosse.

It was during his time at Penn State that his identity became salient. While there, he realized that the football players and wrestlers were the celebrities on campus, and it seemed as if everyone knew who they were. Other athletes, like the lacrosse players, wore the athletic apparel, but while most fellow students knew they were athletes, they did not lavish similar attention upon them. It was surprising that this did not bother Matt, as he knew he was there as a student-athlete, not an athlete who was playing college. While in college, Matt earned multiple accolades. He started all four years and was named captain during his junior and senior seasons, and was named a 2012 United States Intercollegiate Lacrosse Association (USILA) Scholar All-American, meaning he maintained a GPA well above a 3.0. He is considered by some to be one of the best all-around lacrosse players to come from the Big Ten.

In the classroom, he was a quiet student who attended all his classes, sat in the front, and met with professors so he would not be labeled by faculty or peers as just another hotshot athlete playing a sport in college, but recognized as a serious student. Matt knew to take school seriously, as it was instilled early by family and his high school education experience at Malvern Preparatory School. He was aware that after college, opportunities to play lacrosse were limited, and that not everyone would be drafted to play professionally. Those who are drafted to play professional lacrosse must also hold full-time jobs to support themselves. For many, graduation or the last collegiate game is when their identity is reevaluated or altered, as the reality of no longer stepping on the field in a uniform, no more classwork, and no more team meetings becomes apparent (Menke & Germany, 2018).

Matt felt fortunate to be drafted into the MLL to play his early career for the Chesapeake Bayhawks; however, this came with the risk of no longer being identified as one of the best, but now one among the best. He ultimately was traded to the Atlanta Blaze before suffering a significant back injury and concussion during the season-opening game in April 2016. This meant he would not be able to play in the MLL All-Star Game that year and would need time to recover and decide if he was going to continue playing. During his recovery time, he used imagery skills and set a goal to return to the game.

In September 2016, his contract was extended for two years. Blaze general manager Spencer Ford said, "Matt Mackrides, first and foremost, is a first class human being. The Atlanta Blaze is lucky to have a person like Matt helping to grow the organization and lead this young team" (Major League Lacrosse, 2016). Matt was not only a player, but also a leader and mentor to the less seasoned players on the team. Matt continued playing for the Atlanta Blaze in the MLL until March 2019.

Today, Matt trains many youth players, hoping to instill in them a strong sense of identity as lacrosse players, but first as a individuals who care about family, teammates, and long-term goals that may or may not include playing lacrosse. He recognizes the importance of identity formation at an early age, and the difference it makes when later faced with adversity or periods of transition. He reminds kids and parents there is more to playing the game, more than getting a college scholarship; most important is respect for the self and respect for the game. His experiences have helped him teach others to keep things in perspective, trust the process, and not lose yourself in it. It is this positive attitude, strong sense of self-concept and resilience, that have shaped his identity to be the excellent coach he is today.

Matt is the founder and owner of Blue Ox Lacrosse, where he is dedicated to providing the highest quality instruction in lacrosse, with the goal of highlighting southeastern Pennsylvania as a hotbed for lacrosse (Mackrides, personal communication, January 31, 2019). Through Blue Ox, he offers individual, small group, and team training along with summer camps that include other activities besides lacrosse, to help build and enhance the identities of future lacrosse players. He is also the assistant lacrosse coach at his alma mater, Malvern Preparatory School. As Blue Ox owner and assistant coach, Matt creates an environment where kids can be themselves, have fun in the process, and find a salient identity as youth athletes.

Take Home Points

1. Others may label you, but it is how you label yourself that will enhance your identity and performance.
2. There is always room to adjust and grow as a player, teammate, coach, and person.
3. Having a positive mind-set is key.

References

Heird, E., & Steinfeldt, J. (2013). An interpersonal psychotherapy approach to counseling student athletes: Clinical implications of athletic identity. *Journal of College Counseling, 16*, 143–57. doi: 10.1002/j.2161-1882.2013.00033.x

Major League Lacrosse. (2016, September 9). Matt Mackrides signs two-year contract with the Blaze. Retrieved from http://www.majorleaguelacrosse.com/articles/matt-mackrides-signs-extension

Menke, D., & Germany, M. (2018). Reconstructing athletic identity: College athletes and sport retirement, *Journal of Loss and Trauma*, *24*(1), 17–30. doi:10.1080/15325024.2018.1522475

Stephan, Y., & Brewer, B. (2007). Perceived determinants of identification with the athlete role among elite competitors, *Journal of Applied Sport Psychology*, *19*(1), 67–79. doi: 10.1080/10413200600944090

THE VALUE OF A SPORT TRANSITION
Taylor Wise, MS

We'll call the runner in this story Jane. Jane began running in high school and was successful enough to be able to compete at the Division I collegiate level. She trained every day for almost seven years and pursued a premedical degree at a difficult academic university. Although others saw an accomplished student-athlete, Jane saw a never-ending list of things to improve on. She had struggled with anxiety and perfectionism for as long as she could remember, but she began to develop symptoms of depression during her senior year of high school. As she continued on to a competitive athletic and academic university, her symptoms worsened while expectations increased. Her teammates noticed her engaging in self-harm behaviors as a coping mechanism, and after a number of consultations with coaches and medical professionals, Jane was pulled from her sport for safety reasons.

There comes a time when every athlete has to make a transition. Some will transition from one sport to another, others from athlete to coach, and others to a life entirely separate from the athletic world (Brewer & Petitpas, 2017). A change of some sort happens for everyone eventually, but one's experience with it can vary depending on a number of factors (Baillie & Danish, 1992). For Jane, one of the important factors was that she didn't make the decision to leave; it was made for her, and she had no way to prepare for the loss or the changes to come. There are many scenarios wherein athletes may be forced to leave their sport before they are ready, even if they make the ultimate decision themselves. For example, many athletes suffer career-ending injuries; others struggle with their motivation as they realize maintaining permanent peak performance is more of a dream than a reality (Grove, Lavallee, & Gordon, 1997). Of course, there are some athletes who are fortunate enough to reach a point in their athletic careers where they feel they have given everything they have to their sport, and are satisfied enough to move on to new opportunities. The difference for Jane was that she didn't feel as if she had any say in or control over the decision to leave her sport.

Jane wasn't done putting in the work, and with those unmet attempts to succeed, she was faced with the unexpected loss of her athletic identity. Most athletes feel strong personal connections to their sport (Brewer, Van Raalte, & Linder, 1993). In order to be successful, you have to be personally invested in and able to dedicate a great deal of who you are to your pursuit. Some amount of identifying with your sport is beneficial, as it provides a sense of purpose and a connection to an athletic community that can be supportive (Brewer et al., 1993). However, Jane found transitioning to a life separate from her familiar athletic world disorienting. She quickly realized that the personality traits that are admired in the athletic community aren't necessarily admired in other contexts (although they often are). She also found it disorienting to be in a world where her worth wasn't measured by how fast she was or how long she ran. She didn't know how to navigate her environment with such obvious emptiness staring back at her.

There was a six-month period during which Jane's symptoms got worse. She was in denial that her athletic career was over and found it easier to be angry than sad. Although she wasn't forced to leave school, she was required to attend individual and group therapy four times a week to help her develop healthier coping mechanisms to stress. One day she realized that she could approach therapy as she approached training: Attack it like an athlete. She increased her participation in sessions and developed a reward system for herself that acknowledged the days she went without engaging in harmful behaviors. She learned to use the skills she acquired as an athlete—such as dedication, perseverance, and resilience—and apply them to getting healthy again. Just two months after her realization, Jane had stopped hurting herself and began to improve many of her depressive symptoms.

The next challenge for Jane was figuring out who she was. She had identified herself as an athlete her entire life, even before she began running. Getting to know herself outside of sport was extremely difficult, but it was an experience that changed her life forever. She engaged in extensive personal reflection to figure out what it was she valued most in life and about herself. Previously, she would have said she valued success and work ethic, but once the context in which she most recognized those values was removed, she realized how much she also cared about spending time with family, traveling, and the way it feels to be healthy. Through therapy and personal development, Jane began to lean into those values and develop multiple identities in herself. She started to recognize in herself the student, the daughter, the adventurer, and the compassionate friend. She realized an energy that came more from wanting to explore new things rather than attempting to be the best.

Jane has since returned to running, but she's moved from competing on the roads to running for herself on the trails. "Being an athlete will always be part of who I am," she says, "but I'm learning there's a lot more to me that I'm still getting to know." When talking with Jane about her transition away from competition, she says that the biggest thing that could have prepared her was to have a sense of who she was beyond just a runner. She emphasizes that being an athlete is still one of her primary identities, but that she's learned to balance it with other personal qualities and life passions: "There's more to me than just a runner. I just wish I had gotten to know that person earlier."

Take-Home Points

1. When facing a life-changing transition, focus on what you can control and try to think less about what you're losing and more about the opportunities to come.
2. Having an athletic identity has many benefits, but it's also important to develop a balanced sense of self and interests beyond sport (Lally, 2007).
3. When struggling with a loss, remember your personal values and lean into those that give you purpose and bring you happiness.

References

Baillie, P. H. F., & Danish, S. J. (1992). Understanding the career transition of athletes. *Sport Psychologist*, *6*(1), 77–98. doi: 10.1123/tsp.6.1.77

Brewer, B. W., & Petitpas, A. J. (2017). Athletic identity foreclosure. *Current Opinion in Psychology*, *16*, 118–22. doi: 10.1016/j.copsyc.2017.05.004

Brewer, B. W., Van Raalte, J. L., & Linder, D. E. (1993). Athletic identity: Hercules' muscles or Achilles heel? *International Journal of Sport Psychology*, *24*(2), 237–54.

Grove, J. R., Lavallee, D., & Gordon, S. (1997). Coping with retirement from sport: The influence of athletic identity. *Journal of Applied Sport Psychology*, *9*(2), 191–203. doi: 10.1080/10413209708406481

Lally, P. (2007). Identity and athletic retirement: A prospective study. *Psychology of Sport and Exercise*, *8*(1), 85–99. doi: 10.1016/j.psychsport.2006.03.003

LEAVING SPORT WITH A SPINAL CORD INJURY
Derek Zike, MS, and Monna Arvinen-Barrow, PhD

It was January 16, 2009. I (Derek) was sixteen years old, an aspiring collegiate ice hockey player and forward for a competitive youth hockey AAA team. My team and I were in the middle of a top prospect showcase in Michigan, playing against the highest-ranked teams in the United States. It was the third game of the weekend. My linemates and I took our shift and proceeded to attack the puck carrier in the offensive zone. While lining up a check, I lost an edge at a distance too close to allow me to brace for impact, crashing headlong into the dasher boards. With a searing headache and ears ringing, my eyes flashed open and I expected to pop right up to my feet. It was then that I realized I could not move anything. I was in a lot of trouble. I remember being aware of everything, all of the excruciating pain. During the early morning hours, I learned that my crash had resulted in a spinal cord injury at the fifth and sixth cervical vertebrae. I underwent multiple surgeries to stabilize my neck and spent a month in the intensive care unit followed by months of acute inpatient rehabilitation. Four months postinjury I was discharged, returned home, and began outpatient physical rehabilitation and occupational therapy. I never regained full physical function. By the time I was seventeen, I was no longer a competitive ice hockey player. Instead, I was a disabled young man living with quadriplegia.

Losing the ability to play ice hockey was devastating. There was nothing I wanted more than to lace up my skates again and resume playing the sport I loved. Ice hockey was more than just the sport. It was tied to my self-worth, it occupied my world, and it was *the* place where I socialized. At times, this was even at the expense of social roles and relationships outside of sport. The crash and the injury took all that away. After the injury, I battled with my self-worth and found it hard to assume other roles outside of ice hockey. My hockey-related friendships were starkly diminished, as I was unable to assume the role that had facilitated those relationships. I struggled to develop new relationships, as I lacked the tools to assume new roles outside of ice hockey.

There are two things that helped me cope with what was now my new normal: pursuing academic excellence and social support. With the help of my parents, I was able to direct my focus toward school and pursuing a college degree. This, despite the spinal cord injury, allowed me to feel as though I was progressing in life and achieving my goals. Graduating from high school and going to college with my peers provided a sense of normalcy, a feeling of being not so different from my peers despite my disability. Similarly, having significant social support from family and true friends helped me deal with, and overcome, feelings of isolation and loneliness. Having strong support became paramount, particularly in the form of access to typical social situations such as sporting events, theater, concerts, and playing video games. Through enabled access to social situations, I became more comfortable in them, which helped me to make new friendships in the process.

Ten years on, I still love ice hockey and I am currently a second-year doctoral student specializing in psychology of sport injury and rehabilitation. My injury experience steered my career interest toward sport psychology. My goal is to achieve a career in academia, specializing in sport injury–related transitions out of able-bodied sport. My self-worth and social identity have also continued to grow and expand. Had it not been for further education and social support, my transition out of sport due to spinal cord injury would not have been as successful as it has been.

Several intrinsic and extrinsic factors have been identified as having an effect on a person's transition out of competitive sport. Although research on understanding psychosocial aspects of career-ending injuries is rare (Park, Lavallee, & Tod, 2013), it is known that the quality of the transition process is dependent on the presence or absence of a range of contributing variables. My story highlights the role of perception of one's athletic and social self, presence of postinjury career plans, and social support as key factors influencing the quality of career transition, findings that are consistent with existing research (e.g., Arvinen-Barrow, DeGrave, Pack, & Hemmings, 2019; Arvinen-Barrow, Hurley, & Ruiz, 2017; Stoltenburg, Kamphoff, & Bremer, 2011). The above research supports the notion that having a narrow, sport-focused self- and social identity may result in more adjustment difficulties during a career transition, as it did in my case. The research also highlights the importance of having a contingency plan for a career outside of sport and appropriate types of social support from significant others as possible strategies to ease the transition process.

Take-Home Points

1. A diversified self- and social-identity are important when transitioning out of competitive sport due to career-ending injury.
2. Having an existing preretirement plan, career, and/or educational pursuits outside of sport can be beneficial for healthy career transition outcome.
3. Similarly, the role of social support is paramount in helping the injured athlete adjust to a life without sport participation.

References

Arvinen-Barrow, M., DeGrave, K., Pack, S. M., & Hemmings, B. (2019). Transitioning out of sport: The psychosocial impact of career ending non-musculoskeletal injuries among male cricketers from England and Wales. *Journal of Clinical Sport Psychology*, *4*(13), 629–44. doi: https://doi.org/10.1123/jcsp.2017-0040

Arvinen-Barrow, M., Hurley, D., & Ruiz, M. C. (2017). Transitioning out of professional sport: The psychosocial impact of career-ending injuries among elite Irish rugby football union players. *Journal of Clinical Sport Psychology*, *10*(1), 67–84. doi: 10.1123/jcsp.2016-0012

Park, S., Lavallee, D., & Tod, D. (2013). Athletes' career transition out of sport: A systematic review. *International Review of Sport and Exercise Psychology*, *6*(1), 22–53. doi: 10.1080/1750984X.2012.687053

Stoltenburg, A. L., Kamphoff, C. S., & Bremer, K. L. (2011). Transitioning out of sport: The psychosocial effects of collegiate athletes' career-ending injuries. *Athletic Insight: The Online Journal of Sport Psychology*, *13*(2), article 2.

Chapter Four

Mental Training

Imagery, Attentional Focus and Control, Self-Talk, Arousal Control and Energy Management, and Emotion Regulation

Much of performance excellence traditionally focuses on the effective use of various psychological skills such as imagery, attentional control, arousal regulation, self-talk, and so on to achieve success. This is the bread and butter of work by mental performance consultants with athletes and exercisers to help them excel in various performance settings. These various skills and strategies aimed at training the mind and optimizing mental preparation are explored in a wonderful set of stories in this section.

William Brown talks poignantly about the role of anxiety in affecting his performance in baseball. Kevin Burke expands on thoughts about performance to include the performing arts—he is an accomplished thespian and provides us with insights into performance in the theater. Mark Cheney discusses coming back and winning a golf tournament after an amazingly bad score on an early hole. Michael Clark addresses the effective use of imagery in coming back from injury and hurdling successfully. Emily Galvin reviews the power of effective self-talk in running the mile. Alan S. Kornspan talks about imagery and self-talk in Billy Mills's amazing victory in the 10,000m run at the 1964 Olympics. Dora Kurimay discusses the effective use of imagery in a collegiate squash player's success. William Land uses the concept of a physiological stress gauge effectively with a competitive golfer. Karen Lo describes the ebbs and flows of arousal control in a champion jockey in horse racing. Michelle M. McAlarnen reviews various stress and anxiety management strategies for success in skiing. Nikola Milinkovic reviews the various psychological skills and their impact on his journey as a tennis player. Deborah Munch addresses the use of self-talk and verbal cues in successful running performance. Kate Nolt discusses the use of psychological skills in addressing stress and attentional issues brought on by helicopter parents. Maximilian Pollack notes the use of various psychological skills in successful performance in football. Meghan Ramick and Selen Razon review various psychological skills, especially arousal control and self-talk, in synchronized skating. Michael L. Sachs discusses attentional control/focus through the vehicle of the iconic phrase "Be the Ball" from the movie *Caddyshack*. Joann Wakefield discusses effective use of imagery within the context of swimming performance excellence and also discusses emotion regulation and its impact on swimming performance in an elite swimmer. Lastly, Cedric Williams and Matthew D. Powless address the emotional regulation strategies required for successful performance in Army Ranger training.

TRYING TO TAKE IT ONE PITCH AT A TIME
William Brown

I approached my coach and told him I had more than nerves heading into our first game, and he replied, "Don't be a head case; I am expecting a lot from you this year, so you better be on your game." Not exactly how a coach should address someone, especially considering most players are already reluctant to express what is going through their minds before the start of their junior year in high school. Let's fast forward to my junior year of college: I'm up to bat with two people on base and my team is down two runs in the bottom of the ninth inning. I get my pitch and hit it out of the ballpark. Elation should follow—but not so fast! Instead of enjoying my game-winning home run, I immediately start worrying about future at bats and having to live up to that moment. What is being portrayed on the outside does not necessarily reflect how someone is feeling on the inside. I did a good job of hiding my anxiety because I was skilled enough to overcome it most of the time. Then there were times when I made mistakes and could not get over it, leaving people to wonder what could possibly be going on in my head. The problem was that nobody asked how my mental game was, let alone equipped me with tools to work on these problems.

I am a former college baseball player and a former college baseball coach. I am currently a sports performance consultant and I also coach travel baseball teams. My current job might surprise people who knew me when I was younger, who would probably think, "That guy was a great player, but he always seemed to get in his own way!" This is true to an extent, and this has led me to studying and getting a degree in psychology and counseling and furthering my education with a master's degree. I was fascinated about what I went through as an athlete, and I wanted to learn more. After studying psychology and thinking about the problems I had, I soon realized that I had dealt with performance anxiety my whole athletic career. I was good enough to receive full-ride scholarships as well as a chance to try out for some professional teams, but my mind-set is what held me back from reaching my full potential. My purpose in life now is to build relationships with people who want to improve their performance and be able to identify and help them deal with their own mental hurdles. I also want to inform coaches about how to identify these problems in their athletes and the steps they can take to improve their mental performance.

I was good—even great—in games when things were going well. I was in automatic mode, or in the flow, where I did not think about anything and the game came easily. The baseball looked like a volleyball coming to the plate—a ball would be hit to me and I would just react to it with no thought, my body taking care of the rest. When I failed, it was a whole other story. I would start thinking about worst-case scenarios after messing up once. I could have a ten-game hitting streak going, but one 0–4 performance at the plate would put me in a downward spiral. When my coach picked up on my struggles, he would say cliché things like "Relax" or "Concentrate." If only he could have told me how to relax or concentrate by employing a technique like deliberate breathing, which has been shown to improve both stress levels and concentration (Ma et al., 2017). Instead, I would fixate on that strikeout and my mind would make up stories that I believed to be true. I would think about striking out when the scout was in the stands and in my mind's eye see him leaving, scratching me off his list. I would think about how my teammates thought less of me after I failed. I would think about the coach sitting me. I even thought about my girlfriend leaving me if I did not perform well enough. Thinking of these things took my focus off the task at hand. I was always caught up with things I had no control over instead of focusing on what was in my control during the game (Hays, Thomas, Maynard, & Bawden, 2009). I took my bad at bats into the field and did not focus on the next play on defense.

I remember a time when I dropped a ball in the outfield after already having a bad game up to that point. I was literally praying that another ball would not be hit to me. Of course, in baseball, the ball seems to find the person who does not want it hit to him. The ball was hit to me the very next batter. I remember seeing the ball going through the air toward me and thinking I need to move, but my body was literally frozen from anxiety and I could not move. I just looked at the ball fly over my head and eventually I gained control of my body and chased the ball down to throw it back in. Coming into the dugout, I got screamed at by the coaches about my lack of effort and not caring about my teammates. However, this could not be further from the truth. The truth was that I tried to act like I did not care to cover up what was really going on. I felt like nobody would understand and that it was something I had to figure out on my own. I started by researching sport psychology books. I happened to run into a book by Harvey Dorfman called *The Mental Game of Baseball* (Dorfman & Kuehl, 2017), which was referred to as the "baseball bible." This book changed my trajectory because it made me realize I was not the only one with these issues. It was a great resource for me because it gave me suggestions and possible solutions to combat my performance anxiety. The great Hall of Fame pitcher Roy Halliday was also a huge fan of Dorfman's work, and swore by *The Mental Game of Baseball* as critical in helping him achieve success.

There are many athletes dealing with the same issues I dealt with every day. Some of them just take it as the way they are, something they just have to deal with. Others want help, but are afraid of the stigma that goes along with opening up. The landscape is finally starting to change; twenty-seven Major League Baseball (MLB) teams have now hired mental coaches (Nightengale, 2018). It now has to start at the lower levels and make mental training as much the norm as physical training, which is viewed as essential to success. For this to happen, coaches have to do the following:

- Get to know your players and build relationships with them.
- Welcome open communication and have a "door is always open" policy.
- Start integrating mental training techniques into practice. This can include: imagery, goal setting, mindfulness, attention control, building routines, breathing techniques, self-talk, and enhancing confidence.
- Give feedback.
- Show you care more about the person than about winning.

My goal since I was a little kid was to the play in the major leagues. I believed, and others would vouch for it, that I had the talent to do so. What held me back was my mental processes, which could have been fixed. If someone had let me know not only that it was normal to have anxiety in sports, but also that there was a solution to the problem, I might have made it. I now know that my true purpose is to help people who struggle with performance issues so that their dreams won't be denied because of them.

Take-Home Points

1. Responses such as anxiety are natural phenomena in sport.
2. Strategies are available for dealing with anxiety and other issues—seek out help if you are the athlete or offer help if you are the sport psychology consultant.
3. The mental game is a critical part of performance excellence—don't neglect it!

References

Dorfman, H., & Kuehl, K. (2017). *The mental game of baseball: A guide to peak performance* (4th ed.). New York, NY: Lyons Press.

Hays, K., Thomas, O., Maynard, I., & Bawden, M. (2009). The role of confidence in world-class sport performance, *Journal of Sports Sciences, 27*(11), 1185–99, doi: 10.1080/02640410903089798

Ma, X., Yue, Z. Q., Gong, Z. Q., Zhang, H., Duan, N. Y., Shi, Y. T., . . . Li, Y. F. (2017). The effect of diaphragmatic breathing on attention, negative affect and stress in healthy adults. *Frontiers in Psychology, 8*, 874. doi:10.3389/fpsyg.2017.00874

Nightengale, Bob. (2018, April 4). "Why Major League Baseball Is '90% Mental' Now More than Ever." *USA Today*. Retrieved from http://www.usatoday.com/story/sports/mlb/columnist/bob-nightengale/2018/04/03/mlb-mental-health-coaches/482122002/.

ACT IT 'TIL YOU IN-ACT IT
Kevin L. Burke, PhD, Queens University of Charlotte

While most athletes would not wish to hear a teammate say, "Break a leg!" just before taking the field or court, actresses and actors cherish this encouraging statement before each performance. However, even with supportive castmates, family, and friends, experienced performers may suffer psychological challenges when showing their talents. One of the most interesting and befuddling occurrences in acting is when a performer who thoroughly knows his or her lines and has executed them numerous times suffers a mental block during a performance—similar to the "yips" reported by golfers and baseball players (Ankiel & Brown, 2018). The following is an example of the struggle of one actress to overcome this "naggravating" (combination of *nagging* and *aggravating*) phenomenon.

Traci, using her own terms, is a very successful actress. Her acting career began, very typically, in elementary school in various school productions—one of her first roles was a nonspeaking role as a rabbit. Through the years she was cast in more challenging roles, mostly in middle and high school productions. However, she also gained further experience with her involvement in local community theatre shows. Once she reached middle school age, her parents helped her acquire an agent. With assistance from the agent and through her involvement with acting workshops, she was cast in background acting roles, commercials, and smaller roles in independent films. During this time she also had numerous auditions for larger films, television shows, and other commercials. One of Traci's favorite comments is, "Acting is my sport." She even has a T-shirt with this statement printed on it.

Currently, Traci is in her early thirties and still has aspirations—as most actors do—to land a leading role in television or film. However, Traci admits she tends to have the most fun while participating in plays, particularly in community theatre. However, a recent stumbling block occurred on stage that Traci does not remember ever experiencing before. While performing in front of an almost-full house, Traci stumbled on a couple of her lines, saying them in an incorrect order and stuttering some of the lines. Fortunately, this occurred during the second act of the play. However, this disruption in her concentration caused her to drop (forget) several other lines before her appearance at the curtain call. While she has appeared in several other plays since this first occurred, similar experiences continued to happen in other theatre performances. The stumbling and dropping of lines mostly occurs during live performances, yet is not perceived as a problem during rehearsals. Traci describes her experience during these negative episodes as her mind sometimes being completely blank. Sometimes she experiences complete panic, followed by racing thoughts of: "What do I do next?" and "Help me!"—the latter of which she sometimes tries to convey to fellow actors and actresses on stage with the "deer in headlights" gaze at them.

Traci reports that she is experiencing less confidence on stage, has begun to question her overall ability, and is concerned how her potential blunders affect her fellow onstage performers. Also, while she states that "90 percent of her performances are quite good," she fears getting a reputation in which other actors/actresses know they have to be ready for "anything and everything" while on stage with her.

Traci sought assistance from me because we had previously performed together and she knew of my work with other actors and actresses as well as athletes. Traci has dabbled in sport and is quite familiar with sport terminology, yet she does not consider herself an athlete. Therefore, to give her an understandable yet different view of her situation, we utilized sport examples to attack her sudden lack of confidence and heightened anxiety. Traci wants to continue to be a valuable and good teammate for other actresses and actors.

To deal with her "blank mind" episodes and "What am I supposed to say next?" situations, we discussed a few self-talk strategies (Weinberg & Gould, 2019) to give her a game plan during the next onstage occurrences. Traci decided to use the simple cue word *talk*, because it is what she needed to do in those types of situations. To help Traci utilize the simple cue word, we employed guided imagery sessions where she imagined being onstage, forgetting her lines, employing her cue word, and then moving on. We also utilized what I term retro imagery sessions (Vealey & Forelenza, 2014), where she reenacted specific occurrences when she forgot her lines, but during these imagery sessions she thought, "Talk" and began speaking with little to no disruption of the play. While Traci was still a very confident actress, having a plan to deal with these potential situations gave her more self-assurance. Traci was encouraged to practice these imagery sessions as much as she could to continue to build her confidence (Murphy, 2005) and prepare for any upcoming onstage snafus.

Another aspect of our work together that seemed to benefit Traci was my sharing of times where I had similar experiences while onstage. I told her that some of the funniest and most memorable onstage moments can occur during these unplanned, ad-libbed scenes. After our laughter subsided, I pointed out that these experiences make for great future storytelling. I shared with Traci my attitude that while I want to do the play as directed and staged, I love seeing how we actors and actresses get out of them—hopefully without the audience noticing the alternate performance. Having this viewpoint (as just another acting challenge) toward acting miscues makes blunders a more enjoyable experience.

As another part of her mental preparation, I encouraged Traci to get involved with improvisation workshops and/or theatre to get onstage practice dealing with unplanned, spontaneous scenes. Improv generally involves placing actors and actresses in onstage situations with no set lines or blocking (where to stand or move), requiring them to spontaneously speak, react, and move.

By practicing and utilizing appropriate self-talk (cue word), imagery, and further acting training (particularly with improv), Traci was able to lower her stage fright, improve her confidence, and increase the fulfillment she receives from participating in "her sport."

Traci continues to enjoy her acting experiences and is now very open with other actresses and actors about how she dealt with her miscues. Most importantly, Traci, as she described, is having "extreme joy" acting and now looks forward to unplanned challenges.

Take-Home Points

1. Having a mental plan helps one be prepared.
2. Having a realistic, positive attitude toward errors helps overcome the fear of making mistakes.
3. Confidence is self-proclaimed and administered.

References

Ankiel, R., & Brown, T. (2018). *The phenomenon: Pressure, the yips, and the pitch that changed my life*. New York: PublicAffairs.

Murphy, S. (Ed.). (2005). *The sport psych handbook: A complete guide to today's best mental training techniques*. Champaign, IL: Human Kinetics.

Weinberg, R. S., & Gould, D. (2019). *Foundations of sport and exercise psychology* (7th edition). Champaign, IL: Human Kinetics.

Vealey, R. S., & Forlenza, S. T. (2015). Understanding and using imagery in sport. In J. M. Williams & V. Krane (Eds.), *Applied sport psychology: Personal growth to peak performance* (7th edition) (pp. 240–273). New York, NY: McGraw-Hill.

"IT'S NOT A TYPO"
Mark Cheney

Mark Cheney and Sydney Smith after the awards ceremony. *Courtesy of Albert Smith*

These were the first words Sydney Smith said to me on the seventh hole of the 2017 Nevada State High School Girls Golf Championship: "It's not a typo." Nevada utilizes a live scoring system, and my phone showed Sydney with a 13 on the par-4 fifth hole. As her coach, I already knew the score (and how it transpired) thanks to a phone call from a USGA rules official. Sydney had hooked her tee shot into the rocks, thought she could hit it out, and then taken 10 shots to get the ball back in play before chipping onto the green and one-putting for a nonuple bogey. It was a shocking and uncharacteristic play from an experienced veteran of tournament golf.

Coming into the state tournament, I viewed Sydney as one of the five or six girls most likely to contend for the state title. She had surely ruined those chances with the 13. Spotting her rivals (Division I commits like herself) nine shots was not going to get it done. Perhaps she could rebound and make her way back to the top six, earning a state medal. Knowing the importance of maintaining a present moment focus while also acknowledging and accepting the current reality, I chose my response carefully: "I know."

After a few moments, I added, "And you have over three-fourths of the tournament remaining."

To that she replied, "Ugh."

Her response was understandable. Most golfers would have given up after taking a 13. The "ugh" was a by-product of attending to both the memory of the fifth hole as well as the prospect of playing in the tournament with her shot at winning presumably eliminated. I reminded her to focus on the present hole. Believing it could not get any worse, Sydney trusted herself and forged onward. She played the remainder of the first round at four under par, finishing with a 77. All in all, it was a respectable score, but it was also eight strokes behind the tournament leader.

What ensued on the second day of the tournament was a textbook display of concentration. In a sport such as golf, the majority of the time on the course does not involve hitting the ball. Ample time exists for distracting thoughts to arise. As Williams, Nideffer, Wilson, and Sagal (2015) describe, drifting out of the here and now leads to less effectiveness in the present. Through the use of her performance journal, Sydney had recognized a tendency to get ahead of herself and engage in future-oriented thinking. Understanding that self-talk can redirect attentional focus, Sydney drew on her insight to employ instructional self-talk by saying, "One shot at a time. One hole at a time." This freed Sydney's mind to focus on the task at hand (Weinberg & Gould, 2019). Her ability to be fully absorbed in the present, without thoughts of the past or future, facilitated the possibility of exceptional performance (Jackson & Csikszentmihalyi, 1999). Rather than focus on what might have been, she chose to focus on the task before her.

At the start of round two, Sydney said to herself, "What do I have to lose? Let's have fun and enjoy my last round of high school golf." Her round started inauspiciously, with a three-putt par on the opening hole and a disappointing par on the second hole. A birdie and a par brought Sydney back to the fifth hole, the scene of her first-round debacle. Standing on the tee box, she asked me, "What do I hit?" In essence, she was asking, "Do I hit the same club I hit yesterday that put me in a bad spot?" My response was designed to bring her focus back to the present moment, "What would you normally hit?"

"7 wood," she said. The very club that had led to the 13.

"Then let's hit 7 wood. Commit to it."

Her tee shot split the fairway and was followed by an audible and visible sigh of relief. With the demons exorcised, she nearly holed her second shot, and tapped in for birdie. She rolled in four more birdies to shoot a front-nine 30. Continuing her use of self-talk, she said, "Let's keep it going. Stay present." As I observed what was occurring, I said less and less. I did not want to provide any type of distraction from the optimal concentration and performance that was taking place.

Meanwhile, the leaders began to falter with a series of bogeys. Throughout her second round, Sydney never asked about her competition, relying on her attentional cueing instead. The comeback was completed when she took the lead on the sixteenth hole. Feeling confident and present, she finished with a career-low 65, winning the state title by two strokes. After making a 13 on the fifth hole, she had played her final thirty-one holes in an astounding 11 under par. In nineteen years of coaching golf, I have never seen a better demonstration of present-moment focus.

Take-Home Points

1. Internal distracters, such as attending to past or future events, can diminish performers' attentional focus and cause performance decrements.
2. Self-talk can counter internal distracters and enhance a present-moment focus.
3. Confidence and a present-moment focus create the possibility of exceptional performance.

References

Jackson, S. & Csikszentmihalyi, M. (1999). *Flow in sport.* Champaign, IL: Human Kinetics.

Weinberg, R. S., & Gould, D. (2019). *Foundations of sport and exercise psychology* (7th ed.). Champaign, IL: Human Kinetics.

Williams, J. M., Nideffer, R. M., Wilson, V. E., & Sagal, M.-S. (2015). Concentration and strategies for controlling it. In J. M. Williams & V. Krane (Eds.), *Applied sport psychology: Personal growth to peak performance* (7th ed.) (pp. 304–25). New York, NY: McGraw-Hill.

HURDLE BY HURDLE
Michael Clark

Group imagery presentation. *Courtesy of Michael Clark*

According to the National Federation of State High School Associations (NFHS), more than 1 million high school track and field athletes compete each year nationwide (Atkinson, 2016). From running to jumping to throwing, the sport offers the opportunity for thousands of high school student-athletes to compete with their rivals and/or strive for personal bests. No matter how fun and fulfilling the process may be, an unfortunate aspect of the sport is injury. Willem Weigel, an All-Conference hurdler in the state of Wisconsin, shares how he used imagery in the days and hours leading up to what he would later refer to as one of his happiest and most fulfilling days as an athlete following an arduous comeback.

Imagery is the ability to imagine an optimal outcome before ever stepping to the starting line. Cumming and Ramsey (2009) suggest that the most effective imagery results from a vivid mental picture that incorporates as many senses as possible and is seen in real time. If we picture only positive outcomes, the brain rewires to allow that behavior to happen more quickly when attempted in real life. At a neurological level, the brain cannot tell the difference between something that is real and something that is imagined (Pascual-Leone et al., 1995).

Willem suffered what was—at first—considered to be a career-ending injury during his warm-up at the indoor conference championship during his junior year. He got out of the blocks cleanly, but his trail leg caught the top of a hurdle, resulting in a fall that tore his ACL, LCL, and PCL, in addition to spraining his MCL. The athletic trainers on site murmured under their breath that they feared Willem's recovery might take well over a year. Willem was in severe pain and devastated.

Through dedicated rehabilitation following various surgeries, Willem was miraculously strong and technically sound enough to open his senior track season just eleven months after his injury. As if racing the literal hurdles in front of him weren't daunting enough, Willem was assigned the same lane where he had fallen. Willem recounts his ability to use imagery to overcome what felt like a mental barrier leading up to his return to the track:

> Rehab and physical therapy had been going well, and I made the goal of returning to the track in the spring to continue hurdling. After getting to the point that the intermediate hurdles felt pretty smooth, the time was getting closer and closer to practice high hurdling again. One pre-season practice I set up a high hurdle but couldn't get in the right mindset to clear it—I had to go over the side of it a few times before finally getting the courage to just jump over it. It was one of my sloppiest hurdles ever, but I was able to clear it. I focused on the intermediate hurdles in preparation for outdoors, but found myself in a position to compete in the 60m high hurdles in an indoor meet. Going into the meet, I used a lot of imagery which helped me to gain confidence going into competition. I would see myself in the race, going over each hurdle and eventually winning.
>
> I was so nervous on the day of the race. I remember isolating myself to get mentally prepared for the race, just focusing on seeing myself going through warm-ups and the race in my mind. An assistant coach who is our sport psych guy and I went through some deep breathing exercises and used imagery to create a final game plan for the warm-up leading up to the race. We focused on going through all the senses I would experience on the starting line, and ran through the race, hurdle by hurdle, in live time.
>
> Getting through my warmups and into the blocks had made me shaky and anxious, but being able to calm down and reflect on all that I went through the previous 11 months helped me to feel proud to be even able to step to the starting line. I had a clean race and instantly hugged my coaches as I crossed the finish line. I had done it! If there's one thing I will always remember from that day, it was the feeling I got knowing that I wasn't alone in the emotional journey that accompanied my injury.

Willem went on to finish his senior season without injury, facing each practice and competition with poise and confidence. A few weeks into the indoor track season he ran a personal best in the 55m high hurdles and a lifetime best in the 300m intermediate hurdles at the outdoor conference championships. Through his use of imagery, among other mental skills, Willem became a better leader, modeling perseverance and commitment to the sport.

Take-Home Points

1. Use as many senses as possible to make the mental picture as clear and vivid (a polysensory approach).
2. Imagery works best when running the image in real time.
3. Include only optimal outcomes or scenarios where you're overcoming adversity.

References

Atkinson, L. (2016). High school track and field participation continues to increase. Retrieved from https://nfhs.org/articles/high-school-track-and-field-participation-continues-to-increase/

Cumming, J., & Ramsey, R. (2009). Imagery interventions in sport. In S. D. Mellalieu & S. Hanton (Eds.), *Advances in applied sport psychology: A review*, 5–36. London, UK: Routledge.

Pascual-Leone, A., Nguyet, D., Cohen, L. G., Brasil-Neto, J. P., Cammarota, A., et al. (1995). Modulation of muscle responses evoked by transcranial magnetic stimulation during the acquisition of new fine motor skills. *Journal of Neurophysiology*, 74(3), 1037–45.

CONTROLLING A RACING MIND WHILE RACING THE MILE
Emily Galvin

If you have ever competed in a track event or run a marathon or half-marathon, you know that while your feet are moving at one pace, your mind could be running a mile a minute. Often the inability to manage one's thoughts can be an impediment to peak performance. Elite performers are deliberate with the self-talk they employ during training and competition, using it to meet their needs in the moment without letting errant thoughts affect their performance.

Self-talk, simply defined as "athletes' verbalizations that are addressed to themselves" (Hardy, Hall, & Hardy, 2005, p. 905), serves different functions. It can be used to boost confidence (Williams, Zinsser, & Bunker, 2015), manage competitive anxiety (Hardy, Jones, & Gould, 1996), and focus athlete attention (Landin, 1994).

My work with a Division I track and field athlete demonstrates the power of effective self-talk, particularly in directing attention during competitive events. This runner—let's call her Jane—was a highly competitive miler. She excelled her first year as a collegiate runner and placed high expectations on herself to continue dropping time her sophomore year. She was an extremely focused and hardworking athlete who thrived on competition. She was eager to employ mental strategies to help her in her quest for speed. In our sessions, we discussed the obstacles she faced running the mile. At times she struggled with focusing too much on the pain of the race, or found herself worrying about going out too fast and not having enough energy to finish strong. However, she knew she did not want to shift her focus to cues entirely unrelated to the race; that could result in losing precious time by not pushing herself to her limit. Thus, staying focused while avoiding overthinking was her primary concern.

Together, we decided to focus on the self-talk necessary for her to excel. I advised her to break down the mile race into chunks, to identify what she needed to accomplish—or what her purpose was—in each chunk, and to choose one word or one concise phrase to help her focus on that objective. She divided her race into four parts: the first 200 meters, the next 600 meters, then 400 meters, and the final 400 meters. We discussed what she needed to focus on and achieve in each of those chunks. For example, in the first 200 meters, her objective was to start strong in order to get into the best position. She came up with one word for each portion of the race that encapsulated her objectives for that segment. To demonstrate, her self-talk plan was: position, speed, strength, fly.

After making any mental plan, the next step is to put it into action. Jane did so in practice and in races. In practice, she used it during workouts to help her feel prepared and confident to rely on this strategy during competition. She took it upon herself to share her cue words with her coach, and her coach reinforced her efforts by shouting them to her as she ran past him on each lap. (She even shared with me a video of one race where she speeds by going into her final 400 meters and you can hear her coach shout, "Time to fly!" from the side—with *fly* being her cue word for the final lap). We checked in on her progress with the plan during our weekly sessions, focusing on her progress conditioning her body to respond to her cue words.

This progress in practice helped her effectively implement her plan during competitions. It gave Jane something productive to focus on, which alleviated any undue stress from ineffective self-talk or lack of focus before races. When she raced, she kept her mind on her efforts (because losing focus could mean slowing down and losing valuable seconds), but avoided overthinking or thinking too much about the pain of pushing her body. As she started each of her designated chunks, she used her cue word and repeated it to herself like a mantra as she powered through that portion of the race. Using her plan, she took control of the inevitable self-talk running through her head and used it to her advantage.

Jane's commitment to both physical and mental training resulted in a personal record in the mile that season. Her excellent performance outcomes were the result of an effective training process. Identifying the self-talk necessary to thrive in her race, Jane reflected on past successes and failures in races and enhanced her self-awareness. Ultimately, she developed a framework for implementing a deliberate mental race plan that she carried over into other events.

Take-Home Points

1. Self-talk used in competition should be concise and specific to the task at hand.
2. Practice self-talk strategies in training settings to enhance confidence implementing your plan in competition.
3. Share your self-talk plan with coaches, teammates, or support staff who can support your efforts and hold you accountable.

References

Hardy, J., Hall, C. R., & Hardy, L. (2005). Quantifying athlete self-talk. *Journal of Sports Sciences*, 23, 905–17.
Hardy, L., Jones, G., & Gould, D. (1996). *Understanding psychological preparation for sport: Theory and practice of elite performers*. Chichester, UK: Wiley.

Landin, D. (1994). The role of verbal cues in skill learning. *Quest, 46,* 299–313.

Williams, J. M., Zinsser, N., & Bunker, L. (2015). Cognitive techniques for building confidence and enhancing performance. In J. M. Williams (Ed.), *Applied sport psychology: Personal growth to peak performance* (7th ed.) (pp. 274–303). New York, NY: McGraw-Hill.

IMAGINING SUCCESS AND STAYING POSITIVE: ONE LAP AT A TIME
Alan S. Kornspan, University of Akron

Billy Mills was one of the best long-distance runners in the history of the United States (Hersey, 1984). Mills attended the University of Kansas and was a student-athlete on the track and field team. While at the University of Kansas, Mills became a three-time track and field All-American and was a member of the 1959 and 1960 national championship outdoor track and field teams (Hersey, 1984). It has been claimed that "Billy Mills created the greatest upset in Olympic history" (Hicks, 1996).

Mills's story provides an excellent description of how mental training techniques such as imagery, positive affirmations, and journaling can help athletes achieve a high level of success. Imagery is picturing in your mind's eye what you want to see happen. Many athletes use imagery as a motivational tool and a way to stay positive and committed to a long-term goal (Weinberg & Gould, 2019). Closely related to imagery is positive affirmations, in which athletes repeat positive thoughts to themselves. Both imagery and positive self-talk can help athletes enhance their confidence and stay positive. In addition to using these techniques, athletes often maintain training logs and journals so they become aware of how they are improving and what they are thinking about during training and competition (Ravizza & Fifer, 2015).

Mills's story is a great example of an athlete who used mental training techniques to excel in long distance running. In particular, almost four years before Mills won an Olympic gold medal, he was almost two minutes behind world record holder Ron Clarke's best time (Hicks, 1996). So how did Mills do it? How did he win an Olympic gold medal four years later?

Mills continued to train and also utilized mental skills to help him achieve his goal. After college, Mills joined the Marines and met marathon runner Alex Breckenridge, with whom he began training. Throughout his time training with Breckenridge, Mills imagined himself daily competing against Clarke, the 10,000m Olympic champion and world record holder in the 10,000m (Hersey, 1984). In fact, Mills completed every practice by imagining himself sprinting 100 meters and defeating Clarke to win the Olympic gold medal (Bell, 2010). Specifically, during these imagery times, Mills felt like he was a "breath of wind" and he saw himself pass Clarke to win the race (Bell, 2010). Based on Mills's use of imagery, it is not surprising that he believed the subconscious mind could not differentiate between what was being imagined and what was really happening (Hicks, 1996).

In addition to using daily imagery, Mills also used journaling and positive affirmations as he mentally and physically prepared for the 1964 Olympic

Games. Mills noted that six weeks before the Olympics, on September 5, he wrote in his journal, "I am in great shape"; "Starting to have a strong finish"; "I am ready for a 28:25 10,000m run in Tokyo" (Hicks, 1996). Thus, in his journal, he used many positive affirmations to keep himself motivated. These affirmations also included "Must Believe" and "I believe I can run with the best in the world." Through his mental preparation and development of awareness, Mills simplified his thinking to focus on how he could increase his effort for a few seconds in each lap of a twenty-five lap race. He believed that thinking about taking two minutes of time off was a difficult way to begin thinking about the process of getting faster, so he tried to make it much simpler for himself (Hicks, 1996).

During the 10,000m race in the 1964 Olympics, Mills incorporated the mental skills that he had practiced. He explained that with two laps left to go in the race, world champion Ron Clarke looked back and noticed Mills was right behind him. Mills kept his thoughts positive by telling himself that Clarke was worried and that if he just stayed with him he would have a chance to win (Hicks, 1996). As Mills started the last lap, the other competitors boxed him in tightly. Suddenly, Mills was lightly pushed to the side by Clarke's elbow. He thought he was going to fall but was able to keep his balance and remain slightly behind Clarke. Then Mohammed Gammoudi went right between Mills and Clarke and took the lead. At that moment, Mills began to accept that he might finish in third place. As he came to the final curve he heard nothing except his heart pounding (Hicks, 1996). At this point, Gammoudi was in the lead, Clarke was second, and Mills was in third place (Olympic Channel, 2013). In the final stretch in potentially one of the greatest upsets in Olympic history, Mills used his positive affirmations to say to himself, "One more try; one More try." Then Mills's self-talk changed to "I can win; I can win." As he came down the final stretch with 30 yards to go, he started to say to himself, "I won, I won, I won" as he sprinted by his competitors to win the gold medal in the 10,000m (Hicks, 1996).

In reminiscing about his 1964 Olympic victory, Mills stated, "You focus for four years, dozens of times of times a day, visualizing. Reliving the moment the way you want it to be. And then you win. That one moment you know you're the best in the world" (Hicks, 1996).

Take-Home Points

1. Use imagery as part of your mental training while competing in your sport.
2. To stay committed in your sport over a long period of time, use positive affirmations to stay confident and motivated.

3. Use a journal to stay aware of your thoughts and feelings as you continue toward your athletic goals.

References

Bell, R. (2010). *Mental toughness training for golf: Start strong finish strong*. Bloomington, IN: AuthorHouse.

Hersey, M. D. (1984, April 21). Mills' moment. KU History. Retrieved from https://kuhistory.ku.edu/articles/mills-moment

Hicks, S. (Director). (1996). *The ultimate athlete: Pushing the limit* [DVD]. Taipei, Taiwan: King's International Multimedia.

Olympic Channel. (2013, June 11). Incredible moment as underdog Billy Mills wins 10,000m Gold—Tokyo 1964 Olympics [video file]. Retrieved from https://youtu.be/5F5iCsymMj0

Ravizza, K., & Fifer, A. (2015). Increasing awareness for sport performance. In J. M. Williams & V. Krane (Eds.). *Applied sport psychology: Personal growth to peak performance*. (pp. 176–87). Boston, MA: McGraw-Hill.

Weinberg, R. S. & Gould, D. (2019). *Foundations of sport and exercise psychology* (7th ed.). Champaign, IL: Human Kinetics.

SEE IT TO BE IT! HOW SQUASH PLAYER LENARD PUSKI HELPED ST. LAWRENCE UNIVERSITY END A LONG LOSING STREAK AGAINST TRINITY COLLEGE
Dora Kurimay

Lenard Puski got a squash scholarship to study at St. Lawrence University from 2015 to 2019 (n.d.). Lenard had been an elite Hungarian squash player who played for Hungary in the European Team Championships. He also played in the European Individual Championships. Right before he started his studies at St. Lawrence University, he and I worked together for several months in Hungary.

His goals were to create pre-performance routines (Lidor, 2010) to facilitate current rituals and to create new ones if necessary. Pre-performance routines and pre-shot routines or rituals are controlled selections of thoughts and behaviors that are specifically used by athletes prior to their performance to help balance their arousal level and increase their concentration and confidence level. Lenard told me he wanted to increase his confidence and concentration. He wanted to have a good start at St. Lawrence University. It is always hard to go to a new school and/or a new country, where you have to prove yourself all over again. We created an imagery routine (Vealey & Forlenza, 2015; Weinberg & Gould, 2015) for Lenard that included his nonplaying time rituals: pre-performance routines and in-between time rituals such as serve and serve receive rituals, mistake rituals, and breathing techniques as well. Serve and serve receive rituals are how an athlete spends the few seconds right before his or her serve and serve receive happen. For example, the ritual can cover how many times an athlete bounces the ball right before his or her serve and his or her mini physical and mental ritual right before receiving the serve. A mistake ritual is a physical gesture that helps an athlete bounce back right after losing a point. It is a physical pattern that the athlete does consistently when he or she misses a point; for example, turning away from the court and looking up at one point to flush his or her mind. Finally, breathing technique helps to release tension by focusing on the exhalation (Kurimay & Toon, 2014).

He shared with me that the technique of imagery helped him considerably right before his matches because he usually had to play the last match on his team. He was expecting to be the captain and best player on his team, so he felt a great deal of pressure when he went to St. Lawrence University. The technique of imagery helped him to cope with pressure and increase his confidence and concentration right before his matches.

Research indicates that imagining a motor act is similar to performing it. Movements and imagery of movements are functionally equivalent. Functional equivalence theory explains that imagery enhances performance because imagery and performance are the same, so imagery practice is the same as physical practice (Morris, Spittle & Watt, 2005).

Lenard related the following exciting story about a match that occurred in the 2015–2016 season, during his freshman year. This match helped St. Lawrence University end its losing streak against Trinity College. This was its first win against Trinity College since 2009 since the university started having a squash team (St. Lawrence University, 2016). St. Lawrence University hasn't had another win against Trinity since this win. It should be noted that Trinity has won thirteen national championships and is one of intercollegiate sports' all-time dynasties.

According to Lenard,

> My best memory was to win my last match at 4–4 standing against Trinity College. It was a historic moment for my university because we never ever beat Trinity College, the college that didn't have any losses and was leading the first place at the league that time. I had to play the last match and I had a long waiting time before I played against Trinity. I had to watch all my teammates' matches and be able to be ready to play when I stepped on the court. I used visualization 30 minutes before my match and it helped me to keep my focus on my upcoming match, and not get distracted by watching my teammates' matches and with the pressure to win. I was able to win this crucial match, which was a huge accomplishment for me and for my school!

Let me review how he was able to "See It to Be It." We applied the following steps when we created his imagery script before he went to St. Lawrence University:

1. I asked Lenard to choose a match in his memory when he played his best, and I provided him with several questions that helped him write a script about his peak performance experience. The questions helped him to remember what he did right before his match, what he was wearing, how he felt, what he served, how was his footwork, pace, strokes, body language, and what was going through his head, and so on.
2. We watched one of his best matches together to see which rituals were working for him and which he wanted to change.
3. We created (optimized) his already existing rituals based on video analysis and through talking it over. He focused on his serve and serve receive rituals and his mistake ritual.
4. He practiced his rituals and imagery and he tested what worked and what did not. Vividness, clarity, and consistent practice (minimum three times a week) were crucial in this process.

5. We modified the scripts a few times, and he added his warm-up routines and other rituals in the script with music as well. An MP3 that included his scripts and music was rerecorded for him. The goal was that he would be able to do the imagery without the MP3 in the long run and just run it in his head.

Lenard did a great job during his freshman year—he was the Liberty League Rookie of the Year and an All-American. Lenard won his division in the Molloy Division at the College Squash Association (CSA) team nationals and finished ranked in the top twenty nationally. He went 19–2, including 9–2 at four and set the St. Lawrence University single-season record for wins. He continued playing well the rest of his career and the Saints even played in the semifinals of the national championships and got fourth in the nation in 2016 and 2018. Unfortunately, Lenard was injured in his last year. He graduated in 2019 and will start coaching in New York.

Take-Home Points

1. Everything starts with awareness—see what routines and rituals work when an athlete is experiencing his or her peak performance and what has to be changed.
2. Choose the best method that works for your athlete; everyone is different. For example, the technique of imagery as a pre-performance routine worked really well for Lenard right before his matches.
3. Practice, adjust, and sharpen it.
4. In the end, See It to Be It!

References

Kurimay, D., & Toon, K. (2014). *Get your game face on like the pros!* Berkeley, CA: Game Face System.

Lidor, R. (2010). Pre-performance routines. In S. J. Hanrahan & M. B. Andersen (Eds.), *Routledge handbook of applied sport psychology: A comprehensive guide for students and practitioners* (1st ed.) (pp. 537–46). London, UK: Routledge/Taylor & Francis.

Morris, T., Spittle, M. & Watt, A. P. (2005). *Imagery in Sport.* Champaign, IL: Human Kinetics.

St. Lawrence University. (n.d.). Lenard Puski. Retrieved from https://saintsathletics.com/roster.aspx?rp_id=8944

St. Lawrence University. (2016). Saints hand #1 Trinity first loss, 5–4. Men's Squash Athletics News. Retrieved from https://saintsathletics.com/news/2016/2/13/MSQUASH_0213160452.aspx

Vealey, R. S., & Forlenza, S. T. (2015). Understanding and using imagery in sport. In J. M. Williams & V. Krane (Eds.). *Applied sport psychology: Personal growth to peak performance* (7th ed.) (pp. 240–73). New York, NY: McGraw-Hill.

Weinberg, R. S., & Gould, D. (2015). *Foundations of sport and exercise psychology* (6th ed.). Champaign, IL: Human Kinetics.

LEARNING TO READ YOUR PHYSIOLOGICAL STRESS GAUGE
William Land

Any race car driver will tell you that being fast requires more than just knowing how to drive a car. Being a good racer also requires an awareness of the current state of the car. Drivers must use their gauges and monitor aspects of the car's condition such as rpms, engine temperature, oil pressure, and fuel level. Drivers who fail to pay attention to these critical aspects run the risk of damaging their engine, running out of gas, or, more importantly, not winning the race.

The ability to monitor one's current condition is not important only for race car drivers; it is essential for all athletes. Just as race car drivers maintain an awareness of the state of their car, so too must athletes learn to monitor their own mental and physical states during competitions (Land & Tenenbaum, 2014; Ravizza & Fifer, 2005). Situations of heightened performance pressure, such as during competitions, can trigger activation of the body's sympathetic nervous system. This activation results in the release of stress hormones that act to rev up the body, much like stepping on the gas pedal of a car. Physiological changes such as an increase in muscle tension, respiratory rate, and cardiovascular activity occur in order to prepare the body for dealing effectively with the source of stress (Hanton, Mellalieu, & Williams, 2005). These well-orchestrated physiological changes are commonly referred to as the fight-or-flight response, which has evolved in order to help individuals react to life-threatening situations. While these physiological changes under stress may be beneficial when running from an attacking lion, these changes are not always helpful to the performance of sports skills, especially sports skills that require coordination and precision. Consequently, it is imperative that athletes learn how to read their gauges and know what steps to take to cope with physiological changes that may be occurring due to stress.

A perfect example of this comes from a collegiate golfer I had the pleasure of working with. This individual was a very accomplished golfer at a top Division I university known for the sport. During competitions, however, he began struggling to play up to his capability. This was obviously very frustrating for him. In practice he would play fine, but during team qualifying or tournaments, his play would suffer. As I spoke with him, I noticed that when his performance started to deteriorate, it was always accompanied by a particular type of performance error: namely, a slice. In golf, a slice is a type of unwanted shot that curves to the right and off target. I found it important that his poor performance always manifested in a particular type of performance mistake. The golfer believed the slice was due to poor movement technique and attempted to correct the mistake on the course by concentrating on the proper form. However, as indicated by a wealth of research on attentional focus, turning one's focus toward movement execution can be detrimental to performance (Wulf, 2013). Research indicates that a focus on the trajectory of the shot is better for performance than focus on the movement itself (Bell & Hardy, 2009).

My hunch was that the problem this golfer was experiencing under pressure was not due to poor technique per se, but rather was a result of the physiological changes that accompany increases in stress. Specifically, I was concerned that performance pressure was increasing muscle tension, which was interfering with the coordination of the movement, causing the occurrence of the slice and the resultant poor performance. As stated by legendary golfer Bobby Jones, "You must swing smoothly to play golf well, and you must be relaxed to swing smoothly." To explore this hunch, I asked him about any perceived muscle tension during his competitions. Perhaps unsurprisingly, he stated that he never paid attention to muscle tension, and thus did not know if he was feeling tense. I have found in my work with athletes that many athletes are not overtly aware of physiological changes that occur under stress, and thus require specific training so that they can learn to monitor and read their body's gauges.

Based on this golfer's lack of self-awareness of potential physiological changes, I introduced a strategy to teach him how to monitor these changes, starting with muscle tension. To do this, I had him subjectively rate the degree of muscle tension he felt (how stiff his arms felt, how tightly he was holding the club) after each hole of golf. As he recorded his score on the score card, he also provided a score for his muscle tension (from 1 for low tension to 10 for very tense). This process helped the golfer learn to check in and become aware of any changes in muscle tension. The results were eye opening for him. After a bad hole, he could easily see an increase in his muscle tension scores for the next few holes. The golfer also made an insightful observation during this training: He recounted that he observed himself having a "death grip" on the golf flag when removing it from the hole following a poor hole. His growing awareness of his muscle tension allowed us to utilize strategies to cope with and compensate for the muscle tension in order to reduce its negative effect on performance. In particular, we utilized a breathing strategy and muscle relaxation techniques for the arms to help dissipate the unwanted tension. (See Hanton, Mellalieu, & Williams, 2005, for a review of techniques.)

For this golfer, learning to become self-aware of his own physiological changes was eye opening. He could clearly see a relationship between changes in his muscle tension and his performance on the golf course. Without the ability to read one's gauges, it becomes difficult to know when to utilize mental skills that can be useful in effectively ameliorating the potentially harmful effects of heightened physiological arousal (Ravizza & Fifer, 2005). In practice, the use of self-rating scales can be useful for helping athletes gain awareness of various physiological parameters that can impact performance, such as heart rate, respiration rate, and muscle tension. For the golfer in this example, once he learned to recognize the signs of stress, he was able to effectively implement techniques to help control the negative effects of muscle tension. His performance quickly rebounded, and with it came an increase in confidence stemming from the knowledge that he was in control and was not at the mercy of the stress. Just as a race car driver watches the gauges on his car, athletes need to be able to read their own gauges and take corrective actions to keep their bodies performing at their peak.

Take-Home Points

1. It is important to be aware of the physiological changes that occur due to stress (e.g., muscle tension, heart rate, respiration rate, and lack of sleep).
2. Focusing attention on movement technique can be detrimental to skilled athletes during competition.
3. Coaches or sport psychology professionals can help athletes develop strategies to reduce the negative impact of these changes.

References

Bell, J. J., & Hardy, J. (2009). Effects of attentional focus on skilled performance in golf. *Journal of Applied Sport Psychology, 21*, 163–77.

Hanton, S., Mellalieu, S., & Williams, J. M. (2005). Understanding and managing stress in sport. In J. M. Williams & V. Krane (Eds.), *Applied sport psychology: Personal growth to peak performance* (7th ed.) (pp. 207–37). New York, NY: McGraw-Hill.

Land, W. M., & Tenenbaum, G. (2014). Self-awareness theory. In R. J. Eklund & G. T. Tenenbaum (Eds.), *Encyclopedia of sport and exercise psychology* (pp. 617–19). Los Angeles, CA: Sage.

Ravizza, K., & Fifer, A. (2015). Increasing awareness for sport performance. In J. M. Williams & V. Krane (Eds.), *Applied sport psychology: Personal growth to peak performance* (7th ed.) (pp. 176–87). New York, NY: McGraw-Hill.

Wulf, G. (2013). Attentional focus and motor learning: A review of 15 years. *International Review of Sport and Exercise Psychology, 6*, 77–104.

UP AND DOWN THE LADDER:
THE EBBS AND FLOWS OF A CHAMPION JOCKEY
Karen Lo

"There's [number] four, ladies and gentlemen . . . Derek Chan on Star Legend. Predicting another win later," the commentator's voice blared over the PA system. After a short chat with the stewards and the trainer, it was time for Derek to get ready for his seventh race of the day. All eyes were on him as he cantered round the parade ring. I noticed, however, that he looked a little dazed. It was 9:30 p.m. and the crowd was deafening.

He made his way to the gates together with the other jockeys. He kept looking down at his hands; it was an unusual gesture. A few minutes later he was off on Star Legend, while the crowd cheered behind the rails. It was the 2200 meter turf race. "Star legend, Audacity and Happy-Go-Lucky are in the leading pack . . . Star legend comes 10 to 12 around the bend, final stretch 400 meters out . . . here comes Happy-Go-Lucky emerging down the middle, sweeping the lead . . . amazing turn of acceleration . . . folks, it's Happy-Go-Lucky, he's first, Star Legend second, Audacity third!"

Back in my office the next day, Derek showed me the playback, looking very flustered. "I guess I just lost focus," he said. "I was exhausted, and I zoned out the last three races."

I had him describe his prerace routines and how he felt between races. He told me,

I usually hand the horse over for a brush up, weigh in, change my gear for the next race, socialize with horse owners, tell them what the horse's condition is ... then I go and get ready, walk around the parade ring, and head out. There's usually twenty-two minutes in between and I have around ten minutes on my own at the gates. In the first five races I can still function, but once I hit my sixth race for the day, I start feeling flat. I want to get fired up until I complete my eighth race, and finish strong, but I can't." Derek usually does eight races in one evening.

We had a conversation about what "firing up" meant to him. He described it as being at his optimum, feeling excited and on point. Using the Inverted U Theory as a reference (Landers & Arent, 2001; Williams & Gould, 2011), I asked him to rate his optimal level on a scale of 1 to 10, 1 being extremely relaxed, and 10 being extremely psyched. "7 would be my state of readiness, I think," he said. "Things start rolling from 6:30 p.m. and if I were to stay at 7 all evening without shutting down at odd moments, I don't feel present after 10:00 p.m. anymore, and that affects my last three races."

It is important that athletes know how to utilize their energy by switching on and off, especially for those who engage in long hours of competition (Landers & Arent, 2001). This involves a mixture of being aware of one's own optimal arousal level and planning when and how to focus.

It was clear that Derek knew what he wanted: He wanted to switch off when he could. "What stops you from being at a 7 at the gates?" I asked, wanting to confirm the barriers that are keeping him from being ready and performing well.

"Socializing with the owners, and having to remember what to say when I'm being hounded by the press," he said. "It drains me mentally."

We went through his routine again and identified two time slots that he can choose to switch off:

1. Walking around the parade ring, he can relax and get down to a 5 on his arousal scale, where he would like to remain until he gets to the gates.
2. Five minutes prior to the start of the race, he wants to build his momentum back up and get back to a 7 so that he can be ready.

We worked on strategies that could allow him to move up and down the scale. First, he had to think of two scenarios that best represented 5 and 7; second, he had to think of arousal-reduction techniques to slide down from 7 to 5 (what would happen at the parade ring); third, he had to come up with arousal-inducing techniques to go back up from 5 to 7 (what would happen at the gates).

Through incorporating imagery techniques, Derek described 5 as a learning state, where he was present and mindful while sitting inside the stables in full gear, hearing the horses neighing softly, and being at ease. He described 7 as a more alert and ready state; he associated this with something he liked doing often: climbing up the ladder inside one of the stables and peeping through a wall crack, with the sun shining in, breathing in that fresh air and feeling hopeful for the day. When he needed to slide down to a 5, he would imagine climbing down the ladder and sitting back down in the stables; to get back up to 7, he would simply imagine climbing back up the ladder and breathing in that morning air.

Derek tried applying the scale in the next few races and started winning again. Shortly afterward, he accumulated his seventieth win, successfully graduated from the apprentice jockey school, and continued on to embrace life as a senior jockey.

(The names of the horses and jockey in the story have been changed to respect the jockey's confidentiality.)

Take-Home Points

1. Determine your optimal arousal level through remembering past successful experiences or imagining your ideal state of readiness.
2. Be aware when you are not at that optimum state.
3. Think of arousal-inducing and arousal-reduction techniques to get to your optimum when needed.

References

Landers, D. M., & Arent, S. M. (2001). Arousal-performance relationships. In J. M. Williams (Ed.), *Applied sport psychology: Personal growth to peak performance* (6th ed.). New York, NY: McGraw-Hill.

Weinberg, R. S., & Gould, D. (2011). *Foundations of sport and exercise psychology* (5th ed.). Champaign, IL: Human Kinetics.

RIDE IT OUT: STRESS AND ANXIETY MANAGEMENT STRATEGIES ON THE SLOPES
Michelle M. McAlarnen, PhD, CMPC,
Minnesota State University, Mankato

Preparing for the descent. *Courtesy of Michelle M. McAlarnen*

In eighth grade, I skied for the first time on a school field trip. We traveled north to a small ski hill and some people jumped on the chairlifts, whisked away to fresh powder and smooth runs. I joined the morning ski lessons with a few others and found myself awkwardly managing ski poles and skis. The first test was to get off the chairlift. The instructor encouraged us to plant our skis and let the chair push us down the small decline. As I dismounted, I promptly forgot all the instructions and attempted to move my legs to ski down the drop.

I fell face first into the snow, popped my head up, and then lunged to the side to escape the next chair, heading straight for me! I still remember the chairlift operator's surprised face and shout: "Down!" The operator paused the lift, and I shuffled away embarrassed that (a) I fell, (b) I forced the chairlift to stop, (c) everyone saw that debacle, and (d) I was incompetent at this task. Then I realized: I have to ski down this hill and do it all again.

Needless to say, I did not touch skis ever again. I blamed the chaos of skis and poles for my fall and instead adopted snowboarding. Unfortunately, snowboarders also have to get off chairlifts! I snowboarded twice more as a young adult, and apparently I got on and off decently well. I have no memory of these accomplishments. Instead, bottled-up stress and anxiety around ski lifts lurked, waiting to return.

First Lesson

What we resist persists—even (and especially) when we try to change the game (for example, switching from skiing to snowboarding).

In 2015 I moved to Mankato, Minnesota. There is a small ski hill in town, and it seemed to taunt me: "You want to snowboard or are you still scared?" Um, I am still scared, thank you very much! But that February my friend invited me to snowboard and I climbed back onto the chairlift. Aware of my anxieties, he coached me through my quest to conquer my chairlift fears and achieve my dream of snowboarding.

I expressed all the classic symptoms of the stress process and related anxiety (McGrath, 1970; Smith, Smoll, & O'Rourke, 2011; Weinberg & Gould, 2015). There was an environmental demand (getting off the ski lift), which I perceived as challenging and as a threat (to my ego, to my body), and I believed I did not have the resources (physical coordination, skills, and experience) to cope with its demands. This stress response manifested itself in cognitive and somatic state anxiety (Hanton, Neil, & Mellalieu, 2011). My anxious response also peaked because I viewed snowboarding as an important activity with uncertain elements and outcomes. I hoped snowboarding could be a way to enjoy the winter months and spend time with friends. It also was a sport at which I long desired to be proficient. There were many uncertainties, such as navigating the lift, the terrain, and my path down the hill without snowboarding into other people. Thus, as we sat in the chairlift, my muscles tightened, my breath was irregular (too quick or tightened as I held it), and my attention was scattered and lingering on unhelpful external observations and internal dialogue. My mind bounced from thought to thought: jealousy of the kids flying down the hill below me, fear of embarrassing myself in front of everyone, and reprimands for all of these reactions: "You teach sport psychology. Get it together!" Though my avoidant tendencies wanted to retreat back to the warmth of the lodge, there was only one way back, and it was off the ski lift and down the hill.

Second Lesson

Sometimes you need someone to come alongside you and teach you what you teach others.

To work through these anxieties, I did a few things with the help of a friend as we returned to the hill again and again. He began to tell me right before we dismounted, "Ride it out." In other words, do not force anything, just let the momentum take you and be stable in your stance. These cue words calmed me and shifted my focus to what I needed to do instead of all the thoughts whirling in my head. I began to develop a pre-dismount routine that included imagining a clean ride off the chairlift and a few deep breaths, which helped my body reset. My friend noticed that my feet were too narrow when I got off, and I learned to plant my foot closer to my back binding. This placement became a physical cue. Eventually, my ski lift routine and repetitively getting off and back on gave me confidence in my abilities. These strategies are examples of self-instructional training in which individuals adopt attentional techniques and relaxation responses to manage anxiety-provoking situations (Smith et al., 2011; Weinberg & Gould, 2015).

Third Lesson

Develop strategies that match how anxiety presents itself (somatic and/or cognitive) and integrate those strategies into task preparation and execution.

It's been three years and I still wobble at times as I disembark. Anxiety creeps up occasionally, but I try to see it as facilitative instead of debilitative (Hanton et al., 2011). It is reminding me to focus, go through my routine, and recall past successful dismounts, while also acknowledging that this skill is still tricky. The difference is that I have the resources to manage it. My adventures in snowboarding provide the opportunity to be a beginner, with all of the challenges, learning, and moments of glory it offers. As I continue to implement these mental skills techniques along with consistent practice, I notice myself becoming more comfortable on the lift and the slopes. I am slowly transitioning to the next level of snowboarding, taking more chances, riding more smoothly, and remembering to breathe along the way.

Take-Home Points

1. Recognize your stress response process, how anxiety might manifest itself somatically and/or cognitively, and how these responses can shape your behaviors.
2. Develop routines and cues that can help you manage stress and direct your attention and energy to the task. Some examples mentioned include: support from a trusted other, a physical cue and focus phrase, imagery, deep breathing, progressive task practice, and challenging some irrational beliefs around competence.

3. Embrace being a beginner!
4. And ride it out!

References

Hanton, S., Neil, R., & Mellalieu, S. D. (2011). Competitive anxiety and sporting performance. In T. Morris & P. Terry (Eds.), *The new sport and exercise psychology companion* (pp.89–104). Morgantown, WV: Fitness Information Technology.

McGrath, J. E. (1970). Major methodological issues. In J. E. McGrath (Ed.), *Social and psychological factors in stress* (pp. 19–49). New York, NY: Holt, Rinehart, & Winston.

Smith, R. E., Smoll, F. L., & O'Rourke, D. (2011). Anxiety management. In T. Morris & P. Terry (Eds.), *The new sport and exercise psychology companion* (pp. 227–55). Morgantown, WV: Fitness Information Technology.

Weinberg, R. S., & Gould, D. (2015). *Foundations of sport and exercise psychology* (6th ed.). Champaign, IL: Human Kinetics.

A TENNIS JOURNEY
Nikola Milinkovic

I was born and raised in a war-torn country under economic sanctions, strong political turmoil and conflict, but among people historically known to have talent for sports. At an early age, I started playing soccer, as it was a game easily accessible to all and a great way to spend time with friends and find an outlet from daily challenges. It exposed me to the dynamics of teamwork and developing technical skills, and it was fun. I enjoyed playing it but never really imagined myself as an athlete until one day I saw tennis on TV. I thought it was similar to soccer somehow. Both sports require quick explosive movement, tracking the ball, and hand-eye coordination, and both are played in a rectangle. As I was very studious and took school very seriously, there was something mathematical that simply made sense about tennis, although math was far from my favorite subject.

I thought I could be both a student and an athlete, and at the age of eight I decided to join a local tennis club. I improved fairly quickly over the years and was considered a very talented player, but I did not know where to direct that talent. I discovered tournaments were the place exactly for that purpose, but what I did not know was that competing and training were two very different environments (Todd, 2018).

I thought that if I had the technical skills and the physical ability to play tennis, I would always hit the ball well and ultimately win over my opponent. When I stepped on the court to play my first competitive match in the 12s age group, I was suddenly overwhelmed by the presence of family, coaches, teammates, and spectators in the audience. I felt the immediate pressure of a big moment but did not know how to use mental skills—for example, self-talk, breathing, or imagery—to handle the pressure. My feet felt heavy and slow, my muscles felt tense, my heart was pounding, my thoughts were loudly racing, and I felt completely paralyzed (Hanin, 2000).

This experience came as a shock and I felt overwhelmed by the intensity of it. I kept trying to pull my mind into some sort of focus, but the thoughts remained loud, my body remained tense, and a feeling of panic started creeping in. I was aware of what was happening to me, but I did not know what to do with the information my mind and body were sending me (Martens, 1971). Over the next few months, I kept signing up for tournaments, thinking match experience would help me handle the anxiety, but it did not. I reverted to the most common advice I was getting—to pretend that the official match was just practice—but that did not help either. While I continued to compete, I was running out of ideas about how to overcome the anxiety. I started to fear its arrival and felt helpless and trapped under its spell (Clark, 2018). I started to very vividly see myself in the future losing focus, my feet feeling heavy, my heart pounding (Hanin, 2000). These images made me feel extremely uncomfortable as I started to become anxious about becoming anxious.

As I was transitioning into the 14s age group and as the competition was getting better, I noticed that I could not eat or sleep very well the entire week before an event (Fish, 2015). This was the moment when I knew competing was a whole lot more than just being able to technically hit the ball well. It was about training the mind just as much as it was about training the body and technique. I did not know why this was happening or what was causing it. I did not see a way out despite all the well-intentioned advice my parents, teammates, and coaches were giving me. I started to feel alone and hopeless, and thought that I would never in my life win a tournament match. I was tired of fighting my body, my mind, and my emotions every time I stepped onto a court. At age fifteen, after three years of competing against not only my opponents, but my own anxiety as well, I threw in the towel and put my racket down until further notice.

I felt I needed a break from tennis, as I reached a point of total despair. My coaches and parents were fully supportive of my decision and gave me the freedom to do what I thought was right. During this break I continued playing basketball, soccer, and table tennis, sports I really enjoyed playing for fun. This allowed me to keep being active and spend more time with friends. I made no specific plans about going to back to tennis, nor did I know if I would ever play competitively again.

During the next two years, my parents and I moved and to different countries twice due to my mother's international work. I felt liberated, having left tennis and my anxiety behind, thinking I might never have to face either of them again. I started my junior year of high school in an American education system in the Netherlands. One day, as I was walking by the school gym, I noticed a sign for tennis team tryouts. I knew nothing about the American way of playing high school sports or how the system worked. The team aspect of tennis was something I had never heard of before, and suddenly I had a strong feeling of having missed tennis, of somehow being willing to give it another try. At that moment, I knew I had to pick up my racket again.

When team tryouts came around, I felt very nervous, but I was able to focus on the skills I had been developing for years. Picking up a racket again after a long break felt as if I was continuing right where I left off before putting it down, except now I had new energy and motivation. I was able to focus on my game while allowing the nerves to be there. I was more accepting of them and felt them start to dissipate at times and change in intensity throughout tryouts. This new relationship I was developing with my own anxiety allowed me to perform well enough to be invited to varsity (Lloyd, 2018).

The team consisted of international players from all over the world. As we were getting to know each other, I learned about their personal tennis stories and how they perceived tennis in their own ways. Each of my teammates had different self-talk based on their own language and way of thinking about the game. I no longer felt alienated and alone because of my anxiety. I felt accepted and comfortable enough to share my story and learn new self-talk strategies from my teammates and coaches.

In addition to the positive self-talk I was learning, I noticed that I started playing in a more relaxed manner (Martens, Vealey, & Burton, 1990). The fact that we were practicing both doubles and mixed doubles in addition to singles impacted me significantly. All of a sudden, I had a teammate with whom I could share the good and the bad. My anxiety was no longer only mine to keep; there were now two of us helping each other handle it. I felt incredible support and was truly enjoying playing tennis for the very first time in years. The time came to attend our first tournament in Germany, but to my surprise the coach asked me to play singles. He envisioned that we would have the most success as a team if we each played a specific spot. Immediately, I had a flashback of my past thoughts and physical sensations, and felt panic starting to creep in again: "Oh *no*—am I going to go through the same horrific experience as I did in the past?" My mind had taken me into the future and into the outcome of my performance, but this time around I found a space between having these thoughts and responding to them (Fish, 2015). The difference was that now I had a choice: to let anxiety completely overtake me or to focus on my new self-talk, game plan, and what I could control (Hanin, 2000). I wholeheartedly decided to commit to this new mindset no matter how hard it was, and to step back on the court again for the first time in two years.

I won the match!

I was in total disbelief, and for a moment, everything around me became silent as if time was standing still. I stood on the court for the next few minutes all by myself, allowing this new feeling of inner peace and relief to completely flood over me. From that moment on, I started winning more matches and tournaments, peaking in college when my coach suggested I may want to try playing professionally. I knew then that my purpose was to help those who struggle, to lift them up and help them overcome challenges. My anxiety-driven journey was a life-changing experience and was one of the main reasons why I made a decision to combine sports and academics yet again, by attending graduate school in sport psychology.

Take Home Points

1. Talent is like an uncut diamond. It has inner light, but it takes hard work to shape it so it can truly shine. Sometimes it takes hitting rock bottom to

witness our own greatness, learn about ourselves, and discover what we are willing to do to rise back up again.
2. It is necessary that we make a note of those in our corner, of those who will hear us and with whom we can share our deepest challenges.
3. It is okay to feel anxiety. It is a human emotion. We need to be aware of and accept it instead of fighting against it.
4. "It ain't about how hard you hit, it's about how hard you can get hit and keep moving forward" (Stallone, 2006). I learned that my capacity to take the hits was extraordinary. However, we need space to breathe, reflect, recharge, and use mental and emotional skills to keep moving forward.
5. Create drills and game-based competitive scenarios in training. These are important so that we can practice mental and emotional skills in a controlled environment while learning how to use them in real-life situations.

References

Clark, A. H. (2018, October 18). How to harness your anxiety. *New York Times*. Retrieved from https://www.nytimes.com/2018/10/16/well/mind/how-to-harness-your-anxiety.html

Fish, M. (2015, September 1). The weight. *Players' Tribune*. Retrieved from https://www.theplayerstribune.com/en-us/articles/mardy-fish-us-open

Hanin, Y. L. (Ed.). (2000). *Emotions in sport*. Champaign, IL: Human Kinetics.

Lloyd, W. (2018, February 16). Here's why performance anxiety before an Olympic event may not be a bad thing. ABC News. Retrieved from https://abcnews.go.com/beta-story-container/Health/performance-anxiety-olympic-event-bad-thing/story?id=53143148.

Martens, R. (1971). Anxiety and motor behavior: A review. *Journal of Motor Behavior, 3*, 151–79.

Martens, R., Vealey, R. S., & Burton, D. (1990). *Competitive anxiety in sport*. Champaign, IL: Human Kinetics.

Stallone, S. (2006). *Rocky Balboa* [video]. Retrieved from https://www.youtube.com/watch?v=QrmQqEg4isU.

Todd, C. L. (2018, February 22). 6 tips for managing your anxiety from Olympic sports psychologists. *Self*. Retrieved from https://www.self.com/story/6-tips-for-managing-your-anxiety-from-olympic-sports-psychologists?mbid=nl_022518_Daily_Hero6_sl&utm_medium=dailyemail&CNDID=30915080&spMailingID=12997562&spUserID=MTMyNTU0OTU3MTM0S0&spJobID=1342146594&spReportId=MTM0MjE0NjU5NAS2.

"BE THE BEST" VERSUS "BE THE BEST CARLEY"
Deborah Munch

When Carley Lutzow was a freshman runner for Florida Gulf Coast University's cross country team, she wanted to be the best runner on the course. Unfortunately, her freshman year concluded in a less-than-desirable fashion, including an injury that forced Carley to take multiple weeks off in order to fully heal. Carley did not yet realize that her focus of being the best runner on the course was actually placing undue anxiety and tension on her body and mind.

It wasn't until a breakthrough race during her sophomore year where she decided to let go of everything—the pressure, the expectations, and the end result—that she realized the goal of being the best runner at any given competition wasn't working for her. Carley decided to focus more on what she could do in order to run her best, and she let go of comparing herself to other competitors. As a result of this shift in focus, she began to experience progress as a runner in both race results and mental toughness.

As Carley entered her senior year, she started to feel the pressure to make the most of her last year. She needed something to remind herself to take a step back, to assure herself that she was fine no matter what the outcome, and that she had done all the work and now all she had to do is put her best self out there. Carley created a verbal refocus cue: "Be the best Carley." Refocus cues can help the athlete to remain focused on the most beneficial aspect of performance at the present time while also avoiding distracting thoughts and feelings (Schmid, 1982). A refocus cue can be something that you say to yourself (verbal), something you look at (visual), or something you do (physical).

Carley acknowledged that saying this phrase to herself allowed her to "let go of expectations and know that I did the best I could on the course, whatever that was that day, even if I didn't win or run a PR (personal record), it was good enough . . . more than good enough, it's just what anyone could ask for—you can't ask for any more than your best" (C. Lutzow, personal interview, December 31, 2018).

Williams, Nideffer, Wilson, Sagal, and Peper (2010) recommend finding a cue that focuses on the positives rather than the negatives, the present moment rather than the past or the future, and the process rather than the score or outcome. "Be the best Carley" is a versatile refocus cue that embraces these recommendations and can be used in multiple different scenarios. Carley used the cue in practice when she was feeling anxious about hitting certain split times, at the starting line of races when she felt nervous and when negative thoughts began popping up, and even in the last mile of a race when her mind began to drift to the future, thinking about the final kick and whether she'd have enough energy or how her competitors would be feeling. The refocus cue "Be the best Carley" led her to ask herself questions about her best self, such as: *What am I thinking? What am I doing? What can I do right now in the moment?* These questions led Carley to put her energy and focus into positive things she could control in the present moment, and this was the zone where Carley performed at her best. Cue words act to trigger a particular response and can be considered a form of self-talk (Weinberg & Gould, 2019). "Being the best Carley" allowed Carley to partake in positive self-talk that made her feel as if she was enough: confident, at peace, and prepared for whatever came her way.

Carley's competitive running career ended on a high note. She finished with NCAA All-Region honors at the 2018 NCAA South Regional Championship, finishing sixteenth place overall, and was the first Atlantic Sun Conference runner to cross the finish line at the race. She had the second-highest NCAA South Regional Championship finish in the FGCU program. Although her competitive running career has come to an end, Carley says she will continue to use her refocus cue "Be the best Carley." As she moves forward in a career in exercise science, she sometimes recognizes the same distracting thoughts and anxiety creep in that she felt in running, thoughts such as: *Am I good enough?* or *Can I do this?* Carley is now equipped to manage those thoughts; she simply reminds herself to "be the best Carley," and then focuses on how to be her best self with what she has in the given moment.

Take-Home Points

1. A verbal refocus cue could be one word or a short phrase that, when said either out loud or in one's mind, elicits a particular desired response.
2. Approach the process of creating a refocus cue with a spirit of experimentation. Does it help you refocus to what is important in the moment? Does it make you feel the way you want it to feel? If not, think about how you can adjust your cue to help you get the result you want.
3. Refocus cues are personal. What works for one person may not work well for another, and what works now for someone may need to be adapted or changed in the future.

References

Schmid, A. B. (1982). Coach's reaction to Dr. A. B. Frederick's coaching strategies based upon tension research. In L. D. Zaichkowsky & W. E. Sime (Eds.), *Stress management for sport* (pp. 95–100). Reston, VA: AAHPERD.

Weinberg, R. S., & Gould, D. (2019). *Foundations of sport and exercise psychology* (7th ed.). Champaign, IL: Human Kinetics.

Williams, J., Nideffer, R., Wilson, V., Sagal, M., & Peper, E. (2010). Concentration and strategies for controlling it. In J. M. Williams (Ed.), *Applied sport psychology: Personal growth to peak performance* (6th ed.) (pp.336–58). New York, NY: McGraw-Hill.

THE BACKGROUND NOISE OF THE OVERACHIEVING HELICOPTER PARENT
Kate Nolt, MPH, PhD

Sarah and her family lived an extremely privileged life in a wealthy community in Texas. Both her parents were successful doctors and her mother was becoming a highly recognizable politician. Sarah's high school athletic career had been a stellar one. Her performance as a volleyball player had been finely tuned under the watchful eye of her parents as well as highly professional private trainers at top local facilities.

Sarah's athletic career began at a very young age. Her parents' expectations had become her own, so much so that Sarah sought my services as a sport psychologist, seeking to calm disturbing thoughts of potential failure that interfered with her attention, concentration, focus, and, thereby, performance. In addition to this, Sarah felt that her teammates were displaying signs of socially rejecting her because of her perceived attitude of being the best on the team. Coaches often cited Sarah's performance in tournaments as exemplary. While Sarah's parents were very proud, the pressure on Sarah to perform was great. Often, at the behest of her parents, Sarah sought out the toughest training programs to improve her skills in spiking, for example, because of one mistake made during a game. The training regimen would be grueling for most teens, but not Sarah. She would not accept that. Her parents' voices were always subliminally there, pushing her on to higher performance levels. But in fact, her parents were not saying much at all. It was Sarah's own perception of their successes in their careers and their own sport performance that led her to feel as if she had to always measure up.

The intake assessment indicated that Sarah was stressed and anxious! Self-talk measures indicated she did not feel good about herself and that she did not believe that others liked her for who she was. Further, while she could recognize how stressed she was, she did not take time to relax through calming activities. Every day was about peak performance: in academics, socially, and especially in her sport. This level of pressure and stress was working against peak performance and leading to burnout. Sarah was conflicted about continuing with the sport she loved or quitting to gain some control over what she perceived as her life under siege.

When we worked together, Sarah and I focused on improving her performance through blocking out the negative thoughts related to her perception that her hovering parents had expectations she would never meet. Motivation to perform at peak levels was clearly not an issue for Sarah. Rather, positive self-talk and concentration exercises were used. Session aims were to help Sarah calm the negative and stress-inducing pressure that affected her on and off the court. Further, imagery exercises were used to control her breathing and heart rate and to improve focus during a game. Neumann and Piercy (2013) indicate that using appropriate attentional strategies can enhance performance and influence psychological state during competition (p. 329).

A skill-based approach was used to improve Sarah's internal attention during games and tournaments. Sarah began to focus her attention on her body position and actions during a skill in a game. This internally focused approach helped to reduce the focus on her parents' potential disappointment in her performance and improved her concentration on the execution of action in a skill and in the moment. Additionally, mindfulness training was used to elicit more compassionate and acceptance-based self-talk. Mindfulness training, according to Baltzell, Chipman, Hayden, and Bowman (2015), can be an alternative to traditional mental skills training and is a nonjudgmental form of heightening awareness in the moment.

After months of this complementary approach of traditional mental skills and mindfulness training, Sarah was able to reduce her anxiety and improve her focus and concentration. Her performance in her senior year of high school led the team to a championship win in a highly competitive tournament. Sarah also found a way to rethink her approach to her parents' success and to not internalize it as a barometer for her own. We had a session with her parents wherein Sarah felt secure enough to discuss the internal pressures that challenged her, and her parents understood and agreed, but did not apologize, that their busy, high-pressure lives should not create such anxiety and chaos for her.

Sarah graduated high school with honors and proceeded to seek out universities with volleyball teams. She was asked by Division I institutions to try out. When the time came to make up her mind, Sarah declined invitations to a team and retired from her sport, as she wanted to focus on her premed studies. She was burned out. In 2019 I received a call from Sarah after nearly four years. After many pleasantries and catching up on family, Sarah got to the reason for her call. She said, "My parents really want me to go to medical school and I am second-guessing. I haven't liked premed. I don't want the life my parents have. I'm not sure if I should go, and I'm really stressing out!" Back in the saddle.

Take-Home Points

1. Be aware of the signs of burnout, as they can lead to anxiety, depression, and stress that can greatly affect performance.
2. Promote mental and physical breaks that include meditation, positive imagery, and self-awareness exercises for improved overall health and performance.
3. Artistically and openly discuss the value of a healthy balance between daily activities, which fosters stronger attentional control and improved performance.

References

Baltzell, A., Chipman, K., Hayden, L., & Bowman, C. (2015). Qualitative study of MMTS: Coaches' experience. *Journal of Multidisciplinary Research*, *7*(3), 5–20.

Neumann. D. L., & Piercy, A. (2013). The effect of different attentional strategies on physiological and psychological states during running. *Australian Psychologist*, *48*, 329–37.

THESE ARE THE MOMENTS WE LIVE FOR
Maximilian Pollack

Our lives are surrounded with moments of opportunity to challenge ourselves, grow, and ultimately thrive. However, we must find a way to get our minds and bodies primed for impending performances when they matter. The question is: How? There are many approaches and answers to this loaded question, but in one particular story, David defeated Goliath. Here is one example from my personal life that tells that story.

High school football was in full swing and it was my junior year on varsity. The school had a top-ranked recruit on the defensive line, and at the time, I was playing offensive lineman. The coaches called all the players to the center of the practice field for a one-on-one pass rush drill from any defensive lineman and any offensive lineman. The top-ranked recruit stepped up as the first volunteer. I stepped up knowing that this would be a moment to remember, and it was mine for the taking. The team circled up around both of us as the coach explained the instructions. My heart was pounding, my breathing rate started to increase, and I felt the sweat starting to flow. It was go time. I had imagined moments like these many times before, hoping that one day the opportunity would present itself. Here it was.

The coach prompted both of us to listen for his whistle blow, which signaled us to go. My opponent's goal was to reach the quarterback as fast as possible. My goal was to prevent the quarterback from being touched. I quickly pictured three different options that my opponent would likely employ once the whistle blew: bull rush, pass rush, or a mix of the two. For each option, I imagined the step-by-step process of defending against each technique. Right before the whistle blew, I pictured my coach from Pop Warner football giving me the speech from when we lost the championship, which brought my energy up a few notches. My mind cleared and my energy was primed and ready to go. Coach blew his whistle.

Our hands grab hold of each other as our helmets simultaneously slam face mask into face mask. This is where the battle begins. Fighting for position and ultimately control, our hands grab hold of any piece of the shoulder pads or jersey we can leverage. I unleash my strength, pushing against him and keeping my feet moving while trying to maintain a firm position. He begins to lose his center of gravity. I drive him forward and he begins to slip. Within half a second, my opponent is driven into the ground and I am holding him there. The moment I have replayed in so many different ways in my mind has come to life.

We all may be able to search our memory banks for when we either saw or experienced an underdog beat a favorite or overcome the expectations of others. How do those who are presented with pressure-filled moments thrive within those moments? Often, our bodies activate in these moments in many different ways and for a particular purpose. However, our perceptions of why these physiological changes happen can either increase or decrease our state anxiety levels. Competitive state anxiety consists of somatic and cognitive anxiety. Somatic state anxiety is based more on our physiological arousal, which can feel unpleasant, nervous, and at times tense. Cognitive state anxiety is based around negative expectations and concerns regarding the self, the situation, or consequences at play. Anxiety is not always considered debilitative, but rather, if reframed effectively, anxiety can facilitate performance (Vadocz, Hall, & Moritz, 1997).

As suggested by Vadocz, Hall, and Moritz (1997), a strategy that can be used to control anxiety is the implementation of mental imagery, which can serve two functions: motivational and cognitive. Motivational functions include goal-oriented situations such as envisioning successful outcomes within an event and generating images related to physiological and emotional arousal such as experiencing the stress and excitement within one's mind. Cognitive functions incorporate mental practice of general strategies and skills. The use of imagery along with relaxation training has been shown to decrease anxiety within athletes, as found in VanDenberg and Smith's (1993) study with wrestlers. Cognitive state anxiety and somatic state anxiety both decreased. A way in which we can increase the effectiveness of imagery practice is through building imagery ability (Rodgers, Hall, & Buckolz, 1991). This requires practice (Vadoacz, Hall, & Moritz, 1997). The proof is in the pudding. We can enhance our ability to calm our nerves, decrease anxiety, and use imagery to help us perform in the moments all around us. Earlier I stated, "The moment I have replayed in so many different ways in my mind has come to life." In fact that moment did come to life, but why? I routinely created moments such as these in my mind over and over again, imagining every part of the experience so when the moment did show up I would be ready. Here are some suggestions for how we can develop our own imagery practices to prepare each person for these moments.

Building imagery ability can be challenging, and therefore one should consider starting with short, intermittent sessions of imagery rehearsal (Cumming & Eaves, 2018). The images created should emphasize quality as the overall priority. A key to developing high-quality imagery is vividness, which describes the clarity, sharpness, and sensory richness of the image (Runge, Cheung, & D'Angiulli, 2017), and controllability, which is the ability to manipulate or influence the imagery content in one's mind (Cumming & Eaves, 2018). In order to vastly enhance the quality of one's imagery, try to incorporate all of the senses—sight, smell, taste, touch, and sound—and any emotion that would likely be experienced. This way, the experience in the mind can be as close to real as the experience in real life. Imagery ability can be improved through simple practice efforts, but if practiced in more deliberate and systematic ways (Cumming & Hall, 2002), imagery ability will likely reach new heights (Cumming & Eaves, 2018).

The moments we live for are all around us. Whether you're about to face off against a high-level opponent, take a game-winning shot, or simply perform with all you've got, set yourself up for success by taking as much control of arousal and anxiety levels as possible. Envision success and practice doing so. Incorporating all of the aspects that could present in your performance will add to the realism and richness of the performance. Athletes tend to implement the use of motivational imagery the most and typically right before a competition, which can lead to increased confidence (Vadocz, Hall, & Moritz, 1997). When opportunities present themselves, you can choose to either be ready for the opportunities or fall short of readiness. You can discover with proper practice how to create imagined success within our minds so that when the time is right, it yields success in your performance domain. Those moments are yours for the taking, and imagery can help you get there, gain control, enhance confidence, and give it all you've got.

Take-Home Points

1. Use imagery to decrease somatic state anxiety and cognitive state anxiety before a competition.
2. Use different functions of imagery (motivational and cognitive functions can be implemented based on your needs). Motivational imagery is used by athletes to help decrease competitive state anxiety and increase self-confidence.
3. Create a systematic training plan for creating highly vivid and controlled imagery before, during, and after your performances.
4. Seek out a sport psychologist and/or certified mental performance consultant to help you develop effective Imagery practices for competition.

References

Cumming, J., & Eaves, D. L. (2018). The nature, measurement, and development of imagery ability. *Imagination, Cognition, and Personality, 4*(37), 375–93. 1–19. doi: 10.1177/0276236617752439

Cumming, J., & Hall, C. (2002). Deliberate imagery practice: Examining the development of imagery skills in competitive athletes. *Journal of Sport Sciences, 20*, 137–45. doi: 10.1080/026404102317200846

Rodgers, W., Hall, C., & Buckolz, E. (1991). The effects of an imagery training program on imagery ability, imagery use, and figure skating performance. *Journal of Applied Sport Psychology, 3*, 109–25.

Runge, M. S., Cheung, M. W. L., & D'Angiulli, A. (2017). Meta-analytic comparison of trial-versus questionnaire-based vividness reportability across behavioral, cognitive and neural measurements of imagery. *Neuroscience of Consciousness, 3*(1), 1–13. doi: 10.1093/nc/nix006

Vadocz, E. A., Hall, C. R., & Moritz, S. E. (1997). The relationship between competitive anxiety and imagery use. *Journal of Applied Sport Psychology, 9*(2), 241–53. doi: 10.1080/10413209708406485

VanDenberg, L., & Smith, D. E. (1993). *The effects of imagery on competitive anxiety in high school wrestlers.* Presentation at the Annual Conference of the Association for the Advancement of Applied Sport Psychology, Montreal, Quebec, Canada.

MAKE NO MISTAKE: YOUR THOUGHTS BUILD YOUR GAME!
Meghan Ramick and Selen Razon, West Chester University

Synchronized skating is the fourth and newest discipline of figure skating, where between eight and twenty skaters perform on the ice simultaneously while incorporating elements from the other three disciplines of skating: freestyle, pairs, and ice dance. Synchronized skating is unlike most team sports in that there are no distinct positions and all team members perform essentially identical movements at the same time while connected to one another for a good portion of the program. Additionally, there are no time-outs and no halftime where skaters can receive feedback from their coaches, and every movement performed is associated with a point value, so there is little room for error.

Although the goal of synchronized skating is for all skaters to look identical, from their hair and makeup to the height of the extending leg, every skater has a different personality and the ways they prepare themselves to perform are unique to each skater. What works for one skater will not necessarily work for all. I have been skating for twenty-nine years and participated on a synchronized team for twenty-one of those years. My personal approach to performing involves both teamwide and individual rituals that have evolved over those years as a result of my own personal experiences and team dynamics.

While I love the adrenaline rush that comes with performing, as well as the opportunity to work with my teammates to achieve a common goal, controlling my anxiety before major competitions has always been a challenge for me. To that end, sport performance anxiety is seen as a predisposition to experience negative thoughts and/or bodily tension and other forms of somatic arousal in competitive sport settings (Lewthwaite & Scanlan, 1989; O'Rourke, Smith, Smoll, & Cumming, 2011; Smith, Smoll, Cumming, & Grossbard, 2006). Psychological skills are known to help manage competitive anxiety and arousal (Weinberg & Gould, 2018). Over the years, I have learned to manage my arousal and anxiety using a variety of these skills, particularly attention control and mindfulness. Briefly, in performance settings, attention control refers to one's ability to focus and shift attention as needed. Attention control is key to optimal self-regulation under pressure (Luszczynska, Diehl, Gutiérrez-Dona, Kuusinen, & Schwarzer, 2004). Related to attention control, mindfulness is seen as a mental state that results from one's voluntary focus of attention on the present experience in a nonjudgmental and accepting way (Cottraux, 2007).

Specifically related to my use of these skills, a few years ago I was preparing to compete with my team in the Eastern Sectional Championships, a qualifying competition where the top four teams from each division move on to Nationals. Although it was my fifteenth time at this competition with my team, the field was tighter than usual this year, and for the first time, I felt an extreme amount of precompetition anxiety that persisted into the week of competition. I had trouble sleeping, and doubt started to creep into my thoughts. I tried to remind myself of the goals my teammates and I had set earlier that month, such as performing every move to the best of our ability, but I was still worried about what would happen if I couldn't get myself to that mental space on the ice.

Interestingly, however, prior to competition, I came across a cartoon by The Awkward Yeti where his main characters, the Heart and the Brain, were pushing a rock with the words "Self-Doubt" written on it up a hill. On top of the hill was a flag that said "Goal," and the Brain was saying to the Heart, "Maybe it would be easier if we put this down." I remember that right then I made the connection that the only thing standing in my way were my thoughts, and I was responsible for these. I could either give into my debilitative thinking and let the anxiety win, or I could shift my thinking to something I could control, like performing all of my movements to the best of my ability.

Still, at our practice on the morning of the competition, my team held back. We were all a little nervous and we didn't skate to our full potential. Our coaches came into the locker room and said, "Well, you're either going to go out there and do it this afternoon, or you're not." In that moment, I decided that I'd rather step out on the ice confidently and put it all out there than skate tentatively and hold back, as if we were afraid to mess up.

A few hours later in our competition warm-up, where we step through the program on the floor, using attention control and mindfulness, I tried to focus on performing each element to the best of my ability while optimally tuning into my moves. We went out there that afternoon and skated the program of the season and had a wonderful time. We ended up placing third, with the top three teams scoring within one point of each other. We were elated! However, the best part of the experience was being able to overcome my biggest obstacle: my mind, through the conscious control of my attention and mindful monitoring of my performance.

Since then, I have taken these tools and applied them to many other areas of my life. Stress is inevitable, but controlling one's mind and attention are keys to successful performance. Finally, training one's mind can take practice, but is worth it!

Take-Home Points

1. You are in control of your thoughts, so choose where you put your attention and focus on good thoughts only.

2. Be mindful over your performance, and accept instances and events as they are.
3. Focus on having fun! Having fun and enjoying the event makes it easier to go through. When the event feels easier, you will experience less pressure and perform better.

References

Cottraux, J. (2007). *Thérapie cognitive et emotions: La troisième vague* [Cognitive therapy and emotions: The third wave]. Paris: Elsevier Masson.

Lewthwaite, R. & Scanlan, T. K. (1989). Predictors of competitive trait anxiety in male youth sport participants. *Medicine and Science in Sports and Exercise, 21,* 221–229.

Luszczynska, A., Diehl, M., Gutiérrez-Dona, B., Kuusinen, P., & Schwarzer, R. (2004). Measuring one component of dispositional self-regulation: Attention control in goal pursuit. *Personality and Individual Differences, 37,* 555–66.

O'Rourke, D. J., Smith, R. E., Smoll, F. L., & Cumming, S. P. (2011). Trait anxiety in young athletes as a function of parental pressure and motivational climate: Is parental pressure always harmful? *Journal of Applied Sport Psychology, 23,* 398–412.

Smith, R. E., Smoll, F. L., Cumming, S. P., & Grossbard, J. R. (2006). Measurement of multidimensional sport performance anxiety in children and adults: The sport anxiety scale-2. *Journal of Sport and Exercise Psychology, 28,* 479–501.

Weinberg, R. S., & Gould, D. (2018). *Foundations of sport and exercise psychology.* Champaign, IL: Human Kinetics.

BE THE BALL
Michael L. Sachs, PhD

"Be the Ball" is an iconic phrase spoken by Ty Webb (played by Chevy Chase) in the awesome movie *Caddyshack*, directed by Harold Ramis (1980). This Yoda-like advice is given by Ty Webb to a young caddy, Danny, while Webb is hitting the golf ball. The quote is perfect for a discussion of attention/concentration.

Webb says to Danny: "There's a force in the universe that makes things happen, and all you have to do is get in touch with it. Stop thinking . . . let things happen . . . and be the ball."

In discussing attention and concentration, Williams, Nideffer, Wilson, and Sagal (2015) talk eloquently about being in the here and now, being in the present. Nideffer's Model of Attentional Style presents two dimensions: width (broad to narrow) and direction (internal to external). Once an assessment of course conditions (broad external) is completed, along with analysis of club to be selected, type of swing, and so on (broad internal), a brief use of imagery may take place (narrow internal) and then the coup de grâce, the golf stroke itself (narrow external), is completed. This is a closed skill condition, wherein the golf ball is stationary, the environment is stable, and the golfer need only decide when to swing the club. This is perfect for using a mantra such as "Be the Ball" and concentrating totally on the ball and the swing.

There is no need for further analysis once one has gone through the steps described above. Thinking about and analyzing one's swing is detrimental to just letting one's automatic processes unfold and hitting the ball smoothly and comfortably (being the ball). Those interested in the exact movie clip can readily find it on YouTube and/or will enjoy watching the zany comedy itself in its entirety.

Elements of "Be the Ball" relate to current work on mindfulness. For those interested, there are numerous books on mindfulness, including excellent recent ones by Kaufman, Glass, and Pineau (2017), as well as Zizzi and Andersen (2017). Others may be interested in a documentary entitled *Be the Ball* (www.betheballmovie.com/about), which follows on the premise that "people say golf is all about mind over matter."

Take-Home Points

1. Develop a mantra that works for you in facilitating concentration, whether it is "Be the Ball" or "Focus" or "Ball" or something else.
2. Practice the mantra in challenging situations so that using it becomes second nature and works for you!
3. Develop your mindfulness skills so that using a mantra like "Be the Ball" is effective across a variety of situations.

References

Kaufman, K. A., Glass, C. R., & Pineau, T. R. (2017). *Mindful sport performance: Mental training for athletes and coaches*. Washington, DC: American Psychological Association.

Williams, J. M., Nideffer, R. M., Wilson, V. E., & Sagal, M.-S. (2015). Concentration and strategies for controlling it. In J. M. Williams & V. Krane (Eds.), *Applied sport psychology: Personal growth to peak performance* (7th ed.) (pp. 304–25). New York, NY: McGraw-Hill.

Zizzi, S. J., & Andersen, M. B. (Eds.) (2017). *Being mindful in sport and exercise psychology: Pathways for practitioners and students*. Morgantown, WV: Fitness Information Technology.

IMAGINING THE POWER
Joann Wakefield

Marie is a former Division I swimmer who specialized in sprint events at a midwestern university in the United States. She swam competitively for sixteen years at the club, high school, and college levels. Her primary events included sprint and relays. Coach E has successfully coached at the club and collegiate levels for six and a half years, including junior national and national level swimmers.

Marie's imagery story is an incredible example of how dynamic mental skill practice and preparation can be. Imagery is the practice of using the body's senses (e.g., smell, taste, touch, sight, sound, and kinesthetic or movement) to create or re-create an experience (Vealey & Greenleaf, 2010). Imagery offers individuals an opportunity to practice physical skill and prepare for events without physically participating or being at the venue. Honing imagery abilities takes time, practice, and patience.

Two perspectives are utilized when practicing imagery: external and internal. External imagery is equivalent to watching a movie or being a spectator of an event (e.g., watching yourself compete in a race from the deck or stands). Internal imagery is when events are seen and experienced from inside your own body—you are participating (Murphy, 2009; Vealey & Greenleaf, 2010). Important imagery factors include vividness (how clear and detailed an image is) and controllability (imagining what is intended and changing aspects at one's will; Murphy, 2009). Are you able to imagine the colors and smells of a swim meet? Vividness! Are you able to imagine yourself leading the pack in a race *and* making corrections after missing the wall on a flip turn? Controllability! Imagery can help athletes improve motivation, confidence, attention, and focus; find meaning; regulate emotions; and improve performance to a degree (Gregg, Hall, & Nederhof, 2005; Murphy, 2009; Post, Muncie, & Simpson, 2012).

Picture yourself lying down on the pool deck, closing your eyes, and then swimming a personal lifetime best time. Yes, you read that correctly: swimming a best time without even touching the water or wearing a tech suit. Some may think this idea is insanity, but in reality it is the power of imagery. Marie was fortunate enough to have coaches from the club level and higher who dedicated time to the practice of imagery before big meets. As a visual and hands-on learner, Marie welcomed imagery into her race preparation. Marie's college coach, Coach E, introduced her to a new level of imagery practice using a stopwatch.

It was two and a half weeks until the conference championship meet. Coach E instructed everyone to find their own space on the pool deck and lie down in a comfortable position: "Think about your conference events and choose one that means the most. On my prompt, you will imagine every detail possible of this race including swimming your goal time." He then handed out a stopwatch to each swimmer: "I want you to start the watch at the starting beep cue and stop it when you touch the wall to end your race." Coach E prompted the swimmers from stepping off the team bus, walking onto the deck, warming up, preparing behind the block, stepping onto the block, and exploding off the block at the sound of the "beep." Marie chose her 50 freestyle race. At the starting beep, she imagined every detail she could for the race down to her stroke count, breath count, kicks off the wall, atmosphere of the pool, and her personal cue words. Marie surged into the wall and stopped her watch as her palm slammed in the touchpad. After looking up at the scoreboard and seeing her goal time, Marie slowly opened her eyes and sat up. Looking down at the stopwatch she saw a best time, only a few hundredths off her goal time.

Coach E's imagery exercise helped show Marie all of her technical and mental preparation could lead to her goals becoming reality. Marie continued to use imagery all the way up until she dove into the pool for each of her conference races. She imagined the pool area and how she wanted to walk into the venue and prepare for each meet session. Her imagery preparations allowed her to enter the conference meet calm and confident in her season-long preparations and her ability level. Marie achieved or was within hundredths of all her goal times that year. (It is important to note she had been honing her imagery ability since swimming at the club level. The practice was not something she adopted right before the big conference meet.)

Take-Home Points

1. Practice, practice, practice. This level of imagery is most helpful when you have taken the time to practice your imagery abilities (e.g., vividness, controllability).
2. Imagine performances where everything goes right, as well as how you will react and correct if something goes wrong.
3. Try new exercises and techniques to find what helps you mentally prepare best. The possibilities are endless!

References

Gregg, M., Hall, C., & Nederhof, E. (2005). The imagery ability, imagery use, and performance relationship. *Sport Psychologist, 19*, 93–99.

Murphy, S. (2009). *The sport psych handbook*. Champaign, IL: Human Kinetics.

Post, P., Muncie, S., & Simpson, D. (2012). The effects of imagery training on swimming performance: An applied investigation. *Journal of Applied Sport Psychology, 24*, 323–37.

Vealey, R. S., & Greenleaf, C. A. (2010). Seeing is believing: Understanding and using imagery in sport. In J. M. Williams (Ed.), *Applied sport psychology: Personal growth to peak performance* (6th ed.) (pp. 267–304). Boston, MA: McGraw-Hill Higher Education.

POOL OF TEARS: IN THE WATER THEY CAN'T SEE YOU CRY
Joann Wakefield

Marie is a former Division I swimmer who specialized in sprint events at a midwestern university in the United States. She swam competitively for sixteen years at the club, high school, and college levels. Her primary events included sprint and relays. She now enjoys a fruitful career working alongside and inspiring collegiate student athletes to make the most of their academic and athletic careers.

The following story depicts how improperly regulating emotions and utilizing maladaptive coping strategies can lead to negative consequences. Emotion regulation is the use of strategies to trigger, manage, change, or show emotions. These strategies are put in place when there is a discrepancy between one's present and desired emotions (Lane, Beedie, Jones, Uphill, & Devonport, 2012). The aforementioned regulation strategies will lead to positive or negative changes in emotions. A positive emotion change could occur when an athlete is mad about a missed goal kick and then uses a cue word to bring her or his attention back to the game. A negative emotion change could occur when athletes are experiencing stress and negative thoughts, and as a result decide to bury everything inside of themselves without coping. Unregulated emotions in life areas outside of sport can eventually lead to negative impacts on sport performance (Lane et al., 2012; Wagstaff, 2014). There are two types of coping: emotion focused and problem focused. Emotion-focused coping involves regulating emotional responses to the problem, while problem-focused coping involves trying to manage the problem causing stress (Weinberg & Gould, 2011).

Transitioning into college can be stressful and emotional for any incoming freshman, especially those who are student-athletes. Incoming freshmen typically encounter stressors such as living on their own for the first time, adjusting to classes, socializing with a new peer group, and various peer pressures. Student-athletes encounter all the aforementioned in addition to adjusting to a new team dynamic, training style, coaching staff, and position on the team. To say the least, incoming student-athletes face an immense number of potential stressors. Imagine adding a parental divorce, relationship breakup, lackluster freshman season performance, low confidence, and an abrasive team captain into the mix. This is Marie's story:

Marie had the exact freshman experience depicted above. Her parents' divorce tore her apart emotionally. Moving to school was a brief respite from her parents' harsh bickering and their trapping her in the middle, but Marie also felt guilty for leaving her younger sister back home alone to weather the brunt of divorce tensions. Her freshman season performance was soul crushing after a senior high school season full of personal record swims. Marie had a difficult time adjusting to her college coach's training and felt as if she did not belong in the college swimming world. One senior captain often told her she was not trying hard enough or did not care enough in practice. Marie's high school boyfriend was also on the men's swim team. They broke up mere hours after Marie had a disastrous freshman conference meet where she added time in every race. By the end of the season, her personal and swimming confidence had plummeted. Marie spent many practices crying in the water swimming while her goggles hid red, puffy eyes filled with exhaustion and sorrow: "I'd go to swim practice, put my face in the water, and I didn't have to talk to anybody. Swimming was like my escape, but it was also like this huge prison" (Beard & Paley, 2012, p. 24).

Marie developed strong friendships with her fellow freshman teammates but did not feel comfortable divulging all of the emotional toil weighing on her until the very end of the spring semester. She also never spoke a word about any family or personal struggles to her coach until one day in late January. The evening prior, her coach pulled her aside to check in on her after she struggled with a challenging practice. Marie immediately burst into tears and managed to mumble through sobs about her parents' divorce. The coach invited her to meet in the morning to talk about anything on her mind. After many more tears in her coach's office, Marie divulged all of the struggles she was experiencing with her parents' divorce and how it was affecting her emotionally, in the pool, and in the classroom. The coach took the time to share about his own parents' divorce story. He had been in college when his parents were divorcing, too. Marie felt a great relief letting someone into her struggle, especially someone who understood what it felt like to be a young adult with divorcing parents. Finding someone who shared a similar experience intensified her relief, validated her emotions, and showed her there was hope for happiness.

As mentioned earlier, Marie's freshman conference meet was a lackluster performance of added time and disappointing races. Though she had confided in her coach and felt some emotional relief, Marie had not yet worked through all of her thoughts and feelings. She was still holding on to a great deal of grief, anger, hopelessness, frustration, and guilt. It took her another four years to fully work through the negative thoughts and emotions associated with her parents' divorce. Marie slowly learned to focus on things she could control, such as her thoughts, reactions, and motivation; connecting with teammates; and seeking help.

During her sophomore and junior years, she had a renewed sense of self and motivation for training. Both of these seasons resulted in a number of personal records and in-season best times, solidifying her position as a frontrunner in the team lineup. During her senior year, Marie really hit her stride. She had found her love for the sport of swimming again, as well as a positive image of herself and her capabilities. Marie's senior swim season was the pinnacle of her athletic career. She achieved numerous personal records, in-season best times, conference finals, and A relays; continued adjusting to her new family dynamic; strengthened her relationship with her younger sister; and saw herself as a mentally and physically strong young adult.

Take-Home Points

1. Be your own hype (wo)man, not hit(wo)man. Challenge negative thoughts with positive self-talk, cue words, mantras, and visual reminders.
2. Find constructive ways that work best for you to process and release emotions; holding everything in inevitably leads to a flood.
3. Connect with others who have or are going through similar situations. Help reassure yourself you are not alone in the battle.

References

Beard, A., & Paley, R. (2012). *In the water they can't see you cry: A memoir.* New York, NY: Touchstone.

Lane, A. M., Beedie, C. J., Jones, M. V., Uphill, M., & Devonport, T. J. (2012). The BASES expert statement on emotion regulation in sport. *Journal of Sports Sciences, 30*(11), 1189–95.

Wagstaff, C. R. D. (2014). Emotion regulation and sport performance. *Journal of Sport and Exercise Psychology*, *36*, 401–12.

Weinberg, R. S., & Gould, D. (2011). *Foundations of sport and exercise psychology* (5th ed.). Champaign, IL: Human Kinetics.

RANGER UP
Cedric Williams and Matthew D. Powless

The United States Army Ranger School has proven to be the premier leadership course for soldiers since 1951 (US Army, 2019). However, fewer than 1 percent of soldiers in the army at a given time have successfully passed the course. Ranger School is composed of three distinct phases, which require soldiers to persevere through the arduous terrain consisting of woods, mountains, and swamps, with little sleep and food for sixty-one days. On day one, more than four hundred soldiers gather at Fort Benning, Georgia. However, by the end of the first three days, which is known as the Ranger Assessment Phase (RAP week), fewer than three hundred soldiers will remain. Of the three hundred who remain after RAP week, approximately one hundred soldiers will complete Ranger School on the first attempt.

One unique aspect of Ranger School is that every soldier is required to pass prerequisites that were verified by their superior officers prior to arrival. Those officers are Rangers themselves and must provide a written endorsement that the candidate has the physical capacity to complete the course. The first crucible is the Ranger Physical Fitness Test, which includes four events (push-ups, sit-ups, pull-ups, and a five-mile run). Candidates are allotted two attempts at each event except the five-mile run. The standards of each repetition are strict and unwavering. As a graduate of Ranger School, the first author can attest that the individual events of Ranger School are not overwhelming; however, the compounding effect of sleep and food deprivation can make the course feel like the challenge of a lifetime. The push-up event, which is first, eliminates nearly forty candidates within minutes of the official start.

Mitchell Orion (not his real name), was a Ranger candidate who found himself in the no-go corral for failing his first attempt of the push-up test. The no-go corral is a holding area for soldiers who are waiting for their second and final attempt at the designated event. Mitchell looked around the no-go corral and saw it was filled with visibly frustrated and anxious soldiers who were on the verge of failing the course. Some of those soldiers had prepared for years to get an opportunity to become Rangers and may never have the opportunity again. Moreover, some soldiers risk the possibility of losing their duty position from their unit if they are dropped from the course. Mitchell remembered how his previous supervisors instructed him that being prepared for adverse moments would be crucial to complete Ranger School and that the ability to regulate emotions and arousal in such critical moments would be essential. Remembering what he had learned, Mitchell attempted to control his breathing, raised his hands above his head, and attempted to intentionally relax his body.

As with high-performing athletes, soldiers must regulate their emotions to optimize performance and achieve their goals (Lane, Beedie, Devonport, & Stanley, 2011). What constitutes successful emotion regulation (i.e., achieving a desired emotional state) is specific to each individual; however, the more successful individuals are in regulating their emotions, the more likely they are to be pleased with their performance (Friesen et al., 2018). Successful athletes have recalled achieving success while experiencing a wide range of emotional states (e.g., angry, calm; Hanin, 2000) and may utilize a variety of emotion regulation strategies to achieve their optimal emotional states (Lane et al., 2011). In Mitchell's case, noticing the tense, negative emotions of those surrounding him in the no-go corral cued him to regulate his own emotions and achieve a more desirable, tranquil state for himself through controlling his breathing, raising his hands, and focusing on relaxing his body

After engaging in his emotional regulation routine, Mitchell was able to calm himself and successfully complete the push-up event. Mitchell would go on to be the first author's Ranger buddy throughout the duration of Ranger School. They spent many moments in the mountains and swamps exercising emotional regulation. The long hikes with heavy packs, interpersonal conflict among candidates, and continual evaluation by Ranger instructors gave candidates a variety of opportunities to exercise the emotional regulation and resiliency skills essential to success. Mitchell went on to pass the Ranger School and is a noncommissioned officer in the United States Army 75th Ranger Regiment.

Take-Home Points

1. The emotional state(s) needed to be successful will be specific to you; there is no one "right" way to feel before performing.
2. Prepare for adverse situations and what emotion(s) you want to feel in those moments.
3. Enlist the help of a coach, mentor, friend and/or sport and performance psychology professional to develop an emotion regulation strategy that will work for you in difficult circumstances.

References

Friesen, A., Lane, A., Galloway, S., Stanley, D., Nevill, A., & Ruiz, M. C. (2018). Coach-athlete perceived congruence between actual and desired emotions in karate competition and training. *Journal of Applied Sport Psychology, 30*, 288–99. doi: 10.1080/10413200.2017.1388302

Hanin, Y. L. (2000). *Emotions in sport*. Champaign, IL: Human Kinetics.

Lane, A. M., Beedie, C. J., Devonport, T. J., & Stanley, D. M. (2011). Instrumental emotion regulation in sport: Relationships between beliefs about emotion and emotion regulation strategies used by athletes. *Scandinavian Journal of Medicine & Science in Sports, 21*, 1–7. doi: 10.1111/j.1600-0838.2011.01364.x

US Army (2019). Airborne and ranger training brigade. Retrieved from https://www.benning.army.mil/infantry/artb/

Chapter Five

Mind-set

Confidence, Emotion, Mental Toughness, Anxiety/Stress/Pressure, and Staleness/Burnout

One can have all the motivation and resources in the world and be superb at utilizing a variety of psychological skills, but if one doesn't have the right mind-set one will not succeed. The development of confidence; effective regulation of emotion; dealing with anxiety, stress, and pressure; and exploring and optimizing one's mind-set (i.e., attitudes and beliefs, frame of mind and perspective) are all are critical contributors to performance excellence.

Monna Arvinen-Barrow, Amanda Visek, and Amie Barrow provide a wonderful personal example of focusing one's mind-set of enjoyment or having fun. (We advocate this as an essential element of participation in exercise and sport.) Arna Erega addresses effectively dealing with anxiety, stress, and pressure to achieve performance excellence. John Heil and Paul Sotor describe the phenomenon of "deer in the headlights" and how one can address this challenge. Anna-Marie Jaeschke, Michael L. Sachs, Dolores Christensen, and Lauren Tashman discuss the mind-set necessary to deal with potentially not finishing an ultradistance race. Lindsey Keenan poignantly discusses depression in sport from a personal perspective and, more broadly, what can be done to address mental health issues. Jen Schumacher eloquently discusses mind-set in talking about choosing what kind of athlete/professional/person you want to be using the context of open-water swimming. Lauren Tashman discusses confidence in work with a collegiate basketball player and the process of establishing confidence in his performance, and also discusses the concept of mind-set in working with a collegiate golfer.

PIDÄ HAUSKAA—HAVE FUN!
Monna Arvinen-Barrow, PhD;
Amanda J. Visek, PhD; and Amie Barrow

Monna

My daughter, Amie, swims competitively. When she was ten years old, she qualified for finals (top sixteen) in a meet that included swimmers of all ages from three different states. On the Saturday afternoon of the finals, I dropped her off to the warm-ups, leaving her with her coach. As a swim mom does, I headed to the bleachers to watch her perform. Amie swam her race, achieved a new best time, and then headed to the dressing room to change.

While her coach and I waited for Amie to come out from the dressing room, the coach said to me, "*Pidä hauskaa.*" Surprised, I responded, "So Amie's been teaching you Finnish?" The coach nodded and explained, "To kill time between the warm-up and her swim, I asked Amie to teach me a few common phrases in Finnish, like thank you, yes, and no." From Amie's club, only she and one other older swimmer had qualified. This meant that while waiting for her event, she did not have her usual swim friends around to talk to. Her coach went on to say, "I also asked her, how do you say good luck? She hesitated and said, 'I don't know.' Then I asked her, well what does your mom say to you before your swim meets? She responded, '*Pidä hauskaa*—it means have fun.'"

I smiled and nodded:

That's right. I never wish her good luck—instead, to have fun. I don't wish her good luck because it would imply that her own skills are not good enough and that she needs luck in order to succeed. On the other hand, telling her to have fun means that I, as a parent, want her to enjoy swimming and have fun while racing. This way, without added pressure from me, or the sentiment that what she's done to prepare for this race is not enough, she can confidently just do her thing. If she continues to have fun, I know that she will continue to grow in her development as a swimmer.

Amanda

Even though the literature is replete with evidence that fun plays a significant and vital role in the experience of an athlete, its importance cannot be underscored enough. Fun is what keeps young athletes playing (Gardner, Magee, & Vella, 2016)—and, for those with high performance aspirations, it helps fuel them in their pursuit of sport excellence (Snyder, 2014).

According to the fun integration theory's FUN MAPS (Visek et al., 2015), informed and developed directly by young athletes, parents are indeed a contributing source of fun: namely, in the form of the encouragement and support they provide. Importantly, then, what parents say to their young athletes, and when they say it, can be profoundly impactful. For parents, though, knowing what to say to their young athletes before, during, and even after practices and competitions is not always so clear. "*Pidä hauskaa*" illustrates simple yet important messaging consistent with athletes' moment-to-moment sport need—that is, to have fun.

Fun is derived from specific actions and behaviors, of which the FUN MAPS illustrate eighty-one, the majority of which are process-oriented determinants. Among them, young athletes report the most important are those that underpin factors, including *Trying Hard, Positive Team Dynamics*, and *Positive Coaching* (Visek et al., in review). Outcome-oriented determinants, such as winning (*Mental Bonuses*) and earning trophies and medals (*Swag*), though fun, are not what young athletes report as being most important. Instead, it is working hard, competing, playing well, being supported by teammates, and coaching that allows mistakes through learning. These are just some of the fun-determinants that are among the most important to young athletes. For parents, the difference between saying, "Have fun" or "Good luck" (which is focused on the outcome of their performance, rather than the process) and asking them after practice or a meet, "What was fun?" versus asking, "Did you win?" or "How did you place?" sets young athletes' expectations for what they will take away as being of paramount importance to their parents. What parents say and how they say it, whether on the field, on the sidelines, during car rides to and from practices and competitions, and even in the home, will shape a young athlete's sport experience. Simply put, words matter.

Amie

Ever since I can remember, my mom has always said, "*Pidä hauskaa!*" to me before I go to practice, to school, to orchestra concerts, to tumbling practice, or to a swim meet. Everywhere I go, really. Afterward, she asks if I had fun. My mom says that to all my friends, too, when we are giving them a ride to practice or a meet, but usually then she says it in English. I am now fifteen years old and a freshman in high school. I train about sixteen to eighteen hours a week (some days I swim doubles) and this year I qualified for the National Club Swimming Association Junior Nationals held in Orlando. I really like my coach, my swim friends, and swimming. It is just fun. Until now, I don't think I have ever really thought about why my mom says, "*Pidä hauskaa.*" It has always just been that way. But it is nice to know her expectation is that I have fun doing what I do and that medals or best times are not her expectation.

Take-Home Points

1. Fun is an integral part of youth athletes' participation motivation in pursuit of sport excellence.
2. Parents play a pivotal role in cultivating fun in sport and shaping a young athlete's sport experience.
3. Consistent with the fun integration theory's FUN MAPS (Visek et al., 2015), parents should be encouraged to use simple, process-oriented messages with their young athletes.

References

Gardner, L. A., Magee, C. A., & Vella, S. A. (2016). Social climate profiles in adolescent sports: Associations with enjoyment and intention to continue. *Journal of Adolescence*, *52*, 112–23. Retrieved from http://doi.org/10.1016/j.adolescence.2016.08.003

Snyder, C. (2014). The path to excellence: A view on the athletic development of US Olympians who competed from 2000–2012. In S. Riewald (Ed.), *Initial Report of the Talent Identification and Development Questionnaire to U.S. Olympians*. USOC Sport Performance and Coaching Education Divisions.

Visek, A. J., Achrati, S. M., Mannix, H., McDonnell, K., Harris, B. S., & DiPietro, L. (2015). The fun integration theory: Towards sustaining children and adolescents sport participation. *Journal of Physical Activity & Health, 12*(3), 424–33. doi: 10.1123/jpah.2013-0180. PMCID: PMC24770788

Visek, A. J., Mannix, H., Chandran, A., Cleary, S., McDonnell, K., & DiPietro, L. (in review). Toward understanding youth athletes' fun priorities: An investigation of sex, age, and levels of play. *Women in Sport & Physical Activity Journal.*

THE BIG THREE
Arna Erega, MA, LPCA

As a former track athlete, my desire has always been to work with the athletic population so that I may provide them with support and guidance, just as my sports counselor helped me when I first started working with her in high school. I obtained my license as a professional counselor several years ago and have since focused my attention on working with young athletes and collegiate student-athletes.

Over the past few months, the pattern of calls I typically receive has been parents calling and saying something like, "My child is having a mental block," "My son has lost motivation," "My daughter is playing like a slug," or something else that revolves around lack of confidence and motivation. What I find most interesting is that, most of the time, after I meet with the athlete for the first time, I find out there is no issue with confidence or motivation at all. Most of the time I find that the cause of all of the external symptoms parents initially present their child as having is actually anxiety, stress, or pressure, or some combination of these.

We may define anxiety as a perceived threat, when individuals experience feelings of insecurity as a response to some internal or external sources of threat (Bagheri et al., 2018). Stress, on the other hand, is defined as an ongoing process, which involves individuals interacting with the environment, appraising the situations in which they find themselves, and trying to cope with issues as they arise (Garinger, Chow, & Luzzeri, 2018). Baumeister and Showers (1986) defined pressure as the presence of situational incentives for optimal, maximal, or superior performance. Pressure also has a subjective component, where athletes are aware of the incentives for each level of performance.

In my professional experience so far, I have noticed several patterns. One is that the pressure these young athletes place on themselves ultimately leads them to experience anxiety and then stress as they are unable to successfully navigate the amount of pressure they place on themselves. This often leads them to experience anxiety as well. The second pattern is parents who place pressure on young athletes to perform or achieve a certain score or result, causing the children to experience stress. The children also place additional pressure on themselves, such as not wanting to disappoint parents or coaches. The third pattern I've noticed is young athletes experiencing some form of anxiety, most often performance anxiety, which then leads to stress and frustration because they do not experience these issues at practice and cannot seem to understand why things go differently during game or competition time. Lastly, there is a pattern of young athletes experiencing stress outside of the athletic domain, such as concerns in the academic, social, or family domains. Those stressors may also cause anxious feelings or symptoms and prevent athletes from performing at their highest level because they are unable to focus on their performance in the present.

Anxiety, stress, and pressure seem to overlap a great deal, and where there is one, I am likely to find the other two as well. Obviously, there are many approaches that could be taken to help an athlete; however, one I find most helpful is to teach athletes how to develop a relaxation ritual that is specific to them and to their sport (Murphy, 2005). Often athletes pick up very quickly on progressive muscle relaxation that is initially guided, and as the athletes develop skills and gain confidence, they continue to implement it on their own. Creating a precompetition plan is another strategy used to combat stress and anxiety (Murphy, 2005). Helping the athlete to prepare step by step—starting with positive self-talk, because one's self-dialogue is extremely important in managing anxiety—is critical. Then, moving on to the specific point of focus, for instance, rather than thinking, "I have to play well," or, "I have to score points," the athletes ought to shift their focus on a particular task such as, "Let me guard number 23, and never let them out of my sight," or shift the focus outward, from worrying to "How do I feel when I am shooting free-throws at practice?" and maintaining that feeling.

Lastly, it is important to develop and practice competitive routines (Murphy, 2005). A competitive routine can be practiced any time, and athletes are encouraged to practice them at practices or at scrimmage games. The athletes develop steps that help them remain calm and focused, while managing their anxiety. A routine can include deep breathing, while listening to music, listening to a pep talk, or imagining past successful games or a particular play or move.

Development and utilization of these psychological skills—relaxation, positive self-talk, and development of routines—takes time and effort, just like working on strength, speed, and agility takes time. Do not be discouraged if you don't get it on the first try!

Take-Home Points

1. Help the athletes figure out what it is that they are feeling and where it is coming from.
2. Provide psychoeducation to the athlete regarding stress, pressure, and anxiety and the effects of each.
3. Provide the athletes with coping skills and help them to individualize these coping skills.

References

Bagheri, R., Pourhmadi, M. R., Hedayati, R., Safavi-Farokhi, Z., Aminian-far, A., Tavakoli, S., & Bagheri, J. (2018). Relationship between Hoffman reflex parameters, trait stress, and athletic performance. *Perceptual and Motor Skills*, *125*(4), 749–68. doi: 10.1177/0031512518782562

Baumeister, R. F., & Showers, C. J. (1986). A review of paradoxical performance effects: Choking under pressure in sports and mental tests. *European Journal of Social Psychology*, *16*, 361–83.

Garinger, L. M., Chow, G. M., & Luzzeri, M. (2018). The effect of perceived stress and specialization on the relationship between perfectionism and burnout in college athletes. *Anxiety, Stress, & Coping*, *31*(6), 714–27. doi: 10.1080/10615806.2018.1521514

Murphy, S. (2005). *The sport psych handbook*. Champaign, IL: Human Kinetics.

THE EXTREME STUPOR/КРАЙНИЙ СТУПОР
John Heil, DA, and Paul Soter, Fencing Master

I was watching an athlete choke terribly during a world championship in fencing, looking more and more helpless as a once formidable lead dissolved (Frame & Reichin, 2019). A coach standing next to me, making note of the glassy eyed "deer in the headlights" stare, said, "We have a word for this in Russian. It translates as 'the extreme stupor.'"

Strong stimulation is the solution, he said. He recounted a time when he slapped an athlete, making clear that it was a deliberate decision and not done out of anger. He added that the outcome was an excellent one, with a positive effect on performance and no negative impact on the relationship between coach and athlete. He also made mention of using a variation of the method on himself when stuck in a stupor.

This situation could easily be dismissed as abuse, which it superficially appears to be. And perhaps it is. We expect many would see it as such. But beneath the surface, there is a sophisticated and well-intentioned thought process that merits attention and understanding.

I kept the conversation rolling, asking how he believed this "extreme stupor" might influence the fencer in the future. He responded, "Some are very good about forgetting, and some are not." For those who are not, he suggested avoiding mentioning the situation, lest the athlete be further sensitized. He also advised avoiding putting the athlete back in a similar situation if at all possible. He added that he would work to counteract the impact of the experience as subtly as possible (i.e., without actually mentioning the incident) to prepare the athlete for the next time in the event it was unavoidable.

Processing this thinking through the lens of sport psychology, we see a rich tapestry of concepts at work. There is a deliberate use of denial, which in context appears constructive, intended to avoid further sensitization. From a fundamental behavioral perspective, electing to not comment on a situation that might otherwise draw intense negative comment could function in behavioral terms as extinction, diminishing the salience of the experience and its emotional impact and thus reducing its influence on future performance. Pragmatically, the strong stimulation of slapping functions like thought stopping, where an aversive (but not dangerous) stimulus is intentionally used to interrupt a disruptive emotional response (Bakker, 2009).

Back to the idea of slapping as a deliberate intervention for extreme stupor: When considering the intent and underlying rationale and the leveraging of the coach-athlete relationship, it resembles a paradoxical intervention. For those who are unfamiliar, paradoxical interventions are used for treatment-resistant behaviors: that is, those that have not responded to ordinary and customary practices. Paradoxical techniques are directive, typically appear to be counterintuitive, and draw on the emotional currency of the therapist-client relationship (Dowd & Swoboda, 1984). Without a doubt, extreme stupor is a treatment-resistant behavior. When the intent is to be helpful, slapping is counterintuitive. Without a strong bond, slapping is unlikely to work. Its power is a function of the coach-athlete relationship. The stronger the relationship and the more unlikely that the coach would act out against the goals of the athlete, the greater the paradoxical nature of the behavior and potentially the greater its positive impact—and the less likely it will have a negative impact on the coach-athlete relationship.

A number of factors suggest that what has been described as extreme stupor is a traumatic stress response, albeit an atypical one: the psychological immobilization of the athlete, the presence of avoidant behavior, the increased potential for similar circumstances to trigger a traumatic stress response, and the role of sensitization and desensitization in mitigating or exacerbating future behavior. Conspicuously absent from a diagnostic perspective is the actual threat of death. Nonetheless, the cost of failure in a critical event is formidable, especially when exacerbated by the spotlight put on behavior by the public environment of competition. Failure to perform in a key competition can mean the end of a season or the end of a career—a sports death of sorts, metaphorically speaking. This mind-set is reflected in the lexicon of sport, as in "sudden death overtime." Death threats following poor performances are a part of the fandom sports landscape. Death threats were received by University of Virginia basketball player Kyle Guy following what is described as the greatest college basketball upset of all time in 2018. In 2019, he led his team to its first NCAA basketball championship (Souhan, 2019). Fortunately, Guy found a great network of support. But what about athletes who are despondent over a loss and alienated from their support system?

The conversation continued with other coaches whose opinions I respect and who were willing to speak candidly. I found a shared recognition of the problem, a similar struggle for a solution, and a willingness to resort to unconventional measures. One coach admitted to slapping an athlete in circumstances like those described above, with a similar underlying thought process and a favorable result. A second coach spoke of a similar dilemma with an athlete underperforming in the extreme, delivering strong stimulation in the form of threat (without follow-through) of physical harm, again with a favorable outcome. Another discussed using "smelling salts" as a shock to the senses, with a similar purpose in mind (Fleming, 2017). Yet another offered a cautionary perspective, reflecting on a past coach who had used brief bouts of demanding physical training paired with harsh verbal criticism in response to extreme stupor—noting a situation in which it worked and another in which it backfired.

Paul Soter (one of the contributors to the conversation referenced), has integrated the concept of extreme stupor into his coaching practices (Soter, 2019). He poses the question: "Isn't competitive experience just a much milder form of desensitization to overwhelming stimuli?" He continues. This is commonly seen in an embryonic form in young fencers (e.g., Y-10 and Y-12 fencers) in their first or second tournaments. They tend to be like "deer in the headlights" during their first couple of bouts, then they settled into the process and are able to concentrate and perform much more appropriately in later bouts. Is this difference between novice youth and mature athletes more quantitative than qualitative? Of course, it's different when it occurs out of the blue in an experienced world-class athlete. But that is maybe why a trained resetting trigger of the sort discussed above could be effective.

Our discussion concerns the experienced, seasoned, generally pressure-inured competitor who suddenly and without warning lapses into the condition of extreme stupor. These inexperienced young athletes were not seasoned competitors showing signs of choking. Rather, they were beginning competitors learning about the normal pressure of competition and how to deal with it. Letting them fail initially and allowing them to successfully work through their failures as the competition proceeds is the best possible outcome. This is, of course, one of the major sorting mechanisms in the development of competitive athletes. Some athletes never learn to adjust to this background level of pressure and do not develop as competitors. Working to normalize the stress of competition, and identifying a coping strategy for the next time, can proactively defuse the tension of pressure-ridden incidents, enabling athletes to survive these moments and thrive in their aftermath.

In the everyday vernacular of sport, the incident recounted here might be best described as "choking" on the part of the athlete. But it is a clearly an extreme example. In the context of clinical psychology, it is arguably a traumatic stress response, albeit an atypical one. Given the impact on performance during the event itself, as well as its potentially enduring effects, this represents a situation that demands understanding and begs for a solution.

Do extreme problems justify extreme solutions? The ethical questions raised here are compelling, but so is the impact of a formidably poor performance. Does slapping or a similar action constitute an ethical breach, or could it be a timely intervention? To answer this requires an examination of not only the action itself but also its underlying intentions, its impact on performance, and its effect on the coach athlete relationship. Perhaps it is useful to think of this strong stimulation intervention as analogous to the use of a defibrillator in a heart attack—recklessly dangerous under ordinary circumstances but potentially life-saving if properly applied when the situation calls for it.

The incident described was at a world championship event where John Heil was a consultant for USA Fencing and Paul Soter was a national team coach. The conversations described took place at the event, and until now have been known only to the contributors.

Take-Home Points

1. In the everyday vernacular of sport, the incident recounted here might be best described as "choking," albeit an extreme example, on the part of the athlete. Consider options that will work for individual athletes.
2. Consider the ethical questions raised here, but also the impact of a formidably poor performance. Does slapping or a similar action constitute an ethical breach, or could it be a timely intervention? Consider these issues within your own professional and ethical frameworks.

References

Bakker, G. M. (2009). In defence of thought stopping. *Clinical Psychologist*, *13*(2), 59–68. doi: 10.1080/13284200902810452

Dowd, E. T. & Swoboda, J. S. (1984). Paradoxical interventions in behavior therapy. *Journal of Behavior Therapy and Experimental Psychiatry*, *15*(3), 229–34.

Fleming, D. (2017, November 3). Waiting to inhale. *ESPN*. Retrieved from http://www.espn.com/espn/feature/story/_/page/enterpriseSalts/ezekiel-elliott-clay-matthews-just-the-nfl-smelling-salt-users

Frame, W. C. & Reichin, S. (2019). Emotion and sport performance: Stress anxiety, arousal, and choking. In M. Anshel, F. Gardner, E. Labbe, T. Petrie, & S. Petruzzello (Eds.), *APA handbook of sport and exercise psychology*. Washington, DC: APA Books.

Soter, P. (2019, January 29). *Competitive states of mind* [training manual]. San Francisco, CA: Golden Gate Fencing Center.

Souhan, J. (2019, April 9). One shining Kyle Guy can't stop smiling in the redemptive moment. *StarTribune*. Retrieved from http://www.startribune.com/one-shining-kyle-guy-can-t-stop-smiling-in-the-redemptive-moment/508304532/

158   Chapter Five

TO DNF OR NOT TO DNF, THAT IS THE QUESTION . . .
Anna-Marie Jaeschke, Michael L. Sachs,
Dolores Christensen, and Lauren Tashman

Jaeschke and Sachs (2012) explored the concept of mental toughness in a fascinating group of athletes: 408 ultradistance runners. An ultramarathon is defined as any footrace longer than the standard marathon distance (Dillon, 2004). Some in the ultrarunning community take a narrower definition, acknowledging only runs longer than 50 miles (Dillon, 2004; Hanold, 2010; Knechtle, 2012) or longer than six hours in duration (Zaryski & Smith, 2005). Ultramarathon races may also include a timed objective where competitors attempt to run as many miles as possible—usually around a 400m track—within a set time limit of twenty-four, forty-eight, or seventy-two hours. This timed component can extend up to full six-day races where participants strategically eat and sleep next to the track while logging miles (Hanold, 2010). Ultramarathoners are individuals who run at least 50 kilometers (31.069 miles), often in a race; 100K races (62.137 miles) and 100-mile races are common, and there are numerous 200-mile races and even ones at greater distances. In order to complete these distances, one must, of course, be physically prepared, but the mental component of such an event, which takes many, many hours, is a challenge as well.

Mental toughness is a key element in these events, which are often characterized by ebbs and flows in how one feels physically but also in how one experiences the event from a psychological perspective. There are many definitions of mental toughness. One we prefer is the concept of an innate or developed psychological advantage that allows the individual to cope better than one's opponents with the demands of an event (Jones, Hanton, & Connaughton, 2002). Mental toughness also involves "being more consistent and better than an opponent in determination, focus, confidence, and control under pressure" (Jaeschke & Sachs, 2012, p. 45). It is proposed to be the characteristic that determines how we perceive and respond to demanding situations we encounter as we pursue our goals (Gucciardi, Gordon, & Dimmock, 2009). Thus it is multidimensional in nature, encompassing a variety of psychological skills and coping mechanisms (Crust, 2007).

Of course, one doesn't need to compete against someone else. Competition is often viewed as having four potential opponents: others, oneself, standards/records, and nature/the environment. One of the beauties of ultradistance events is that they can encompass all these aspects of competition. One may indeed be racing against other individuals, especially if one is good enough to win a race or place in one's age group. But often one is simply competing against oneself, perhaps just to finish the race or to achieve a personal record/personal best. Occasionally there are standards/records to be challenged—perhaps an age group record or, in some races, a need to finish the course in a certain time limit (such as twenty-four hours). In the Western States 100, one must finish within thirty hours to receive a commemorative bronze belt buckle; within twenty-four hours and the buckle is silver. Finally, many of these ultra-endurance events require challenging nature—while nature "always wins," the long distance and often changes in elevation and weather conditions increase the degree of difficulty in completing the distance.

One of the interesting elements of running such long distances is that there are times when one cannot finish the event. (This can happen in shorter races as well.) The initialism commonly used within the ultrarunning community is DNF—did not finish. A DNF often has a physical component; perhaps one is injured and one's body simply cannot physically traverse the additional distance required. Related to injury can be dehydration, exhaustion, or other physiological responses that are not injuries per se but nonetheless compromise the body's ability to complete the event. At times, DNF can be more psychological, although this is often tied into one's physiological state—one would be less likely to want to continue if one is injured or feeling terrible. Marcora, Staiano, and Manning (2009), for example, found evidence to suggest that mental fatigue (i.e., perception of effort) may play a greater role than actual physical exertion in exercise tolerance.

The microculture of ultradistance running, however, suggests that if one starts a race, one finishes the race, no matter what happens. Christensen, Hutchinson, and Brewer (2014) interviewed five experienced ultramarathon runners and found evidence for an "existential crisis" in which the runners were faced with a point in their race where the desire to stop running and cease the experience of fatigue and pain became overwhelming. However, the authors found that the runners chose to persist in the pursuit of a "mind-full" running experience, a greater personal challenge, and the finish line. It is hard for the average person to conceive of getting injured (e.g., knee, ankle, etc.) at mile 60 of a 100-mile race and simply toughing it out for another 40 miles.

Deciding to DNF within this microculture is extremely stressful. In a qualitative study of 100K and 100-mile runners, Christensen (2017) found that many runners declared their early commitment to finishing the race at all costs the moment they signed up for the race online, some six to eight months prior to race weekend. The race itself became the "giant white whale" they spent months chasing. One runner noted that finishing his first 100-mile race "became certain in my mind when I signed up and I had begun the duties of work necessary that would make sure that would happen over the six months prior." Another 100-mile runner echoed this mind-set in describing that the race was "a race that I was really committed to, no matter what's going to happen I [was] just going to keep on going through." One experienced 100-mile runner stated that during his race he "never had a thought about not finishing—ever."

Additionally, many runners reported being influenced by the previous ultraraces and stated that these experiences were important for repeating success or finding redemption from past failed attempts. One runner shared her experience of a DNF at another 100-mile race earlier that summer and how that DNF gave her a mind-set that "there was no way that I wasn't going to finish. . . . Unless, you know, I twisted a knee or sprained an ankle or something like that. So, it was a completely different mind-set and it wasn't just a mind-set that I decided at the start of the race" (Christensen, 2017).

However, some runners will, at such a point during their ultrarace, logically assess their situation and realize that they can stop now, hopefully recover within a few weeks, and be back running again, or continue on and finish but then perhaps be laid up for months rehabilitating an injury they have exacerbated for hours. In the Christensen (2017) study, runners described engaging in "calculations" and cost-benefit analyses with regard to finishing their race. One 100K runner stated that she considered "a way to make this work to get me to the finish . . . and then I'll deal with it, whatever the repercussions are." Another 100-mile runner reported that during the final 25 miles of his race he was "fully willing to finish acknowledging that that might do damage to myself that would require time afterward. I had, late in the race, come to that finishing was almost a matter of honor so that not doing so didn't seem like really something that was an option."

Given the ultrarunning cultural imperative to finish, not finishing can be seen as a "scarlet letter" to be borne by the runner. This could be due, in part, to the tendency for individuals in this culture to have more autonomous forms of motivation fueling their participation (e.g., identified regulation, integrated regulation, intrinsic motivation; Ryan & Deci, 2000). In examining mental toughness, Jaeschke and Sachs (2012) found numerous elements, one under the category of persistence/perseverance. There, the concept of never DNFing was presented. One runner noted the following:

> 20 100-mile race starts, and 20 finishes. No DNF, aka Did Not Finish. Very unusual ratio. For an accomplished runner to attempt this distance, the question is not "Can I"? The right question is "Will I"? (p. 56).

Even more poignantly, this was wonderfully encapsulated by another runner:

> Mental toughness comes down to two main areas: can you keep moving when something hurts—when it hits you how stupid it is to run for another 10 hours, do you have what it takes to understand that the pain of DNF is much worse than the pain of the next 10 hours? (p. 56).

Ultrarunners in the study by Christensen (2017) described vulnerability to considering thoughts of dropping out of the 100-mile race:

> It was like an overwhelming feeling of, "How am I going to do this? Feeling like I feel?" And it was kind of a combination of that. I look back now and, really, I didn't have much reason to be in a dark place. Like, other than the fact that I was just feeling tired, I think. And it's funny that I now think about that because . . . it was almost like there was despair.

However, despite these terrible lows described by the runners, many also affirmed a strong belief in accepting that these lows were part of the ultrarunning experience. The runners further expressed serious trust that the low point would eventually pass. For Maria, during her low point she maintained that

> [i]n the back of my head, I'm like, "Ugh, ok, how are we going to finish this?" and I kept telling myself, "Maria, we are going to finish this. We are going to do this. Just keep pushing. One step in front of the other." I mean, ultrarunning is about the pain. And if you go into ultrarunning and not expecting pain then you shouldn't even be there. So, I knew it was going to happen.

Although there were some runners whose mantra was "Death before DNF," many expressed the need to "run smart" and consider the ramifications of continuing to run if a logical analysis suggested otherwise. One runner in the Christensen (2017) study had to withdraw from the 100-mile race due to an ankle injury and described renewed determination from the events of his race during his postrace interview:

> Now I immediately switch my mind to determination to get healthy as fast as I can. I'm signed up for a race six weeks from now? Five weeks from now? And I want to be healthy for it. I do not want to miss it because of an injury here.

In working with ultradistance runners, "one should also consider the mental toughness associated with choosing to DNF; runners talk about how it is harder to quit than to decide to continue, despite extreme fatigue and pain" (Jaeschke & Sachs, 2012, p. 67).

The Application of Mental Skills to Ultrarunning

Previous research has demonstrated the use of a diverse array of mental skills in ultrarunning (Acevedo, Dzewaltowski, Gill, & Noble, 1992; Bull, 1989; Holt, Lee, Kim, & Klein, 2014; Sacks, Milvy, Perry, & Sherman, 1981; Simpson, Post, Young, & Jensen, 2014; Tharion et al., 1989), but specifics about which mental skills are most useful in which types of running events remains elusive. The ultrarunners interviewed by Christensen, Hutchinson, and Brewer (2014) reported the use of mental skills such as self-talk, visualization, goal setting, and the acceptance of pain. Other ultrarunners in 100K and 100-mile races reported experiencing a wide stream of consciousness that included race strategy at the beginning of the race, continued efforts to plan ahead and be efficient at aid stations as the race went on, and use of mental skills, such as self-talk, energy management, positivity and humor, mantras, goal-setting, and a reward system (Christensen, 2017). It is noteworthy that the runners in the Christensen (2017) study never explicitly identified use of mental skills as a planned piece of their race; rather, the skills were simply something the runners did as needed to manage what was going on at the time.

One should use the various psychological skills at the runner's disposal (e.g., self-talk, attentional control, goal setting) to develop a prerace plan for implementation, if needed, during the race if physical/psychological factors arise that would result in consideration of a DNF. The runner should have a strategy/plan for "running smart" and make the best decision possible, including having the mental toughness to DNF if that is the best answer to the question "to DNF or not DNF?"

It is critical for sport psychology professionals to understand that ultrarunning is a unique subset of running in general and is not the same as marathon running. Sport psychology professionals working in a consulting capacity with ultramarathon runners (see Bull, 1989) should become familiar with the culture of ultrarunning, perhaps through attending an ultramarathon event—

or better yet, volunteering at one—to learn the intricacies of the sport first and foremost. Reading the available research on ultrarunners would also benefit a sport psychology practitioner interested in this sport, as would attention to common ultrarunning blogs, websites, and podcasts. At the same time, it is important to point out that this distinction between ultrarunning and marathon running, in addition to the distinction between road and trail running, has not been empirically tested as of yet and further study is warranted.

Take-Home Points

1. Consider the individual's immersion in the ultradistance microculture in working with the runner.
2. Prior to the race weekend, discuss the runner's investment in finishing the race. Is DNFing an option?
3. Tap into the runners' decision-making skills and need to "run smart" in making the best decision during a race whether to DNF or not DNF.
4. Use all psychological skills at one's disposal to make the run as positive an experience as possible.
5. Consider implementing a psychological and emotional debriefing with the runners following their race.

References

Acevedo, E. O., Dzewaltowski, D. A., Gill, D. L., & Noble, J. M. (1992). Cognitive orientations of ultramarathoners. *Sport Psychologist, 6*, 242–52.

Bull, S. J. (1989). The role of the sport psychology consultant: A case study of ultra-distance running. *Sport Psychologist, 3*, 254–64.

Christensen, D. A., Hutchinson, J. C., & Brewer, B. W. (2014, October). *"Like pushing the bullet through your head with your finger": A phenomenological examination of ultramarathon running.* Paper presented at the annual meeting of the Association for Applied Sport Psychology, Las Vegas, NV.

Christensen, D. A. (2017). *Over the mountains and through the woods: Psychological processes of ultramarathon runners.* Unpublished doctoral dissertation, Springfield College, Springfield, MA.

Crust, L. (2007). Mental toughness in sport: A review. *International Journal of Sport and Exercise Psychology, 5*, 270–90.

Dillon, D. (2004, November). A marathoner's next frontier. *Marathon and Beyond*, 41–50.

Gucciardi, D. F., Gordon, S., & Dimmock, J. A. (2009). Advancing mental toughness research and theory using personal construct theory. *International Review of Sport and Exercise Psychology, 2*(1), 54–72.

Hanold, M. T. (2010). Beyond the marathon: (De)construction of female ultrarunning bodies. *Sociology of Sport Journal, 27*, 160–77.

Holt, N. L., Lee, H., Kim, Y., & Klein, K. (2014). Exploring experiences of running an ultramarathon. *Sport Psychologist, 28*, 22–35.

Jaeschke, A.-M., & Sachs, M. (2012). 1,000,000 miles closer to a definition of mental toughness. *Marathon & Beyond, 16*(5), 44–67.

Jones, G., Hanton, S., and Connaughton, D. (2002). What is this thing called mental toughness? An investigation with elite sport performers. *Journal of Applied Sport Psychology, 14*(3), 205–18.

Knechtle, B. (2012). Ultramarathon runners: Nature or nurture? *International Journal of Sports Physiology and Performance, 7*, 310–12.

Marcora, S. M., Staiano, W., & Manning, V. (2009). Mental fatigue impairs physical performance in humans. *Journal of Applied Physiology, 106*(3), 857–64.

Ryan, R. M., & Deci, E. L. (2000). Intrinsic and extrinsic motivations: Classic definitions and new directions. *Contemporary Educational Psychology, 25*, 54–67.

Sacks, M. H., Milvy, P., Perry, S. W., & Sherman, L. R. (1981). Mental status and psychological coping during a 100-mile race. In M. H. Sacks & M. L. Sachs (Eds.), *Psychology of running* (pp. 166–75). Champaign, IL: Human Kinetics.

Simpson, D., Post, P. G., Young, G., & Jensen, P. J. (2014). "It's not about taking the easy road": The experiences of ultramarathon runners. *Sport Psychologist, 28*, 176–85.

Tharion, W. J., Terry, A. L., McMenemy, D. J., Rauch, T. M., Shukitt, B. L., Gallego, E., & Gowenlock, L. (1989). *Psychological attributes, coping strategies, and other factors associated with ultramarathon performance* (Tech. Rep. TS-S9). Natick, MA: US Army Research Institute of Environmental Medicine.

Zaryski, C., & Smith, D. J. (2005). Training principles and issues for ultra-endurance athletes. *Current Sports Medicine Reports, 4*, 165–70.

DOWN BUT NOT OUT
Lindsey C. Keenan, PhD, LAT, ATC

Moving from high school to college is a major life transition for students. This transition is filled with unbound experiences: a new home, new peers, new schedule, new routine, and new responsibilities—including doing your own laundry. Add to that being a student-athlete, with a new team, new coach, new expectations, and new standards, and it's easy to understand the stress college students and student-athletes are under during this time. It is not unexpected, then, that the statistics related to mental health distress college student-athletes experience during this transition are daunting: The prevalence of clinically relevant depression symptoms in collegiate student-athletes during preparticipation exams has been reported as high as 23 percent through anonymous screening (Wolanin, Hong, Marks, Panchoo, & Gross, 2016). Conversely, research has also demonstrated prevalence rates of depression as low as 1.1 percent in student-athletes when screening non-anonymously (McGuire, Ingram, Sachs, & Tierney, 2017). These differences should raise concerns over symptom reporting and help-seeking behaviors, but may not be surprising given the mental toughness and stigmatizing mental health culture of competitive sports (Lopez & Levy, 2013).

Competitive athletes are accustomed to high pressure situations and often are taught to "play through the pain," "ignore the hurt," "push through it," "suck it up," "toughen up," and "get over it." These expressions are so common they are woven into the fabric of athletics; I recall seeing the phrase "Pain is weakness leaving the body" printed on the back of a T-shirt for sale at an youth soccer tournament for eight- to ten-year-olds. Research has suggested these sentiments assist in creating a "win at all costs" environment in which athletes may fear being perceived as weak if they seek mental health help (Lopez & Levy, 2013). Despite the obvious relationship between stigma and help-seeking behavior, what is not obvious is the extent to which mental health distress is recognized by athletes themselves. Consider this story of a collegiate athlete:

> It was the first semester of my freshman year of college and I was excited to be there. I was living with two childhood friends who were also joining the women's lacrosse team with me, crammed into a two-person dorm room. It was everything I had imagined college would be: the nervousness of meeting new friends, the excitement of college parties, the eagerness to get into my major. Things were going well—until they weren't. My long-distance boyfriend had ended our relationship just a few months into starting college, and my grandmother passed away, both within a short time frame of each other. I was grieving, which both I and my best friends understood. What we did not understand

was how long that grieving should last. I found myself completely lost and experiencing what I only recognized as continued grief for months on end; I had trouble getting out of bed and I didn't want to go to classes. I forced myself to go to practice and put on a fake smile while I counted down the minutes until I could retreat to our dorm room, which my roommates jokingly called "the crying room" because I could not stop crying once I was finally back home. I felt trapped, hopeless, and as though I had lost touch with every piece of me that ever experienced joy. I didn't want to die, but I also did not want to live—not with how I was feeling.

Most adults can recognize these signs and symptoms. Clearly I was depressed. But I—and both of my roommates, who were my teammates and best friends—had no idea. I would ruminate: "Am I just still sad about my relationship ending? I think I hate college here. That must be it—I should transfer. And maybe play field hockey somewhere else, instead of lacrosse. I'm just in the wrong place." I would try to convince myself that if I changed scenes, it would change how I felt.

In hindsight, all I needed at that time was guidance. I had not even considered approaching a coach, athletic trainer, or adviser. That was not something that was discussed during orientation or the start of our fall season. And certainly I had not considered counseling. I was wholeheartedly unaware my negative feelings and behavior were related to a mental health issue until I attended one specific Health class. It was a Monday 7–10 p.m. class, and our professor asked us to turn to a page in our textbook that outlined a checklist of depression symptoms. I remember my eyes welling up as I checked "yes" to every single symptom. I was scared, but also relieved, as my heart raced and my brain buzzed with understanding. I was depressed, and had been so for nearly three months, but I had no idea until this moment. Thankfully, I have supportive parents, whom I quickly called to share my revelation. They connected me with the on-campus counseling center, where I immediately started therapy and a road to adjustment, coping skills, and recovery.

A twist you may not expect: This women's lacrosse athlete was me. It wasn't until years later, practicing as a certified athletic trainer, that I realized how the structure of our athletics program at that time had failed me. As a student-athlete, I was never educated about mental health, I was never informed of resources, and I never had a captain, coach, adviser, administrator, or athletic trainer ask me—really ask me—if I was okay. I never had someone tell me it was okay to not be okay. As an athlete, I never knew that was an option. Ultimately, I set out to change that story for future athletes. I continued my graduate education with a PhD in exercise and sport psychology, and my research has focused on the mental health of student-athletes. My goal is to encourage all key stakeholders in student-athlete success and well-being to play a role in changing this narrative for every athlete with whom they work.

I wonder what my experience as a freshman in college might have looked like if mental health were a topic of conversation during my athletic experience. Maybe I would not have sought help as willingly as I did once I was seriously suffering. But I cannot help believe I would not have suffered as long as I did. Therapy changed me, and changed the course of my career and life. Connecting to therapy sooner would have saved me a lot of a stress, time, and struggle on and off the field. And, inevitably, it potentially saved my life.

It is highly likely a mental health screening and early referral to counseling would have prevented me from getting to the place where my depression symptoms were so severe I was thinking about death. Thankfully, organized sport is moving in that direction. The National Athletic Trainers' Association (Neal et al., 2013) and the National Collegiate Athletic Association (2016) have both published consensus papers on psychological considerations in collegiate student-athletes. These recommendations lay the framework for athletic trainers and sport psychologists, as well as team physicians, coaches, athletic directors, and other sports-related professionals, to face and tackle mental health concerns in student-athletes. In professional sport, public statements such as those by NBA All-Star player Kevin Love (2018) are helping destigmatize the conversation around mental health. The best recommendations? Start talking about mental health, implement screening with your athletic trainers and/or sport psychologists, and have a referral protocol in place. You will be surprised how many athletes tell you they are not okay when given the opportunity.

Take-Home Points

1. Check in with the athletes with whom you work. Ask how they are doing and recognize they may not even understand what they are struggling with.
2. Work with the athletic trainers and sports medicine professionals who provide healthcare to your athletes. Do you have a mental health management plan (screening & referral protocol) in place (see Neal et al., 2013)?
3. Work with the available mental health clinicians and resources on and off campus, including licensed sport psychologists, to begin changing the conversation around mental toughness and mental health in sports.

References

Lopez, R., & Levy, J. (2013). Student athletes' perceived barriers to and preferences for seeking counseling. *Journal of College Counseling, 16*(1), 19–31.

Love, K. (2018, March 6). Everyone is going through something. *Players' Tribune*. Retrieved from www.theplayerstribune.com/en-us/articles/kevin-love-everyone-is-going-through-something

McGuire, L., Ingram, Y., Sachs, M., & Tierney, R. (2017). Temporal changes in depression symptoms in male and female collegiate student-athletes. *Journal of Clinical Sport Psychology*, *11*(4), 337–51.

National Collegiate Athletic Association. (2016). Inter-association consensus document: Best practices for understanding and supporting student-athlete mental wellness. Retrieved from https://www.ncaa.org/sites/default/files/HS_Mental-Health-Best-Practices_20160317.pdf

Neal, T. L., Diamond, A. B., Goldman, S., Klossner, D., Morse, E. D., Pajak, D. E., . . . Welzant, V. (2013). Inter-association recommendations for developing a plan to recognize and refer student-athletes with psychological concerns at the collegiate level: An executive summary of a consensus statement. *Journal of Athletic Training*, *48*(5), 716–20.

Wolanin, A., Hong, E., Marks, D., Panchoo, K., & Gross, M. (2016). Prevalence of clinically elevated depressive symptoms in college athletes and differences by gender and sport. *British Journal of Sports Medicine*, *50*(3), 167–71.

YOU GET TO CHOOSE
Jen Schumacher, MS, CMPC

It was the summer of 2009 in Southern California and I had just decided to train for my first channel crossing—I was signed up to swim the Catalina Channel later that August. The twenty-one-mile stretch of Pacific that spans over ocean depths greater than three thousand feet had been crossed only 163 times. The water temperature can range from 58 to 72°F, and most swims begin at midnight to avoid choppy surface conditions from afternoon winds (Catalina Channel Swimming Federation, 2017). Swimmers are not permitted to benefit from any sort of aid, including wetsuits, fins, or resting on the escort boat or kayak that accompanies them. Finally, swims are scheduled well in advance of the actual crossing date, so aside from historical weather data, the conditions of one's swim are relatively unknown.

Given this, I had begun training in earnest a year before my scheduled crossing date by training daily, alternating between the pool and the ocean, even through the winter. I trained in cold water, at night, while sleep deprived, in rough conditions, and with kayakers in order to simulate as many performance conditions as possible. My favorite beaches to train at were Corona del Mar and Laguna Beach in Southern California. As my weekend distances increased throughout the summer, it only made sense to swim the seven-mile stretch between these two beaches. My colleague and friend

Lenny Wiersma agreed to kayak and met me and my training partner and uncle, Dan Schumacher, at Corona del Mar.

When we got to the beach, the conditions were bleak: gray skies unleashing a constant spattering from the sky and howling winds whipping the sea into endless whitecaps. I quickly reframed the challenging conditions, turned to Dan, and remarked, "This will be great training!" Effective self-talk plays a significant role in enhancing performance, and cognitive restructuring, or altering those thoughts in order to view a situation more favorably, can help athletes to find the benefits in adverse situations (Greenspan & Feltz, 1989; Hatzigeorgiadis, Zourbanos, Mpoumpaki, & Theodorakis, 2009). This form of reframing is also essential for controlling emotions in sport (Jones, 2003). "Training for what?!" he quipped back. I had forgotten that unlike me, he was not training for Catalina and was just there for support. I was reminded of the selfless support around my effort and grateful for him, Lenny, and countless others who had volunteered to help me train.

Our swim was off—Lenny in the kayak and Dan and I in the water, battling surface chop and a strong head current. Our progress was slow and steady, our goal clear: Laguna Beach or bust. We anticipated this seven-mile swim to take just over three hours and had prepared accordingly. Every thirty minutes, Lenny raised his paddle to give us the signal to stop, swim over to the kayak, and take in energy-dense fluid while treading water, called a *feeding* in channel-swimming terminology. Like clockwork, the best channel swimmers keep their head down and swim until they get the signal, then feed on the half hour quickly and without complaint. However, as we began closing in on the two-hour mark, I noticed we were hardly halfway. An ominous bluff rose out of the water, a cliff I was so familiar with, and seemed to stay next to us for eternity. I was convinced we were not moving anywhere. Although I had not received the signal, I stopped and asked Lenny if we were making any headway. He replied that we were and to just keep on swimming. I plodded on, not entirely certain we could make it, and again, without being told to, picked my head up and asked if we were making progress. Lenny's patience waned, but he reiterated that we were and that we had to just keep swimming. What I would later find out is that for each of my unscheduled stops, we were being whipped backward by the head current and losing precious ground.

I was tired, sore, cranky, and desperately wanted the swim to be over as we closed in on three hours. We should have been rounding the buoy at Laguna, but instead we were still stuck next to the overbearing cliff. I stopped yet again, without being told to, and asked Lenny if he was sure we were going anywhere. The response was as sharp as it was blunt: "Jen, you get to choose what kind of swimmer you want to be."

And there it was: the ultimate reframe that I had been incapable of doing for myself. I was still frustrated and angry, so I put my head down and swam. Fortunately, I had nothing but time to ponder the wisdom of my kayaker. The more I reflected, the more I understood he was exactly right: I had no control over the conditions of my crossing date, which had been set last December. The weather could be exactly as it was that day, and if that happened, what kind of swimmer would I be? Would I whine and wish the weather away, or would I charge full steam ahead, knowing I had places to go? Would I stop and agonize, bringing others' moods down with me, or would I remind myself that I get to be here and I'm pursuing a dream? I got to make those decisions in that moment. And in that moment, an overwhelming sense of clarity overcame me: It did not matter if we needed to pull out the glow sticks and get in some nighttime training, we were going to get to Laguna Beach. And five hours and forty-five minutes later, we did.

What that swim taught me was the importance of understanding your why and choosing to keep that front and center (Ravizza, 2002). Each day you get to choose what type of athlete, performer, teammate, and leader you want to be. Your behavior in training determines what you can expect from yourself come game day, which underscores the importance of choosing your mind-set, reframing ineffective self-talk, and coming back to your why. And it was more than just swimming—that day I got to decide what kind of educator, friend, and person I wanted to be. I reflected on that day throughout my Catalina Channel crossing later that summer, and in various other challenges thereafter both in the ocean and on land. Although the conditions on my crossing were ideal, I went into the challenge with every ounce of confidence that I could handle anything that was thrown our way. Later, when I went on to complete other, more arduous marathon swims, my thesis, and various personal and professional challenges, I was able to reflect back on this experience and remind myself of how I respond to adversity. So the next time you find yourself stuck in adversity, remind yourself, "You get to choose what kind of _____ you want to be."

Take-Home Points

1. Reframe challenges as opportunities for growth and development.
2. You must train the mind-set you plan to have on game day in training, every day.
3. Know why you are doing what you are doing and keep that front and center.

References

Catalina Channel Swimming Federation (2017). Retrieved from https://swimcatalina.org/

Greenspan, M. J., & Feltz, D. L. (1989). Psychological interventions with athletes in competitive situations: A review. *Sport Psychologist, 3*(3), 219–36.

Hatzigeorgiadis, A., Zourbanos, N., Mpoumpaki, S., & Theodorakis, Y. (2009). Mechanisms underlying the self-talk–performance relationship: The effects of motivational self-talk on self-confidence and anxiety. *Psychology of Sport and Exercise, 10*(1), 186–92.

Jones, M. V. (2003). Controlling emotions in sport. *Sport Psychologist, 17*(4), 471–86.

Ravizza, K. H. (2002). A philosophical construct: A framework for performance enhancement. *International Journal of Sport Psychology, 33*(1), 4–18.

CONFIDENCE: A MIND-SET NOT A FEELING
Lauren S. Tashman, PhD, CMPC, Align Performance, LLC

Where do you get your confidence from? What do you go to when you don't feel confident? Matt, a sophomore Division II men's basketball player, wasn't feeling confident. He vented that he was really struggling because he believed that he should be a starter on his team, but he felt his coaches weren't supportive and didn't believe in him or his capabilities. He felt the coaches had favorites and he wasn't one of them, and he was questioning whether he should transfer. Most importantly, he was questioning his capabilities. In our initial discussion about his presenting problem, we discovered that the main source for his confidence prior to college was his high school coach. He knew that his former coach believed in him, and they had a great relationship. For example, he told a story about when he was coming back from a shoulder surgery and he found unexpectedly that his coach was being a bit negative with him. He brought this up to the coach, who returned to his positive and supportive ways. The overwhelming support from this former coach fueled performance excellence in Matt. However, Matt wasn't playing for this coach anymore, so he needed to find a way to reclaim his confidence.

According to Bandura (1986) in his work on self-efficacy and Dweck (2006) in her work on fixed versus growth mind-sets, our beliefs about our capabilities play a large role in our experiences and performance outcomes.

Further, Bandura (1977) proposed that while we may have beliefs about the implications of a particular behavior on an outcome (i.e., outcome expectations), it is the conviction in our belief about our ability to successfully carry out a behavior or navigate a situation (i.e., efficacy expectations) that will determine whether we avoid or approach a situation as well as whether we initiate and persist with a necessary behavior. In order to derive these efficacy expectations, we can look to various sources in general (Bandura, 1986) and specific to sport (Vealey, Walter-Hayashi, Garner-Holman, & Giacobbi, 1998). Ultimately, the aim of working with clients on confidence should be to explore and enhance their efficacy expectations (i.e., increase trait and state confidence and focus on confidence as a belief system—mind-set—rather than a felt emotion), but also should aim to help the client develop robust sport confidence (i.e., a multidimensional and enduring belief system; Thomas, Lane, & Kingston, 2011).

Consistent with Keegan's (2016) proposal of Education-Acquisition-Practice as a progression for mental coaching (*Note: I use the terminology Education-Application-Integration*), we began with some education on mind-set, the power of belief, confidence, and sources of confidence. Further, consistent with my consulting approach and philosophy, education involves both education about the psychology of the mind and performance and also about oneself (i.e., self-awareness). Thus, we did a confidence profile (Hays, Thomas, Butt, & Maynard, 2010) to help him get a more multidimensional viewpoint on his confidence as well as identify a broader range of sources he could use to support his confidence.

The next phase of the process involved applying (i.e., identifying, practicing, and implementing) some confidence-building strategies. To take more ownership over his confidence he started a confidence journal that consisted of brainstorming and keeping a log of the following, inspired by the conceptualizations discussed above of sources of confidence: accomplishments, things he had mastered or was working on mastering, small wins, challenges he had overcome, his strengths, verbal persuasion from others beyond just his high school coach, the qualities of one of his role models that he wanted to emulate, his preparation, and things he was grateful for. We also analyzed his performance emotions, identifying those that were obstacles to his performance and those that were keys to optimal performance (see Kamphoff, 2018, MVP profile exercise for an example of a similar process). In addition, we profiled and worked on optimizing his self-talk. Through keeping a self-talk log he found that his self-talk got him to feel defeated and negative. Thus, we practiced shifting his unhelpful self-talk to more helpful self-talk. Next we clarified his core values to refocus him back onto who/how he wanted to be as an athlete rather than outcomes/goals he wanted to achieve. As Gardner and Moore (2007) stated, "Consistent, values-directed choices and behaviors (not emotion-directed behaviors) are the essence of the elusive mental toughness that athletes and elite performers want so badly to achieve" (p. 107). He reviewed several value words, selected those that stood out to him relative to the questions of what was most important to him and who he wanted to be as a basketball player, and narrowed down his list until he identified the four core values he wanted to epitomize: make an impact, strive for consistency, demonstrate discipline, and focus on excellence. Lastly, we explored and discussed his mindset and implemented a mind-set mantra—he chose one of his values: impact—that he could use as part of his self-talk to help him refocus on what matters most and who/how he wanted to be as an athlete (e.g., Berkovich-Ohana, Wilf, Kahana, Arieli, & Malach, 2015; Radha, 2005).

The last phase of the process involved helping him to integrate these strategies into his day-to-day mental preparation and performance. We optimized his routines to include the mental skills and strategies we had worked on and did some if/then planning for how he would make use of his self-talk, mind-set mantra, and sources of confidence. We also implemented a check in process on his values alignment so that he was using that as a consistent guide for focusing on what's most important.

After our last meeting, Matt dropped by to tell me that he had decided to transfer to a different school and team going into his junior year. He felt good about the coach and program he was going to be a part of and said he would continue to use everything we had worked on. During fall of the next school year, I got an e-mail from Matt; he reported that he was still utilizing everything we worked on and it was having an enduring impact on his confidence, which was translating to his making a greater contribution to his new team on the court and as a leader of the team. He mentioned that he didn't always feel confident, but he knew how to fuel his confidence and have a confident mind-set, which was making all the difference for him and his team.

Take-Home Points

1. Help athletes to focus away from needing to feel confident and instead develop a confident mind-set supported by a robust and enduring belief system.
2. The confidence profile procedure helps athletes take a multidimensional perspective on their performance and roles as well as potential sources of confidence rather than looking at confidence in a more general or narrow way.
3. Help athletes own their confidence by fostering self-awareness, teaching them about confidence, and helping them utilize strategies that put them

in control of and in a better position to leverage their beliefs about their capabilities.

References

Bandura, A. (1977). Self-efficacy: Toward a unifying theory of behavioral change. *Psychological Review, 84*(2), 191–215.

Bandura, A. (1986). *Social foundations of thought and action: A social cognitive theory*. Englewood Cliffs, NJ: Prentice Hall.

Berkovich-Ohana, A., Wilf, M., Kahana, R., Arieli, A., & Malach, R. (2015). Repetitive speech elicits widespread deactivation in the human cortex: The "Mantra" effect? *Brain and Behavior, 5*(7), e00346. doi: 10.1002/brb3.346

Dweck, C. S. (2006). *Mindset: The new psychology of success*. New York, NY: Random House.

Gardner, F. L., & Moore, Z. E. (2007). *The psychology of enhancing human performance: The mindfulness-acceptance-commitment (MAC) approach*. New York, NY: Springer.

Hays, K., Thomas, O., Butt, J., & Maynard, I. (2010). The development of confidence profiling for sport. *Sport Psychologist, 18*, 373–92.

Kamphoff, C. (2018). *Beyond grit: Ten powerful practices to gain the high-performance edge*. Minneapolis, MN: Wise Ink.

Keegan, R. (2016). *Being a sport psychologist*. London, UK: Palgrave.

Radha, S. S. (2005). *Mantras: Words of power*. Spokane, WA: Timeless Books.

Thomas, O., Lane, A., & Kingston, K. (2011). Developing and contextualizing robust sport confidence. *Journal of Applied Sport Psychology, 23*, 189–208.

Vealey, R. S., Walter-Hayashi, S., Garner-Holman, M., & Giacobbi, P. (1998). Sources of sport-confidence: Conceptualization and instrument development. *Journal of Sport & Exercise Psychology, 20*, 54–80.

TEEING UP FOR SUCCESS BY EXPLORING AND SHIFTING MIND-SET
Lauren S. Tashman, PhD, CMPC, Align Performance, LLC

Collegiate golf is interesting; it's an individual sport played as a team sport in which a small number of athletes are on the team yet all of them do not get the chance to participate in (or even attend) each competition. While this might sound similar to the notion of being a starter versus a nonstarter, it's actually very different. In general, the determination of who gets to attend and compete in each golf tournament is made by each golfer on the team participating in one or more qualifying rounds leading up to the tournament. Thus, the golfers must navigate three types of performance contexts: practice, qualifying rounds, and tournaments.

This story is about Sarah (not her real name), a sophomore Division I golfer who came onto the team as one of the top athletes in her country and now, as a sophomore, is struggling to qualify for any of the team's tournaments. This team is extremely impressive in its recruitment of athletes, so while it might not have been expected that she be a top standout performer on the team, the coach was surprised about her performance and expected more from her this year. Sarah started mental coaching meetings toward the end of her sophomore year. While some research has shown that female individual-sport collegiate athletes may be more open to psychological skills training (e.g., Wrisberg, Simpson, Loberg, & Reed, 2009), her timing could have been indicative of the role of cultural factors (e.g., Ong & Harwood, 2019) and readiness for change (e.g., Massey, Gnacinski, & Meyer, 2015). In the first several meetings with Sarah, it became clear that there were two important mind-set-related factors at play: (1) Her mind-set as a freshman on the team was different than her mind-set as a sophomore and (2) she had different mind-sets about practice, qualifying rounds, and competition that were not helping her to perform optimally in any of those contexts.

What is mind-set? As a basic definition it can be thought of as one's outlook or perspective on oneself, a given situation, the world, and so on. According to Buchanan and Kern (2017) one's mind-set acts as a "puppet master" and "reflects personally distinguishable attitudes, beliefs, and values, which influence one's ability to learn and lead, and to achieve and contribute" (p. 1). As a freshman, Sarah approached her time on the team carefree. This enabled her to perform well without expectation and look at everything as an opportunity for growth that would support her throughout her collegiate career and beyond. However, when she became a sophomore, the transition brought with it a shift in mind-set that no longer supported her optimally. In a case such as this, understanding transitions in general as well as specific to sport is essential (see Tashman, 2019). Further, while student transition research has focused mainly on the transition in and out of college, the sophomore experience is also important to understand (e.g., Tobolowsky, 2008). For Sarah, this transition brought with it an expectation associated with her performance, and as a self-proclaimed perfectionist, not performing optimally was not okay in her eyes (i.e., self-oriented perfectionism), nor did she perceive it was okay in her coach's eyes (i.e., socially prescribed perfectionism; see Hewitt & Flett, 1991).

"With appropriate ability and conditions, we can consciously shift our mindsets" (Buchanan & Kern, 2017, p.1). Thus, to work on her overall mindset, we worked on (re)defining success, setting goals for the year, and incorporating reflective practice into her daily evaluations. In order to help her (re) define success we first focused on identifying and commitment to acting in alignment with her core values (Smith, Leeming, Forman, & Hayes, 2019). I gave Sarah a long list of potential value words and asked her between sessions to review the list and circle which ones stood out to her when keeping the following three questions in mind: (1) What is most important to me? (2) What do I want to be known for? (3) Regardless of the result, what do I want to be characteristic of my golf performance? Then, in our next session we reviewed her list together and she explained why she chose each word. We narrowed that list down until she arrived at three core values—grit, bold, process—and discussed what these looked like in practice, qualifying rounds, and tournaments (i.e., behaviors and actions that would demonstrate these values in action). Committing to acting in alignment with her values was integrated into her daily routine as focus cues leading into each practice/round, as a check in throughout each practice/round (for rounds, she wrote her three values on her scorecard and checked in on alignment in segments of three holes), and as a reflection following each practice/round. Sarah started keeping a journal, and each day she wrote a short reflection on her alignment with her values and any actions she wanted to focus on or take the next day in order to align with them.

In order to shift her mind-set using goals, we used the GOTE framework that comes from the world of acting (Cohen, 2007). First, we discussed her goals (What did she really want for her sophomore year?) and the obstacles she was already encountering or might encounter. Then we discussed the tactics she would implement (the daily processes/actions she would focus on or take). Lastly, we discussed her expectations: What did she expect out of herself? What did her coach expect of her and how would she integrate this by focusing on what she could control? Why was she playing, what excited her about this year and her goals? As a final initiative to help her shift her sophomore mind-set, we implemented a reflection tool for her to use each day when she was reviewing and evaluating her performance. Each day the coach had the golfers keep track of their performance metrics and scores (he had a sheet they filled out in binders they kept), so we added a stop-start-continue to this process so that she was focusing on process and feeding forward her performance rather than getting caught up in focusing only on results (e.g., Ryan, 2012).

In order to optimize her mind-set in practice, qualifying rounds, and competition, we first profiled them utilizing the cognitive behavioral therapy belief-driven formulation process (see Psychology Tools, n.d.). We explored her thoughts, feelings (body sensations, emotions), behaviors, and underlying beliefs for each of the three performance contexts. Through this process we noticed various things about her habits of thinking and responding, her keys to success, and the mental skills that could be implemented or optimized. Most notably, we were able to uncover and discuss her differing mind-sets for these three contexts. Her mind-set in practice was still that carefree outlook she had taken freshmen year, while her mind-set in qualifying rounds was a pressure to perform coupled with a fear of not doing so. Interestingly, utilizing the team's home tournament she played in that year, her mind-set was an attitude of excitement. Thus, she became aware that her mind-set in qualifying rounds needed to be shifted, and her mind-set in practice also could be optimized in order to help her more effectively mentally prepare for qualifying and, ultimately, competition. In order to make these mental shifts, we utilized a list of emotion words to help her identify the mind-set she wanted to bring into these contexts. She arrived at *fierce* for qualifying and *challenge* for practice. Finally, to support her in bringing these mind-sets into action, we identified, practiced, and integrated other mental skills strategies, such as self-talk, focus cues, and routines.

These sessions, activities, and strategies ultimately helped her to shift not only her mind-set but also her performance. The shifts didn't happen quickly, nor did the changes in performance come immediately. However, during her junior year she qualified for and competed in several tournaments for the team and also represented her home country in a few tournaments that year. Most importantly, it wasn't just her performance that shifted, *she* also shifted: She was noticeably lighter and happier, and she enjoyed her collegiate athletic experience more because of the work she did to explore and optimize her mind-set as well as implement mental skills strategies.

Take-Home Points

1. Mind-set matters. Exploring mind-sets and the implications of them on habits of thinking and responding as well as performance are important

first steps to being able to help athletes identify and shift nonoptimal mind-sets.
2. Clearly identifying one's target mind-set(s) helps create clarity of what one is trying to espouse and achieve.
3. Implementing mental skills strategies helps athletes put their targeted mind-set(s) into action, train their minds, and mentally prepare to perform optimally.
4. Take into consideration the research and theory underlying readiness for change when working with athletes and designing interventions.

References

Buchanan, A., & Kern, M. L. (2017). The benefit mindset: The psychology of contribution and everyday leadership. *International Journal of Wellbeing*, *7*(1), 1–11.

Cohen, R. (2007). *Acting one* (5th ed.). New York, NY: McGraw-Hill.

Hewitt, P. L., & Flett, G. L. (1991). Perfectionism in the self and social contexts: Conceptualization, assessment, and association with psychopathology. *Journal of Personality and Social Psychology*, *60*(3), 456–70.

Massey, W., Gnacinski, S. L., & Meyer, B. B. (2015). Psychological skills training in NCAA Division I athletics: Are athletes ready for change? *Journal of Clinical Sport Psychology*, *9*(4), 317–34.

Ong, N. C. H., & Harwood, C. G. (2018). Attitudes toward sport psychology consulting in athletes: Understanding the role of culture and personality. *Sport, Exercise, and Performance Psychology*, *7*(1), 46–59.

Psychology Tools. (n.d.). Belief driven formulation. Retrieved from https://www.psychologytools.com/worksheet/belief-driven-formulation/

Ryan, R. M. (2012). The facilitation of reflection within an online course. *Reflective Practice*, *13*, 709–18.

Smith, P., Leeming, E., Forman, M., & Hayes, S. C. (2019). From form to function: Values and committed action strengthen mindful practices with context and direction. *Journal of Sport Psychology in Action*. doi: 10.1080/21520704.2018.1557773

Tashman, L. S. (2019). The evolution of a career: Navigating through and adapting to transitions in sport, exercise, and performance. In A. Mugford & J. G. Cremades (Eds.), *Sport, exercise, and performance psychology: Theories and applications* (pp. 175–203). New York, NY: Routledge.

Tobolowsky, B. F. (2008). Sophomores in transition: The forgotten year. *New Directions for Higher Education*, *144*, 59–67.

Wrisberg, C. A., Simpson, D., Loberg, L. A., & Reed, A. (2009). NCAA Division-I student-athletes receptivity to mental skills training by sport psychology consultants. *Sport Psychologist*, *23*(4), 470–86.

Chapter Six

Facing and Overcoming Challenges

Mental Toughness, Anxiety/ Stress/Pressure, Staleness/Burnout, Resilience, and Rehabilitation from Injury

Achieving performance excellence almost always comes with challenges. These may be having to cope with injuries and rehabilitation; dealing with perceived anxiety, stress, and pressure in various situations and performance contexts; coping with staleness and burnout; or needing to effectively use one's resources of mental toughness and resilience. The athlete and exercisers who can successfully cope with these challenges and overcome them are more likely to achieve success and the level of performance excellence they desire.

Megan Buning and Tiffany M. Kasdorf discuss overcoming injury to achieve a successful career in collegiate softball. Damien Clement and Monna Arvinen-Barrow review the role of deep breathing and prayer in successfully coping with injury in an athlete. Tami Eggleston provides a wonderful story of grit in a racer and family in drag racing. Kerry Guest provides a personal perspective on overcoming challenges in life to be successful. John Heil notes the importance of a sport psychologist in a challenging situation with a fencer. Laura Miele uses her personal experience as an injured athlete to discuss working with athletes on injury rehabilitation. Kate L. Nolt addresses the role of running in helping her cope with a challenging family environment. Selen Razon talks about the challenges of maintaining a slim physique in the face of a family history of obesity and, with Meghan Ramick, address challenges associated with a life changing medical diagnosis and future performance. Shaya Schaedler discusses the role of goal setting in coping with a serious injury and dealing with the challenges of coming back in her swimming career. Tshepang Tshube, Karin Jeffery, and Stephanie Hanrahan address the power of making successful changes in oneself in overcoming challenges in an elite sprinter's career. Taylor Wise eloquently discusses her personal journey through injury to achieve success in collegiate swimming. Anna Weltman talks about the challenges of returning to cycling after a crash. Lindsay Woodford poignantly describes her journey in dealing with the challenges of overtraining syndrome in lightweight rowing.

MORE THAN THAT, I WAS NEVER JUST...
Megan M. Buning and Tiffany M. Kasdorf

Tiffany McDonald Kasdorf was a record-breaking softball pitcher for the Florida State University (FSU) Seminoles from 2004 to 2008. Tiffany joined the Seminoles after a stellar high school career with North Mason High School in Belfair, Washington. As a two-sport standout, Tiffany ultimately fell in love with pitching. The result was a prep career highlighted by numerous accolades, including the league's most valuable player, double digit no-hitters, and a minuscule earned run average (0.30) her senior year. An uncommitted pitcher until October of her senior year, she was propelled by her efforts to the top of her recruiting class and caught the attention of one of the premier college teams in the country. The Seminoles were hot and knocking on the door of the Women's College World Series. Tiffany became a Nole in October of her senior year. Tiffany entered her senior year season content and ready to end her prep career with a bang. However, her body had other plans.

At the start of her senior season, Tiffany started experiencing a nagging pain in her pitching elbow. The pain was so severe that she was not able to pitch her last game in the state championship tournament. On top of missing the most important tournament of her prep career, Tiffany was worried the pain meant something more serious was happening. How would this affect her scholarship offer from FSU? A series of doctors' visits confirmed Tiffany had a partial tear of the ulnar collateral ligament in her pitching elbow. To throwing athletes, this is often the kiss of death, as this type of injury often requires reconstructive surgery (i.e., Tommy John). Tiffany was devastated and scared, but she had no choice but to inform FSU of her injury and decide next steps for her future.

It should be noted that Tiffany was not immediately sold on FSU during recruitment. Her West Coast roots pulled her to stay, but her initial contact with Dr. Joann Graf, then the head coach, changed her mind. Coach Graf made sure Tiffany felt valued as a person first (over athlete), and since their initial contact during the fall of Tiffany's senior year, Coach Graf had laid the groundwork and built a relationship with Tiffany. Tiffany had begun to trust Coach Graf and believed that she truly valued Tiffany's well-being over anything else. Although Tiffany was scared to tell Coach Graf of her elbow injury, she also had a sense of peace because of the relationship. Tiffany rested over the summer before heading to Tallahassee. Upon arrival, she met me, her new pitching coach.

Tiffany was replacing the reigning National Player of the Year, and I was told I would need to reteach her how to pitch with more fundamentally sound mechanics. On top of the fact that Tiffany was not permitted to pitch fully until the spring season, she and I were stressed in different ways. As a young, inexperienced coach, I was not sure of much, but Tiffany was. She remembers distinctly how I was similar to Coach Graf in that I made her believe her well-being and health was a priority. Tiffany shares, "I remember you not making my injury into a big deal. You just said, 'Okay, here's what we're going to do' then you laid out a plan." This helped build a trusting relationship very early on and reaffirms the important role coaches play in shaping athletes' experiences and perceptions (Jowett, 2007; Jowett & Cramer, 2010; Wang, Koh, & Chatzisarantis, 2009). In Tiffany's situation, the importance of the relationship was critical to her continued performance and provides support for Jowett's 3+1Cs relationship model (2007), along with other coach-athlete relationship literature (e.g., Buning & Thompson, 2015).

Tiffany experienced the first part of her freshman year as an injured athlete. She was able to avoid surgery, but the rehabilitation process would consume her entire freshman year. Although highly self-determined, she still struggled with feeling inadequate and left out of the team dynamic. To help her during the course of our journey together during this critical freshman fall, I always had tasks for Tiffany to complete related to her pitching. Tiffany shares that this was a big reason she was able to progress: "You always gave me something to do. I was never just sitting around being the injured girl. These tasks gave me goals and made me feel just as a part of the team as anybody else." Although she was recovering from an injury, Tiffany contributed to her craft and the team. Giving her meaningful activities and tasks helped her develop a sense of purpose and belonging. This speaks to the importance of coaches creating performance-oriented team climates that incorporate mastery goal strategies (Roberts, Treasure, & Conroy, 2012).

That fall was tough, but Tiffany shares one last action that helped her overcome her injury: "It was our last practice before winter break and the first day I could really pitch. You invited our best hitter to the field and had me pitch to her under the lights. You could have done it ten different ways, but you chose to let me pitch to that hitter at that time of day. And that just meant so much to me." This decision to have Tiffany pitch under the lights to the best hitter on the team (and top in the country) was to show Tiffany I had confidence in her ability and a reward for hard work. The outcome was that the hitter was out seven of ten practice at bats that night. It would have been more convenient to have Tiffany pitch to the most available hitter at team practice. But this singular action confirmed to Tiffany that she was valued, appreciated, and ready. Her interpretation and experience of this situation went a long way in her developing adaptive strategies in the future (Treasure, 1997). Tiffany went on to be one of the most prolific pitchers at FSU and still holds numerous spots in the FSU record books. Her freshman season alone resulted in the ACC's Freshman of the Year award paired with All-Tournament and All-Conference honors. She finished her career as the all-time strikeouts leader (939) for FSU, and finished her senior year second nationally in appearances (57) and innings pitched (329.1), all the while ranking in the top ten for wins (30) and top twenty for single-season strikeouts (312). In conclusion, Tiffany was a special athlete. Her inherent self-determined approach, coupled with a growth mind-set, helped her overcome what could have been a career-ending injury. Her success was bolstered by a committed, involved coach. Together, we were able to lay the foundation for an incredible career for Tiffany.

Take-Home Points

1. Work hard and early to establish trust with the athlete.
2. Devise a plan with the athlete and coaches that will allow injured athletes to stay involved with the team yet still contribute to their craft.
3. Go the extra mile to show the athletes they matter to you. Provide opportunities to show your confidence in their ability.

References

Buning, M. M., & Thompson, M. A. (2015). Coaching behaviors and athlete motivation: Female softball athletes' perspectives. *Sport Science Review*, *24*(5–6), 345–70.

Jowett, S. (2007). Interdependence analysis and the 3+1Cs in the coach-athlete relationship. In S. Jowett & D. Lavallee (Eds.), *Social psychology in sport* (pp. 15–27). Champaign, IL: Human Kinetics.

Jowett, S., & Cramer, D. (2010). The prediction of young athletes' physical self from perceptions of relationships with parents and coaches. *Psychology of Sport and Exercise*, *11*, 140–47.

Roberts, G. C., Treasure, D. C., & Conroy, D. E. (2012). Understanding the dynamics of motivation in sport and physical activity: An achievement goal interpretation. In G. Tenenbaum & R. C. Eklund (Eds.), *Handbook of sport psychology* (3rd ed.) (pp. 3–30). Hoboken, NJ: Wiley.

Treasure, D. C. (1997). Perceptions of the motivational climate and elementary school children's cognitive and affective response. *Journal of Sport and Exercise Psychology*, *19*, 278–90.

Wang, J. C. K., Koh, K. T., & Chatzisarantis, N. (2009). An intra-individual analysis of players' perceived coaching behaviors, psychological needs, and achievement goals. *International Journal of Sports Science & Coaching*, *4*(2), 177–92.

COPING WITH INJURY: DEEP BREATHING AND PRAYING
Damien Clement and Monna Arvinen-Barrow

Tamaya was a walk-on striker on her Division I collegiate soccer team. Two weeks into her freshman season, she sustained a grade II lateral ankle sprain while challenging for a header during a training session. This was Tamaya's first major injury. When the injury occurred, all her hard work flashed before her eyes: "What is happening? Is my career over before it even started? Why is God doing this to me?" Tamaya's religious upbringing prevented her from seeking medical treatment or taking medication, but as per team policy, she needed to meet with her athletic trainer for initial evaluation. Tamaya was reluctant to talk to the team athletic trainer: "I am sorry, it's not you. . . . I just know you cannot help me. I know the pain will go away, God willing."

A few days later, Tamaya was feeling worse. She felt like the pain in her ankle was literally controlling her life. She couldn't walk; she couldn't sleep; she could barely hold a conversation with someone because of the pain. Her athletic trainer noticed Tamaya's discomfort when she happened to hobble by the athletic training room, and asked if Tamaya would be willing to try nonmedical approaches to help her cope with her injury. Tamaya reluctantly agreed: "I know you want to help me, and I do want to return back to the soccer field soon. Right now, I am in so much pain and feel lost. I keep praying, and hoping God will show me my path. I trust him, and I know he will guide me. It is just hard, with the pain you know. So if you have some ideas that do not conflict with my convictions, I am willing to listen and try."

The athletic trainer listened and expressed positive regard for Tamaya's concerns. She told Tamaya that she understood her position and respected her decision not to seek medical care: "Tamaya, what I think could help is deep breathing, particularly when it feels like the pain is taking over. Correct me if I am wrong, but using deep breathing to cope with the pain better should be okay and in line with your convictions and values." With Tamaya nodding in confirmation, the athletic trainer introduced her to an easy deep breathing app on her phone: "Let's download this app for you. It is called Pranayama, developed by Saagara. They claim it's the most popular breathing app in the world, and I agree—it's awesome. The app is designed to teach your body how to use breathing effectively. By using it consistently, you can teach your body to breathe at its full capacity, which can help you cope with pain, among other health benefits. And it's free! Also, knowing how important your faith is for you, I would also encourage you to continue to pray as you normally do. Research has shown that prayer can help athletes deal with stress and anxiety, and there is no doubt in my mind that this injury, and the pain it is causing, is stressing you out."

Tamaya decided to give the trainer's suggestions a go, and to her surprise, using the breathing app systematically several times a day appeared to ease her pain. She noticed significant positive changes in her pain levels, sleep, and mood: "With rest, breathing, and prayer, I found myself feeling better one day, one week at the time. Getting back to the field was amazing. I thank God for giving me the strength to overcome this experience."

Tamaya's story highlights the importance of client-specific coping strategies during sport injury rehabilitation. It is evident from the story that religion and prayer play a significant role in Tamaya's life. When applied to the sport injury context, belief in God (i.e., a type of cognitive appraisal) and prayer (i.e., a form of behavioral coping) can influence and be influenced by one's emotional responses to injury (Clement, LaGuerre, & Arvinen-Barrow, 2019). It is known that some injured athletes do rely on prayer as a means of coping with their injuries (Arvinen-Barrow et al., 2015), particularly in dealing with stress and anxiety often associated with injury (Park, 2000).

Broadly defined as an "intentional control of the breath, consciously inhaling, retaining, and exhaling the breath slowly and deeply" (Scotland-Coogan & Davis, 2016, p. 437), deep breathing can be also beneficial for individuals like Tamaya. Research has found that deep breathing stimulates blood flow and releases endorphins, which act as the body's natural pain medication (Busch, Magerl, Kern, Haas, Hajak, & Eichhammer, 2012). Deep breathing also helps reduce stress and anxiety and increase a sense of calm, both of which most likely helped Tamaya cope better with pain. Providing Tamaya with a smartphone app for deep breathing was also an effective way to increase her sense of control over her situation and help her set goals, as well as increase her confidence, motivation, and intentions to be healthy (Crookston et al., 2017).

Take-Home Points

1. As a practitioner, it is important to respect clients' religious coping strategies and be able to reflect on one's own strengths, weaknesses, and potential biases related to religion and spirituality.
2. Use of deep breathing and prayer can facilitate injured athletes' coping with pain, injury, and the overall rehabilitation and recovery process.
3. When used appropriately with the right client, smartphone apps can be very beneficial in facilitating better coping with injury.

References

Arvinen-Barrow, M., Clement, D., Hamson-Utley, J. J., Zakrajsek, R. A., Kamphoff, C. S., Lee, S.-M., . . . Martin, S. B. (2015). Athletes' use of mental skills during sport injury rehabilitation. *Journal of Sport Rehabilitation*, *24*(2), 189–97.

Busch, V., Magerl, W., Kern, U., Haas, J., Hajak, G., & Eichhammer, P. (2012). The effect of deep and slow breathing on pain perception, autonomic activity, and mood processing-an experimental study. *Pain Medicine, 13*(2), 215–28.

Clement, D., LaGuerre, D., & Arvinen-Barrow, M. (2019). Role of religion and spirituality in sport injury rehabilitation. In B. Hemmings, N. J. Watson, & A. Parker (Eds.), *Sport, psychology and christianity: Welfare, performance and consultancy* (pp. 71–86). Abingdon, UK: Routledge.

Crookston, B. T., West, J. H., Hall, P. C., Dahle, K. M., Heaton, T. L., Beck, R. N., & Muralidharan, C. (2017). Mental and emotional self-help technology apps: Cross-sectional study of theory, technology, and mental health behaviors. *JMIR Mental Health, 4*(4), e45. doi: 10.2196/mental.7262

Park, J. (2000). Coping strategies by Korean national athletes. *Sport Psychologist, 14*, 63–80.

Scotland-Coogan, D., & Davis, E. (2016). Relaxation techniques for trauma. *Journal of Evidence Informed Social Work, 13*, 434–41.

GRIT AT 335 MILES PER HOUR: A DRAG RACING STORY OF GUTS, RESILIENCE, INITIATIVE, AND TENACITY
Tami J. Eggleston

We all like an underdog story. It is the American dream—the local hometown boy makes it big. In the world of professional auto racing, many of the elite racers come from racing families and are people who own large racing businesses. There are many types of auto racing, but the most prestigious drag racing organization is the National Hot Rod Association (NHRA) and the top of the NHRA drag racing classes is Top Fuel. Top Fuel dragsters are the quickest accelerating racing cars in the world, reaching speeds of 335 miles per hour and completing the thousand-foot race in less than four seconds! What follows in this essay is a story about a drag racing hero and his mental grit. In the sport psychology literature, the concepts of grit, resilience, mental toughness, and tenacity are often used interchangeably. An athlete may show mental toughness during a competition by not losing focus and playing strong the entire game. Grit, resilience, and tenacity seem to require overcoming greater obstacles and even suffering over the long term (Duckworth, 2016). Clay Millican embodies guts, resilience, initiative, and tenacity combined to make grit.

Guts

It takes guts to play any sport, but it takes a special kind of guts to strap into a race car capable of 10,000 horsepower. Just being able to drive and handle the g-force and speed of these cars is impressive. But this isn't just a story of a man of humble beginnings going on to race in this amazing sport; it is the story of a man who just never gives up. So let's start with Clay Millican, a forklift driver at a Kroger supermarket in Tennessee who had the guts, with the support of his family, to quit his job and become a professional drag racer. Clay found sponsors and financial support to start his dream. In 1998 Clay got his Top Fuel license and made his NHRA debut with a White Sox–sponsored dragster at his first race at Chicago. (This would come full circle when Clay again got a White Sox sponsorship for his race in Chicago in 2019.) Outside of the world of drag racing, few people know him or his story, but in the world of drag racing he is a legend and a hero for his drag racing ability—and more importantly, for his smile, heart, and never-say-never spirit. Clay had the guts to dream big and the guts to work hard to make his dream a reality.

Resilience

Clay possesses what Duckworth (2016) calls grit, defined as a combination of passion, perseverance, hard work, and overcoming obstacles and never giving up. Part of having grit is being resilient and overcoming challenges and losses. According to Duckworth, people can truly embrace grit only if they have suffered. Millican had to struggle just to become a professional racer, then he achieved great success in the International Hot Rod Association (IHRA). The IHRA is a professional drag racing association, but it doesn't have the financial resources, the speed, or the publicity compared to the NHRA. Clay went on to become a multiple-time IHRA Top Fuel World Champion, with numerous IHRA national event wins, and is one of the greatest drivers in the history of IHRA, but he wanted to take his program to the NHRA. Clay was not satisfied with success at a very high level when he knew there was still one more challenge for him—an NHRA national event win.

When Clay made the step to NHRA, he did not have the funding to run an entire season, and he often struggled just to be able to qualify to make the field in the NHRA. But still he kept finding the right people and securing sponsorships—and he never gave up. Due to his winning personality, huge fan support, and ability to make connections, in 2009 he earned the sponsorship of Parts Plus, which has been a loyal sponsor through the ups and the downs.

On the drag strip, Millican has had his share of adversity and struggles, but his greatest suffering happened in August 2015, when Clay and his wife, Donna, lost their twenty-two-year-old son Dalton in a tragic motorcycle accident. Dalton was following in his father's footsteps and had a successful career in ATV racing and monster truck. Just a few days after his son's funeral, Clay was back at the drag strip trying to win an NHRA trophy—the legendary Wally Trophy, named after Wally Parks, the founder of the NHRA.

Going through difficult times on and off the track has made Clay stronger and better. Rotella (2015) states that if your dream to accomplish something is awesome and important, then it won't be easy. Clay went through the fire, but he didn't lose his confidence, his faith, or his ability to keep moving forward, toward his dream.

Initiative

Clay and his family used the loss of his son as motivation and inspiration for a variety of causes. First, Clay raises funds to support Paws and Claws to spay female pit bulls. Clay also joined forces with auto racer Doug Herbert to put on safe teen driving classes through the Be Responsible and Keep Everyone Safe (BRAKES) Foundation. Clay and Donna took their heartbreak and turned it into initiatives to help others and keep Dalton's memory alive. Clay also used this suffering to remind him to keep smiling and make the most of his opportunity as a professional drag racer.

Clay did not allow setbacks in his personal life or in his drag racing profession to stop him. He simply doesn't give up. Clay keeps working hard. He uses setbacks to remind him about what really matters in his life, and he keeps moving toward his goals. Clay views his drag racing and his intense will to win as his purpose, his calling. It is in his DNA.

Tenacity

If grit is made up of guts, resilience, initiative, and tenacity, Clay Millican embodies all of them, but he is as tenacious as the pit bulls and bull terriers his family loves so much. Although Clay had unparalleled success in the IHRA, he struggled to find his way to the winner's circle and that Wally Trophy in the NHRA.

Duckworth (2016) states that tenacity—the ability to fall down and get back up—is more important than talent or luck. Clay doesn't even think about giving up because his purpose, passion, and goals keep him moving forward. Somehow Clay managed to keep a positive attitude for years in the NHRA without winning a single national event or that Wally Trophy. He won some rounds—he got very close—but he didn't reach his ultimate goal. Most drivers would not have had the tenacity and drive (pun intended!) to just keep going from 1998 to 2016 without an NHRA national event win. Think about that: almost twenty years and over 250 races of working, sacrificing, learning, and struggling for that one goal!

But finally it all came together for Clay. On Sunday, June 18, 2017, almost two years after the loss of Dalton, on Father's Day at Bristol Raceway in his beloved home state of Tennessee in front of a huge crowd, Clay's grit finally paid off as he got his first win! As the crowd sang "Rocky Top," Clay and his family and crew hoisted that Wally, and there wasn't a dry eye watching! We all want to see the good guy win and see tragedy turned to triumph and a happy ending.

Wolf (2018) summarizes what Brian Lohnes, an NHRA Mello Yello Series broadcaster, said: "Clay is as kind and fiercely competitive a man as you'll ever meet. You don't go from being a forklift operator to a Top Fuel racer on luck. You do it on guts, heart, and ability. Clay and his wife Donna suffered a nightmarish tragedy and they have handled it in only the way they could. You do not have to have ever given one errant thought about drag racing to appreciate the story of a father and of a man who has achieved and suffered in ways few of us will ever know."

When asked how he keeps such a positive can-do—or "Milli-can"—attitude, Clay says, "I know I am very blessed to do what I do. And with that blessing I am driven to work as hard as I can to make the most of every opportunity given to me" (C. Millican, personal communication, January 26, 2019). Even during the challenges on the track and the personal loss in his own life, he still has a sense of gratitude. He is always pushing and wants more in the future, yet he is simultaneously content in the present. Clay has read Eckhart Tolle's books and tries to live by the mantra: "Realize deeply that the present moment is all you ever have. Make the now the primary focus of your life" (Tolle, 1999, p. 35).

Clay certainly lived in the moment on that special day in June 2017 when he won his first Wally after almost twenty years spent working toward that goal. As of the writing of this chapter, Clay has gone on to win two more Wallys in 2018 and is pursuing more wins with the same level of intensity, passion, and gratitude. The Clay Millican story is an amazing story of grit, mental toughness, guts, resiliency, initiative, tenacity—and also a story of love, family, friendship, teamwork, and faith; The fact that he does it all at 335 miles per hour just adds to the legend!

Take-Home Points

1. Grit takes guts, resilience, initiative, and tenacity. These qualities can be learned, but one has to be willing to work hard, sacrifice, and dream big enough.
2. Going through the fire makes you stronger.
3. Through the good and bad times of sport and life, live life with joy, kindness, a smile, and gratitude.
4. Having a clear goal and desired outcome as well as supportive family (and crew or team) helps you stay focused and resilient to keep moving forward.
5. While working for your dreams and planning for the future, be engaged and present in the now.

References

Duckworth, A. (2016). *Grit: The power of passion and perseverance.* New York, NY: Scribner/Simon & Schuster.
Rotella, B. (2015). *How Champions Think.* New York, NY: Simon & Schuster.
Tolle, E. (1999). *The Power of Now.* Vancouver, BC: Namaste.
Wolf, A. (2018) Must-watch: Clay Millican's storybook tragedy to triumph story. *Dragzine.* Retrieved from https://www.dragzine.com/news/must-watch-clay-millicans-storybook-tragedy-to-triumph-story/

FAILING FORWARD
Kerry Guest

Growing up the youngest of five in a single-parent household in one of the nation's notoriously violent and poverty-stricken areas, Metro-East St. Louis, I learned to covet the psychological skills necessary to navigate through these challenges. Motivated by the sport platform as a way out of hardship, at a young age I utilized the transferability of such mental skills in social, school, and performance encounters. It is this belief that has fueled my passion and purpose-driven behavior, both academically and professionally.

As a young African American male athlete in adolescence, I was conditioned with praise that corresponded with identifying only as an athlete. After all, professional sport is mistakenly embraced as the only way out of financial and economic hardship in communities of lesser affluence (Manswell & Barnicle, 2018). Fortunately, understanding the complexity of my personal developmental context, I was able to nurture an identity of cognitive and physical potential rather than physical ability alone. Ultimately, I discovered transferable cognitive skills related to resilience that assisted in avoiding the trap of athletic identity foreclosure, escaping prematurely committing to a specific identity (Brewer & Petitpas, 2017). Exploring how the skills developed through athletics could serve in alternative spaces maximizes productivity far beyond the conclusion of sport participation. The trials of economic hardship, in conjunction with the trials of sport, allowed for plenty of practice at overcoming adversity.

Resilience is the self-evaluated ability to withstand and thrive through adversity and stress encounters (Fletcher & Sarkar, 2016). Our previous exposure to adversity may, over time, assist unconsciously in the ability to address conflict and formulate solutions if we perceive that we have an ability to do so. Past research has clearly shown the importance of resilience for coping responses to adversity and increases in perceived self-efficacy and compassion. Self-evaluating the successful navigation of previous adversity specific to an individual's journey inside—and outside—the sport experience is a pivotal step in discovering resilient characteristics that you may already subconsciously possess. Although resilience is not fundamentally a fixed trait, as a proactive and transferable skill set it can unlock a higher ability to learn and reflect, enhance sport function, and develop a greater appreciation for life (Howells, Sarkar, & Fletcher, 2017).

As an undergraduate student at Illinois State University, I built my foundation of knowledge in psychology and competed at the NCAA Division I FCS level in football. Navigating college as a first-generation traditional student with limited support was mentally and physically challenging, yet during this time I learned substantially, both as a student and young man. Like many college football players, my aspiration was to play in the National Football League. However, to ensure my efforts to elude generational poverty would not be in vain, I continued to explore alternative options. Recognizing that I was given access to education through the platform of sport, I began practicing an identity outside of sport, utilizing the skills I fostered from participating in sport. That was reflected in my acceptance of leadership roles in small-group class assignments as I had done within my sport position group, nurturing public speaking skills through practice, and approaching first impressions with a professor as I would with a professional scout.

The threat of sudden change is ever present. Being flexible and embracing the actions required to overcome each challenge is a key to life's encounters as well as sport, no matter the circumstance. Despite suffering a career-ending back injury to my sciatic nerve prior to my senior year of competition, I was able to lean on my past experiences, which were replete with self-identified resilient moments, to be effective through sudden change. I took this perceptible resilience opportunity and practiced cognitive skills into the professional field of psychology. Despite graduating with an unremarkable 2.61 grade point average, I decided to focus on building a new primary identity in academia, leveraging personal experiences and sport-nurtured skills through adversity.

I spent two years serving as a mental health professional and mental skills coach, targeting the facilitation of resilience and civic participation in communities of color across the sport and academic settings. This proved to be a pivotal part of my life as I gained clear insight into my passions and the power of self-reflection. From coordinating Special Olympics events for athletes with disabilities to coaching Division I football recruits on the gridiron, I was able to craft a skill set that would further serve my aspirations. These experiences inspired me to strengthen my theoretical knowledge in psychology by pursuing a master's degree in sport and exercise psychology at Southern Illinois University Edwardsville. Here, I had the invaluable opportunity to lead undergraduate kinesiology and health education courses as a graduate assistant. Although there was a lack of academic accolades in my previous undergraduate performance, I was determined to maximize the graduate experience by doing great work and learning from both my successes and my shortcomings of the past. This willingness to systematically approach challenge served me greatly throughout my higher education. Upon graduation I was honored as the School of Education Outstanding Graduate Student of the Year, with a 4.0 grade point average. Ultimately, this momentous accomplishment hat solidified my identity as a student, utilizing what I gleaned as a student-athlete across various socioeconomic demographics.

Feelings are deceptive. I didn't feel confident that I would finish atop my cohort nor that I even belonged in the same room with many of my classmates, but that didn't matter. Instead of being handcuffed by my past performance or triggered by sudden change, I was directed day to day by efforts to perform my best in the moment. Today, resourcefully responding to adversity continues to serve me in my life after ball. From a role at IMG Academy, one of the premier boarding schools for athletes in the world, serving as a mental conditioning coach on the Athletic and Personal Development Team promoting transferable cognitive skills for amateur to professional competitors, to being chosen as an Indiana University Graduate Fellow for the counseling psychology PhD program, I have been honored to share this message across academic and sport platforms.

Just like the first time you shoot a basketball or swing a golf club, the performance results of mental practice aren't instantaneous. We build resilience through continued self-evaluation and acknowledgment. Take time to check in with yourself during trying times, ask yourself what new information you can take forward in your journey, and establish a call to action. When attempting to rise to new levels of confidence through adversity, actions come first, then feelings follow. Acknowledge the action or actions that bring you closer to a desired performance or identity goal and create winning streaks—a daily tally that allows you to track the days that you successfully met your expectations with action. This can be recorded on a cell phone notes app or an office whiteboard to serve as a visual cue. Taking this approach will allow you to focus on the present-day process while highlighting the continuation of growth and progress.

Throughout your athletic, academic, and/or professional career, you will be faced with many challenge opportunities associated with overcoming adversity. You won't always "feel" confident in these moments. The key is to direct your attention to daily actions through the threat of sudden change and emotions. A great place to start is to identify a mentor who serves or has served in the position you desire to pursue professionally or is professionally trained to be an asset to your pursuits. This can be an academic counselor, administrator, organizational leader, or mental performance coach, to name a few resources. Regardless of the nature of the connection, enter this relationship as a learner to maximize the information, insight, and direction you need to be triumphant in both mundane and trying times. With faith in your resilient ability to accomplish challenging goals and the courage to embrace your growth with this systematic approach, your desired identity and performance outcomes are within reach.

Take-Home Points

1. Fail forward. Take time to check in with yourself during trying times. Ask what new information you can take forward in your journey and what tools have been helpful in the past; establish a call to action.
2. Focus on successful actions over feelings of confidence. Establish winning steaks (a system to track consecutive days when action matches expectation toward your desired performance outcome) and leverage mentors for direction to resourcefully respond to challenge. The actions of confidence come first; the feelings follow.

References

Brewer, B. W., & Petitpas, A. J. (2017). Athletic identity foreclosure. *Current Opinion in Psychology, 16,* 118–22.

Fletcher, D., & Sarkar, M. (2016). Mental fortitude training: An evidence-based approach to developing psychological resilience for sustained success. *Journal of Sport Psychology in Action, 7,* 135–57.

Howells, K., Sarkar, M., & Fletcher, D. (2017). Can athletes benefit from difficulty? A systematic review of growth following adversity in competitive sport. *Progress in Brain Research, 234,* 117–59.

Manswell, M., & Barnicle, S. (2018). Athletic identity and the transition out of sport among Division I football players. *Journal of Sports Research, 5,* 12–17.

BEING THERE
John Heil, DA

A sport psychologist, a coach, an athletic trainer, and a fencing equipment technician (actually called an armorer) go into a bar. This is not a joke, but there is a punchline: The sport psychologist sees things that others don't—or at least should. Actually, the sport psychologist, coach, trainer, and the armorer go into the hotel lobby, with a bar to the side. Question: Who notices the cadre member in distress? It is the sport psychologist. This takes place at a world championship, with the sport psychologist as a member of the USA cadre, a term referring to a large and loosely affiliated contingent of athletes, coaches, parents, and administrators, many of whom in this instance are not well acquainted with one another.

A cadre member (who was unfamiliar to me at the time, and whom I will refer to as CM) had been robbed and injured, and was standing at the hotel desk trying to contact the local police. From across the lobby, I could see CM's body language of distress, which on closer examination was even more apparent in facial expression. I veered away from the group and toward CM to see if I could render aid. Further conversation revealed that the anxiety surrounding the incident was heightened by its occurrence at night in a foreign city, and by a language and cultural barrier that became apparent in efforts to seek help.

CM was clearly appreciative of the concern expressed and the assistance provided, which likely muted the initial sense of shock and helplessness that is typical of a traumatic event. The effectiveness of this simple intervention was likely enhanced by its timeliness and ease of accessibility, provided without an overt appeal for help. This pragmatic approach to stress intervention, which focuses on simple aid and comfort, is the philosophy of psychological first aid, which is recommended as a first line of approach in unfolding traumatic events (National Center for PTSD, 2006).

CM and I met later that evening while the athletic trainer attended to the injuries. We discussed the robbery and assault, providing support, defusing emotional tension, and reinforcing that safety had been restored. We spoke by phone after returning to the United States, working through the distress, which was diminished but ongoing. CM expressed appreciation for my efforts in helping reconcile the event and move forward.

Humor and fortuitous encounters aside, this anecdote raises questions about the role of the sport psychologist in a team setting, particularly in regard to competence and boundary issues (Watson & Etzel, 2019). In the 24/7 context of the team travel setting, personal boundaries are relatively porous and the psychologist's role is potentially expansive. This requires sport psychologists to frame their role and take action in a way that simultaneously considers not only professional skills and abilities but also expectations that the cadre may have of the psychologist. Cadre expectations and sense of personal boundaries may or may not be realistic or otherwise congruent with the way psychologists typically function. This disconnect can compound the challenge of service delivery and may require on-the-spot education regarding professional roles.

In the ideal situation, the sport psychologist will be prepared to fill the void when a need arises, especially when timeliness is a critical element and other professional services may not be readily accessible. Ravizza's (1988) thoughts on team consulting endure as both an excellent resource and set of recommendations: establishing trust and respect so that cadre are receptive to services and becoming knowledgeable of team dynamics to understand when, how, and with whom to intervene.

It should not be a surprise that the sport psychologist (who in this case happened to be me) would pick up on behavior that escapes the coach, the trainer, and the armorer. For sport psychologists to add value to the cadre, they need to bring something unique to the team environment, something not provided by other professional staff. The ability to provide this intangible element is at the core of the value added proposition of a sport psychologist, especially in a team setting.

This event occurred while I was serving as a consultant to USA Fencing.

Take-Home Points

1. Being a team sport psychologist means looking after others' welfare, on and off the field of play, in a way that reflects need and opportunity and that leverages professional roles and existing relationships. This relies on psychological mindedness and an awareness of the environment and the people in it.
2. The team setting raises questions of role, of competence, and of boundaries. Conventional wisdom suggests that sport psychologists need to clarify their role and clearly identify who is the client, but practical reality suggests that the sport psychologist traveling with the team needs to be prepared to step into a void when the need arises.

References

National Center for PTSD (2006). *Psychological first aid: Field operations guide.* Washington, DC: National Child Traumatic Stress Network and National Center for PTSD. Retrieved from https://www.ptsd.va.gov/professional/treat/type/psych_firstaid_manual.asp

Ravizza, K. (1988). Gaining entry with athletic personnel for season-long consulting. *Sport Psychologist*, *2*(3), 243–54. doi: 10.1123/tsp.2.3.24

Watson, J. C., & Etzel, E. F. (2019). Ethical and legal issues in sport and performance psychology. In M. Anshel, F. Gardner, E. Labbe, T. Petrie, & S. Petruzzello (Eds.), *APA handbook of sport and exercise psychology* (pp. 821–38). Washington, DC: APA Books.

PSYCHE OF THE INJURED ATHLETE
Laura Miele, PhD

To me, there is no better place to be than on a court with a basketball in my hand. To explain this is very difficult. It was a passion and a dream. . . . Now, there is just passion and a different dream.

The blissful mental state of being on the court or the playing field is like no other feeling in the world. For most, being an athlete becomes their identity; being an athlete is imbedded in their soul. It is an inner life, an inner fire. When people yearn for something, they sacrifice all they can to achieve success. It is not only about the success; the fact that individuals can truly create something within themselves that lifts their self-worth makes athletes willing to give up everything (family/social life) and reach for nothing more.

When an athlete with a promising future succumbs to a career-ending injury, it can be devastating. It has been hypothesized that individuals who derive their self-worth solely from their identity as athletes are at increased risk for depression after experiencing an athletic injury (Brewer, Van Raalte, & Linder, 1993; Heil, 1993). The range of emotions they experience is tumultuous at best. I know this because I was one of those athletes. You go to a dark place; the physical and mental pain takes you into a world you have never been.

When I injured my back and was in rehabilitation back in the 1990s, my physical therapist did not know how to deal with the myriad emotions I was expressing. For me, it was a trying time. I was scared and lost and uncertain of my promising basketball career. My physical therapist tried to help me, but he was not equipped with the skill set at that time to assist me with the psychological obstacles I was facing.

Years later, when I went back to my university to visit, I got to speak with my physical therapist and thank him for all he had done for me. He told me that it used to break his heart that he could not do more for me when I was struggling and that he wished he had learned more about psychology of injury through his studies.

Rehabilitation is a process for some athletes in terms of getting back from the division between the mind and body. Most people do not realize that when you are injured, your body and mind go through a separation period and need to be reunited in order to heal on all levels. This took me a long time to achieve after I was injured and was in rehabilitation for years with my back injury. During that time, I struggled with all the rehabilitation and felt like I was never going to be the same. What I did not realize was that the pain I was feeling was more psychological. Incapable of getting back on the basketball court, my mind-set just was not right, and it hindered my capacity to find the fight within myself to get back to playing. I lost my mind-body connection at that time. This held me back. No one who was working with me at the time was able to identify the situational depression that was taking over my psyche.

I remember being in the athletic training room at Arizona State University, going through physical (emotionally trying) therapy, and one of my buddies—a basketball player who had been trying to recover from an ACL blowout—looked at me and said, "Nobody knows what we are going through—nobody knows!" That was not a "woe is me" cry; it was the true internal pain of an athlete. This was an athlete with a shot at the NBA. It was a valid statement that I, the physical therapist, and trainers knew and were aware of—but could they really understand? More often than not, in order for something to be fixed on the outside it needs to be fixed on the inside. However, help from a trained professional can expedite the healing process as they have the knowledge and expertise to provide the tools for an injured athlete's mental toolbox.

"Without appreciating the psychological aspects of injury and recovery, the injured athlete is unlikely to attain optimum healing, conditioning and early return to function" (Heil, 1993, p. 25). For the past twenty years, I have studied and worked with injured athletes. After a career-ending injury, these athletes frequently fall into depression and suffer moderate anxiety that encompasses thoughts about their physical recovery and what kind of future lies ahead. "Depression occurs with events that disrupt roles by which people define their worth, if these people lack alternative sources of self-worth" (Heil, 1993, p. 342). While working with injured athletes, I tell them to remember what made them an athlete in the first place and move forward by setting one goal at a time. As a motivational tool, goal setting allows athletes to translate commitment into specific and relevant actions (Ford & Gordon, 1997). Goal setting can empower an injured athlete as long as the goals are realistic and short term. The acquisition of small successes, such as getting stronger physically, leads to becoming stronger mentally. This journey takes time.

When working with injured athletes, I teach the philosophy of positive self-talk and creating a mantra that one can speak to every day and live by. I have found in my experience with injured athletes that the strength they can generate from within will assist with the physical recovery.

Working with injured athletes takes patience. They need not only physical assistance, but also social and emotional support. When something so personal, something you have dedicated such hard work and sacrificed so much for is taken away, it is a loss like no other. It is a death, a divorce, a loss of oneself. "Sometimes an athlete can fall prey not just to the injury itself, but to the emotional trauma that surrounds it" (Heil, 1993, p.34).

The transition to becoming a noncompetitive athlete was traumatic. The loss of a sports career, no matter the type of sport or how early or late in a career, feels as if the carpet has been pulled right out from under the athlete's feet without warning, like hitting a brick wall. Today, recovery is not just about overcoming the physical injury itself; getting over the mental and emotional injury amongst athletes is also a common problem. Recovery takes time; it takes great strength to move on and to let go. These are not always easy tasks for individuals who were—or felt they were—on their way to a plush athletic career. The athlete experiences loss at all levels; not only does a career get lost, but the friendships and the camaraderie that were built along the way disappear as well.

"Without sports to help define or evaluate themselves, many athletes are left confused as to their identities, low in self-esteem and confidence" (Crook & Robertson, 1991, p. 119). Sport psychologists should understand that the end of an athletic career is a traumatic transition; goals must be set to create hope and avoid situational depression that can become chronic. Athletes have a fire and a passion within themselves; their energy needs to be channeled in a positive capacity for them to realize they still have limitless potential, even if it is not on a court or a playing field.

Take-Home Points

1. Athletes do not lose their motivation if directed and reminded that even though there was a loss, there still is so much to gain. There can always be a different or parallel dream with even more to gain.
2. Identifying when athletes have lost themselves, either by a coach, friend, and/or sport psychologist, will happen before the athletes even know it themselves.
3. The mind will only be defeated if it fails to identify its strengths.

References

Brewer, B., Van Raalte, J., & Linder, D. (1993). Athletic identity: Hercules' muscles or Achilles heel? *International Journal of Sport Psychology*, 24, 237–54.

Crook, J., & Robertson, S. (1991). Transitions out of elite sport. *International Journal of Sport Psychology*, 22, 115–21.

Ford, J., & Gordon, S. (1997). Perspectives of sport physiotherapists on the frequency and significance of psychological factors in professional practice; Implications for curriculum design in professional training. *Australian Journal of Science and Medicine in Sport*, 29, 34–40.

Heil, J. (1993). *Psychology of sport injury*. Champaign, IL: Human Kinetics.

RUNNING TO COPE OR RUNNING AWAY—HOW MUCH IS TOO MUCH?
Kate L. Nolt, MPH, PhD

I began to run when I was twelve years old. Growing up in Birmingham, Alabama, during the 1960s and 1970s, I never felt that I lacked anything important. I had a stable home, brothers and sisters I played with, and lots of family and friends. My father traveled a lot and left us at home with domestic help and a stepmother, known as Mom growing up, who was less than thrilled with her life. She took her frustrations out on us all—mostly me, as I was the middle child, sensitive and close with my father. I adored my father, who died in 1998, even though he was away a lot. My relationship with my mother deteriorated over the years.

In the late 1970s my grandfather, aging and possibly suffering from dementia, sold the family business right out from underneath my father, the company president. Our family was plunged into a difficult set of financial circumstances, which led to our having to relocate to Baltimore, Maryland. When we arrived in Baltimore, we were shocked by the difference between urban living and southern living! There were kids in my middle school who were from diverse racial backgrounds (as opposed to the homogenous white childhood I'd had up until then). While diversity was never an issue for me in terms of acceptance, the degree to which my mother's unhappiness grew was something much harder to accept. This was because her own health was deteriorating and she had little support from my father. She then turned to me, a thirteen-year-old girl, to take care of her and her demanding need for attention.

As a coping mechanism for the emotional roller-coaster I was on, including an abusive relationship from my mother, I began to run. Run and run I did, every day, sometimes twice a day. It was a subtle evolution from running to cope, to running because I couldn't live without it. I ran to get out of the house when my unhappy mother unleashed her negativity and anger. The environment in the house was tense. I ran because I experienced anxiety when I went to school and then came home. Running saved me from a complete breakdown and yet led to a dependence on the exercise to live. This went on for nearly five years. Eventually, I added doing forty-five minutes of an exercise video each day to running twice a day. I even began to sacrifice taking time to eat a meal for a quick run. I didn't realize it at the time, but I went from running to cope to running away without ever leaving my home. I suffered from exercise addiction (Sachs, 2018), and yet my performance, to me, was Olympian. Running was also a way to reduce the risk that I would engage in even riskier behaviors to cope, such as drugs, alcohol, and promiscuity, all of which were much more socially accepted then. To me, these were not an option.

I recall that one day—and this was a time when we did not have an app to measure this—I ran twelve miles without even noticing. Most of that run I cried. After this run, when I returned home, I became aware of the fact that I felt good! My mother was in a fit of anger, and yet I felt mentally alert, clear, and relaxed. I began to realize there were some excellent benefits to running. With enthusiasm, I absorbed issues, old and new, of *Runners World* and became engrossed in the stats of others, articles about proper body alignment during a run, breathing technique, footfall, and the facts about how mental health was improved as much as physical health by running. We can't forget the articles about the shoes! I absorbed it all.

I noticed that I began to care more about my personal best performance in a noncompetitive, more recreational manner. I began to build self-confidence, something my mother's presence always worked to tear down. While my self-image was on shaky ground because of the spiteful nature of my mother's influence over the years, I began to realize that my performance in running went from being extrinsically motivated by my need to cope to being intrinsically motivated by the healthy feeling and confidence I had after a run. Ersöz (2016) discusses this as controlled motivation (extrinsic) versus autonomous motivation (intrinsic). The controlled motivation in my circumstances comprised the anxiety and stress caused by the tense and abusive environment in my home. The autonomous motivation came when I began to realize that what started as a healthier coping mechanism (rather than alcohol and other drugs) had evolved into an exercise in becoming and staying healthy and feeling good about myself.

I used imagery to enhance my performance. I recall imagining I was an Olympic running star. The streets would be lined with people cheering me to a stellar finish. I successfully ran marathon after marathon—in my imagery, each time my personal best record improved. I imagined beach running (which I do today), with a sunrise so peaceful and beautiful that Claude Monet would find it worthy of painting. As my confidence in running grew, my endurance improved, and I gave myself over to what I now know is flow, that state of feeling like your feet barely touch the ground, like you are floating on air. Yoshida et al. (2018) report that flow state involves "people [being] so intensely involved in an activity that nothing else seems to matter" (p. 184). I began to heal. Slowly but surely, I found the courage to heal and seek the help that I needed from therapy and good friends. All the while, I maintained a level of running that serves me well to this day.

While I still run today, as a fifty-five-year-old woman, I have a much healthier approach both mentally and physically toward exercise and my performance. I still have not run a marathon, and I don't plan to. I haven't spoken to my mother in years, and I still tend to shy away from races as I never wished to insert the competitive nature of a race into something that I do for the enjoyment and health benefits of it. I never wanted the positive mental state that resulted from the benefits of running to be hijacked by either my personal best record, a stressful training schedule, or the need to finish first. I don't regret this. I do see others who gain fulfillment from these things in their running careers, and I salute them. It has just never been for me. While I no longer have a need to cry during a run, I acknowledge that my performance in running has changed a lot through the years (a sub-eight-minute mile is now a thirteen-minute mile). Happily, I still derive much from the imagery of an Olympic performance and the streets lined with people cheering me on to the finish. However, now those faces are less a crowded blur and more the faces of those I love and who mean so much to me.

Take-Home Points

1. Running—or other activities—can serve as critical coping mechanisms for stressful life events/circumstances.
2. Even though these activities are quite positive, addiction to these activities is possible. Be aware of the signs and symptoms of exercise addiction and how to respond appropriately.

3. Focus on enjoyment of these physical activities, for the exceptional physical and mental health benefits they can provide.

References

Ersöz, G. (2016). An examination of motivational regulations, dispositional flow and Social physique anxiety among college students for exercise: A self-determination theory approach. *College Student Journal, 50*(2), 159–70.

Sachs, M. L. (2018). Exercise addiction. In S. Razon and M. L. Sachs (Eds.), *Applied exercise psychology: The challenging journey from motivation to adherence*. New York, NY: Routledge.

Yoshida, K., Ogawab, K., Mototanib, T., Inagakib, Y., Sawamurac, D., Ikomad, K., & Sakaia, S. (2018). Flow experience enhances the effectiveness of attentional training: A pilot randomized controlled trial of patients with attention deficits after traumatic brain injury. *NeuroRehabilitation, 43,* 183–93.

DEFYING THE ODDS
Selen Razon, PhD

Alison was born into a family with four obese siblings. Due to both genetics and poor eating habits in the family, it did not take her too long to realize that her chances of being slim and remaining slim were . . . slim. Alison was perceptive and made a decision to be healthier than the rest of her family, but she really did not know where to start. She just was not used to seeing any healthy behavior around her. In fact, as she was growing up, all she could see was that her family was extremely sedentary and had a diet very low in nutritional value and very high in saturated fats.

Eventually, and perhaps not surprisingly, she saw her family go through health troubles, which further reinforced her decision to separate herself from the bad habits she unwillingly acquired while living with them. Alison was able to change her life and become uncharacteristically healthy in comparison to the rest of her family. Today she is a very successful yoga teacher. Students have a hard time finding spots in her classes, and many think she is inspirational. Her slimness exudes not only health, but also confidence in a body that is extremely flexible—often much more so than the very young students who are taking her classes. Looking at her, one can never imagine that she actually comes from a very different place and the very high odds she beat to end up where she is today.

When I asked Alison how she defied the odds, her recounting aligned with the tenets of self-determination theory (SDT; Deci & Ryan, 2008). SDT is a key theory in performance psychology. In a nutshell, SDT stipulates that one's self-determination to achieve any goal (e.g., sport success, behavior change, etc.) is tied to meeting three psychological needs: the need for competence, the need for autonomy, and the need for relatedness.

Of these, the need for competence pertains to our need to feel mastery over the outcomes of what we are undertaking. The need for relatedness has to do with our need to interact, connect, and care for others. Finally, the need for autonomy has to do with our need to have an integrated self where we feel self-sufficient and not dependent on others in our choices and actions (Gagné, 2014).

Consistent with the tenets of the theory, when she was first introduced to yoga, Alison was a shy adolescent who did not feel particularly attracted to any type of physical activity, regardless of how much she wanted to be active. However, she was motivated to find something to stick with. Based on Alison's recollections, when she first started doing yoga thirty-nine years ago, she felt an immediate sense of mastery (i.e., that she could learn how to do the poses correctly if she worked on them). Unlike many other undertakings she had previously engaged in, she did not feel as if this was above her; she felt challenged, but in a realistic way. Alison also felt considerable relatedness—there was a great deal of connection in her yoga community and a true sense of caring and being there for each other with others who were practicing yoga. Alison apparently had not felt this in the activities she previously practiced.

Finally, she also recounted that she felt a true sense of autonomy (i.e., a sense of self-sufficiency and independence in an environment where her input was valued and actively sought). Much aligned with the theory; after years of searching, Alison felt for the first time the intrinsic motivation to stick with a physical activity that would save her from her sedentary upbringing and help her achieve a healthy life against all odds. Intrinsic motivation is the proclivity to engage in a task because the task is perceived as inherently enjoyable or even as a reward in itself (Kinnafick, Thøgersen-Ntoumani, & Duda, 2014; Ryan & Deci, 2000). As fueled by her intrinsic motivation, Alison's long-term practice of yoga eventually translated into healthy eating habits and an overall exemplary lifestyle.

Alison's story is important, especially for those of us aiming for permanent behavior changes or long-term success in our athletes and clients. Change and success that are permanent or even inspiring to others, as in Alison's case, require intrinsic motivation. Therefore, when we aim for real change in others we need to remember to appeal to their intrinsic motivation, for once intrinsic motivation is there, one can defy the odds!

Take-Home Points

1. As best as you can, make sure your athletes or clients feel some kind of mastery over the skills they are learning. You do not have to make things too easy, but too high levels of difficulty will also impede the experience of mastery. Make it challenging but manageable.
2. Athletes and clients will thrive in settings where they feel connected to others. Pay attention in creating atmospheres where people can relate to and care for each other.
3. Have your athletes and clients make some of the decisions during their training regimen. Intrinsic motivation happens when people feel like they have a say in what happens to them.

References

Deci, E. L., & Ryan, R. M. (2008). Self-determination theory: A macrotheory of human motivation, development, and health. *Canadian Psychology/Psychologie Canadienne, 49*, 182–85.

Gagné, M. (Ed.). (2014). *The Oxford handbook of work engagement, motivation, and self-determination theory*. New York, NY: Oxford University Press.

Kinnafick, F. E., Thøgersen-Ntoumani, C., & Duda, J. L. (2014). Physical activity adoption to adherence, lapse, and dropout: A self-determination theory perspective. *Qualitative Health Research, 24*, 706–18.

Ryan, R. M., & Deci, E. L. (2000). Intrinsic and extrinsic motivations: Classic definitions and new directions. *Contemporary Educational Psychology, 25*, 54–67.

DO NOT QUIT!
Selen Razon, PhD, and Meghan Ramick, PhD

This is a story of mental toughness and persistence. This story does not belong specifically to sport, but the lessons from this story are applicable to all walks of life, including other performance fields. Furthermore, the protagonist of this story, Maggie, could be any of us.

Maggie was a medical doctor, a specialist in infectious disease. She was very successful in her field; in fact, when she was diagnosed with a very rare autoimmune condition called Behcet's disease, she was only in her forties and on her way to assuming bigger and better positions in her hospital. The Mayo Clinic defines Bechet's disease as a rare disorder that causes blood vessel inflammation throughout the body. It is an autoimmune disorder in which the body's immune system mistakenly attacks some of its own healthy cells. As such, those who have it eventually develop inflammation-related symptoms around their mouth, skin, genital areas, eyes, joints, blood vessel, digestive system, and brain. There is no cure for the disease, but medication can help reduce signs and symptoms (Mayo Clinic, n.d.).

The news came as a shock at first. Upon medical advice, Maggie left her position and started a new life in which her husband would be the sole breadwinner for the family and she would have to take care of herself at home. However, as disastrous as the prospect looked, Maggie was mentally tough. Mental toughness combines cognitive, affective, and behavioral qualities that allow individuals to persist in the pursuit of their goals despite setbacks and stressors (Gucciardi, Gordan, & Dimmock, 2008). As such, despite the considerable anxiety and stress that her new reality presented, Maggie was determined not to give up and looked for other ways to still have a meaningful life.

Fast forward many years: Maggie's persistence led her to discover and practice a new way of being that is anchored in her family and faith. Today, in her seventies, despite the ever-present and increasing symptoms of her condition, she leads several groups and charities that give back to people in need. Maggie organizes classes and gatherings at her place to share knowledge and wisdom with others, raises her grandchildren from all over the world, and receives frequent awards and recognitions for her accomplishments. But most importantly, Maggie is happy and content and almost grateful to the medical condition that allowed her to find a new way of being and being happy.

When we asked Maggie how she made it so well after what happened, she recounted two things that are extremely relevant to all performance situations, especially when performing under anxiety and stress. She told us that first, when she realized the amount of work she had to do to change her life in order to survive, she tapped into her confidence. Self-confidence is as an important part of successful performance in sports and life in general, positively influencing behaviors, attitudes, and goal attainment (Cox, Shannon, McGuire, & McBride, 2010). At first Maggie was challenged with having enough self-confidence, but then she consistently reminded herself that she had overcome other obstacles and told herself she would overcome this one as well. Related to the notion of confidence, she also underlined the importance of believing in something bigger and stronger than she is. In fact, there is research from performance psychology that also shows that individuals' belief systems and faith can often help them, especially in the face of difficulties (Egli & Fisher, 2017).

Take-Home Points

1. In facing any stressful events, as bad as they can seem at first, do not let your athletes give up. Find ways to tap into their confidence. Help them build confidence if they are challenged with it.
2. Faith and belief are personal, but be open to your athletes' beliefs to the extent that they can be major sources of motivation to perform well when faced with difficult situations.
3. Similar to confidence, mental toughness predicts success in resilience and success in the face of adversity (Hart, Brannan, & De Chesnay, 2014). Help your athletes get mentally though. They will likely need it!

References

Cox, R., Shannon, J., McGuire, R., & McBride, A. (2010). Predicting subjective athletic performance from psychological skills after controlling for sex and sport. *Journal of Sport Behavior, 33*, 129–45.

Egli, T. J., & Fisher, L. A. (2017). Christianity and sport psychology: One aspect of cultural competence. *Journal of the Christian Society for Kinesiology, Leisure, and Sport Studies, 4*, 19–27.

Gucciardi, D. F., Gordan, S., & Dimmock, J. A. (2008). Towards an understanding of mental toughness in Australian Football. *Journal of Applied Sport Psychology, 20*, 261–82.

Hart, P. L., Brannan, J. D., & De Chesnay, M. (2014). Resilience in nurses: An integrative review. *Journal of Nursing Management, 22*, 720–34.

Mayo Clinic. (n.d.) Behcet's disease. Retrieved from https://www.mayoclinic.org/diseases-conditions/behcets-disease/symptoms-causes/syc-20351326

COMING BACK FROM INJURY
Shaya Schaedler, MEd

I was an All-American swimmer in high school. At the end of my senior year, I was diagnosed with Cushing's disease and required endoscopic brain surgery to remove a tumor. Twelve days before I started college on a full-ride swimming scholarship, the surgery took place. While not a typical injury, the disease and surgery were jarring to my athletic career and involved unique challenges and physical rehabilitation before I could get back into the pool. I feared I would never have the athletic success in college that I had prior to brain surgery. I am not alone in thinking so. Researchers have identified concerns of inability to perform as a common barrier many athletes face in returning from injury (Podlog, Dimmock, & Miller, 2011). Some of my doubts came from not being in the pool for almost a year. I had never been out of swimming for that long, and it was terrifying to think about the possibility of underperforming. However, the people around me also drove some of these doubts. The apprehension of my doctors and my parents swirled around in my mind, telling me more than once I should consider ending my athletic career due to the length and difficulty of recovery. This led to conflicting thoughts and doubts surrounding my competence and my ability to make a comeback.

Using smart goals can be a useful first step in recovery. Implementing realistic short-, intermediate-, and long-term goals can aid in building confidence in returning to sport (Podlog et al., 2011). Athletes are not simply machines. We have thoughts, feelings, and beliefs about ourselves in relation to competence. It may not be enough to only use smart goals and rehabilitation exercises. It is not possible to separate feelings from the process of recovery. Using common counseling practices such as cognitive behavioral therapy may be useful in addressing competence concerns. As outlined by Fenn and Byrne (2013), cognitive behavioral theory assumes that an event (i.e., an injury) occurs and we have thoughts in response to this event such as "I'll never be the same." These thoughts may lead to feeling incompetent or worthless, which influences how we behave. We may not stick to a recovery regimen or may question our athletic identity.

Mental health professionals provide the knowledge and expertise to address these maladaptive thoughts through cognitive reframing, which includes providing alternative ways of viewing the situation and challenging negative thoughts with logic. For example, instead of thinking, "I'll never be the same," reframing may look like: "Stop. I am being irrational. I have come back from adversity before. I am working hard and it will take time to get back in shape. I am doing this because I love this sport and am excited to get back to it." (Podlog et al., 2011). Providing an alternate framework with less negativity can decrease negative thought patterns and feelings. To address competency concerns, it is not enough just to implement goals surrounding recovery and then stop there. We must also address thoughts and feelings surrounding recovery. We have the ability to control our thoughts, and the first step is becoming aware of them. From there, we can actively challenge the negativity with logic and instill healthier thought patterns.

Ultimately, self-confidence and belief surrounding the ability to come back from our injuries must come from within. However, it may be hard for athletes to admit they are struggling in the first place, as help-seeking behaviors are often seen as weakness (Watson, 2005). After all, how many times have coaches told us to toughen up? Athletes are less likely than nonathletes to engage in help seeking behaviors due to fear of loss of prestige and stigmatization (Watson, 2005). In my own recovery process, I feared letting anyone know how much I doubted myself; I didn't want anyone to think I was weak, and this fear kept me from utilizing adequate resources. I insisted on handling my recovery on my own, and while I was able to bounce back well, I ended up pushing myself too hard, too soon, trying to prove a point. I wanted to be tough because, after all, athletes build their brand on being the toughest, on working the hardest, on the ultimate comeback. No one wants to hear about—or be—an athlete who took years to come back from injuries; everyone wants to be the athlete who came back sooner than expected, the athlete who is straight grit. However, this attitude ultimately led to many frustrating setbacks and only reinforced my self-doubt because I was physically unable to accomplish what I was demanding of my body on the time line I created for myself based on this "tough" mentality. Although I was able to finally swim best times by my junior year and reach the final at the Pac-12 conference championships, I never felt fully competent in my swimming abilities again. This hindered much of my recovery process, simply because I was afraid to ask for help. Coaches and mental health practitioners can play an integral role in destigmatizing help-seeking behaviors. Normalizing the fact that recovery is difficult and that struggling with competence is a common concern in injury rehabilitation may allow athletes to feel more comfortable opening up and may allow them to seek the help they need.

Take-Home Points

1. Using SMART (e.g., specific, measurable, action-oriented, realistic, and time-bound) goals can help athletes with building confidence.
2. Using cognitive behavioral therapy techniques may provide a framework for athletes to challenge their self-doubts.

3. Athletes are less likely than nonathletes to seek help. Normalizing the difficulties of the recovery process and attempting to destigmatize help-seeking behaviors may encourage them to utilize appropriate services.

References

Fenn, K., & Byrne, M. (2013). The key principles of cognitive behavioral therapy. *InnovAI*, *6*(9), 579–85.

Podlog, L., Dimmock, J., & Miller, J. (2011). A review of return to sport concerns following injury rehabilitation: Practitioner strategies for enhancing recovery outcomes. *Physical Therapy in Sport*, *12*(1), 36–42.

Watson, J. C. (2005). College student-athletes' attitudes toward help-seeking behavior and expectations of counseling services. *Journal of College Student Development*, *46*(4), 442–49.

LIFE CHANGES FOR ATHLETIC EXCELLENCE
Tshepang Tshube, Karin Jeffery, and Stephanie Hanrahan,
University of Botswana, San José State University,
and the University of Queensland

This is a story in two parts. The first part describes how Isaac Makwala, an elite sprinter from Botswana, improved his performance by deliberately changing his behavior on and off the track. The second part tells how this new Isaac overcame highly adverse circumstances to make history in the International Association of Athletics Federations (IAAF) World Championships in 2017.

Isaac Makwala holds Botswana's sprint records in the 100m, 200m, and 400m. He is also the second-fastest 400m African athlete of all time. Born in 1986 in the small village of Tutume, he grew up herding goats and cattle. In 2006 the Francistown Athletics Club, a military-based and military-supported track and field club, recognized his athletic gifts and recruited him. That same year he qualified for the 2007 All-Africa Games and other international meets. His first international competition was in Eindhoven, Netherlands, where he ran a personal best of 46.48 seconds in the 400m.

After these initial successes, however, Isaac's performance began to deteriorate. He qualified for the 2012 Olympic games but was eliminated in the first round. His off-track behavior saw a corresponding decline; at various international training centers, he was frequently reprimanded for bullying younger athletes and other disruptive behaviors. Stressed, frustrated, and confused, he did not know how to deal with his feelings other than by taking them out on those around him.

Painful as his struggle was, it was consistent with a larger pattern in African runners as described by Yomi Omogbeja, editor of the website AthleticsAfrica.com. According to Omogbeja, most African athletes run well in small meets in Africa and Europe, but fail to perform on the larger stage due to anxiety, intimidation, pressure, and general lack of experience with ultra-high-profile international competition. These athletes need more exposure to the highest levels of international competition in order to express their talents (Omogbeja, quoted in Sibanda, 2014).

Isaac himself recognized that he needed to make some changes. Although he had not read Dweck's (2009) work on growth mind-set, he instinctively understood that he was not a fully formed individual and that he had the ability to change those characteristics that limited his success. However, he also recognized that, with his relative inexperience, he did not know exactly what he should focus on changing. This is where Justice "Coach JD" Dipeba became a critical influence. Dipeba, himself a former Olympian, knew how to help runners get faster. But even more importantly, he recognized that Isaac had to substantially change some of his behaviors both on and off the track. Coach JD espoused a "3D philosophy" of discipline, dedication, and determination. This philosophy helped Isaac to understand the relationships between all the dimensions of his life and specifically how to enhance his athletic performance by raising his behavioral standards off the track. Isaac accepted Coach JD's philosophy, and their relationship both on and off the track grew into a strong bond (Tshube & Hanrahan, 2018), one that continues today.

At the same time, the 2014–2015 season saw a significant change in Isaac's behavior. He became more introspective, focusing on his own abilities, and reported being happier. In a marked reversal from his previous behavior, he even began mentoring younger athletes. That same season, he beat his previous 400m personal best (45.25 seconds) more than ten times, setting national records in the 100m, 200m, and 400m. He also broke the African record for the 400m, which had endured for the previous ten years. Isaac acknowledged his coach's role in these successes, stating, "I must thank my coach, Justice Dipeba who always tells me to . . . give my best" (Makwala, quoted in Sibanda, 2014).

Following these successes, Isaac attracted a huge national and international following on social media. As an international track star from Botswana, he felt obliged to be available to his fans. However, under the pressure of their expectations and frequently negative feedback, his performances again deteriorated sharply. Once again, Isaac and Coach JD saw the need for a major change. Isaac decided to give up his social media presence and shut down all his accounts. He switched his focus from his public persona to his personal life and family. He became more actively involved in caring for his infant daughter. That same season he won the Diamond League (an annual series of international elite track and field meets) and ran the 400m in under 44 seconds three times. He also became the first man in the world to break a 20-second 200m and a 44-second 400m *during the same meet*, an astonishing feat.

Isaac's new focus and discipline were sorely tested during the norovirus outbreak in the 2017 IAAF World Championships in London. This virus causes extreme gastric distress and is notoriously contagious. Therefore, when athletes and staff began exhibiting symptoms, quarantines were swiftly imposed. Despite limited symptoms, Isaac was barred from both the 400m finals and the 200m heats. Feeling well enough to compete, he attempted to enter the stadium for the 400m, but guards blocked him and escorted him away. Understandably upset at missing this chance for a medal, he stated that his mind was "broken." However, when his quarantine period ended and he was still symptom free, he was allowed to run a solo 200m time trial. On a freezing, rainy day, Isaac made history by qualifying for the 200m finals while running completely alone. He ultimately placed sixth in the finals with a time of 20:44, which was relatively slow for him. The last-minute schedule changes did not allow him enough recovery between races, thus adding physical fatigue to his other stressors. Given these circumstances, Coach JD was still happy with his runner, saying, "I think the performance was brilliant" (J. Dipeba, personal conversation, July 26, 2019).

Isaac thus overcame two extremely adverse experiences in 2017: being physically barred from the track in the 400m and having to run his 200m qualifying heat with no competition. Either factor by itself could have crushed his morale. As before, he credited his triumph over adversity to his character-changing work with Coach JD. Together, Isaac and Coach JD have formed one of the most successful partnerships in track and field, in Africa, or anywhere else in the world.

As Dweck (2009) asserts, we need not assume that "we are what we are," or that we are "stuck" with the characteristics that limit our growth and success. Isaac Makwala's story illustrates that we do have the power to make substantial changes in ourselves, particularly in our responses to stress and adversity (Dweck & Leggett, 1988; Potgieter & Steyn, 2010). It further shows how this process is enhanced when a willing athlete and a skilled coach combine their talents to work toward a mutual goal.

Take-Home Points

1. Behavior off the track (or field or court) affects athletes' performance on the track (or field or court).
2. Structured self-reflection, particularly about discipline, dedication, and determination, can help athletes change their attitudes and behaviors.
3. Shutting down (or severely limiting) one's social media presence can enhance focus and provide time for other activities.

References

Dweck, C. S. (2009). Mindsets: Developing talent through a growth mindset. *Olympic Coach, 21*, 4–7.

Dweck, C. S., & Leggett, E. L. (1988). A social-cognitive approach to motivation and personality. *Psychological Review, 95*, 256–73.

Potgieter, R. D., & Steyn, B. J. M. (2010). Goal orientation, self-theories and reactions to success and failure in competitive sport: psychological perspectives. *African Journal for Physical Health Education, Recreation and Dance, 16*, 635–47.

Tshube, T., & Hanrahan, S. J. (2018). Southern African Olympian perspectives of the coach-athlete relationship. *International Journal of Sport Psychology, 49*(3), 224–39.

Sibanda, A. (2014). Makwala: Africa's fastest in 400 metres. *Daily News Botswana*. Retrieved from http://www.dailynews.gov.bw/news-details.php?nid=12735

UNCONVENTIONAL SUCCESS THROUGH INJURY
Taylor Wise, MS

I started competitive USA swimming at the age of six. For fifteen years, I swam six to seven days a week, between three and eight hours a day, for fifty weeks out of the year. Although I didn't always love swimming, I always loved the pursuit of excellence. However, that pursuit came with a cost.

Most people think of swimming as relatively low impact compared to other sports. Most people would be correct, but swimming as frequently as I did from such a young age meant that I took thousands of strokes a day long before my body finished developing. I also tended to do the "rougher" events—such as butterfly and the individual medley—as a kid. These events are particularly hard on the body. By the time I was nine years old, I was having pains in my shoulders. Before high school, when my training intensified to approximately seven hours a day, I had reached a point where I could no longer lift my arms from my sides.

Most athletes are taught to fight through pain (Orlick, 2008). Grit and perseverance are considered good traits in an athlete. Although such traits often lead to enhanced performance, they can also be very damaging to the body (Thompson & Sherman, 1999). Had I addressed the issues with my shoulders when I was young, I may not have reached the point of no return. Nonetheless, I persisted. As a state hopeful in one of the most competitive states for high school swimming, I was determined to figure out a way to continue at the level I was reaching. My parents and I consulted with at least four doctors, all of whom told me that my shoulders were the worst they had ever seen and that my only hope—not only for swimming but also for a regular life without pain—was immediate surgery. The problem was that they would have to repair so much damage that it was unlikely I would swim fast ever again.

I had no interest in swimming without the potential to reach my goals. We kept looking. Finally, after a few recommendations from experienced athletes, I was fortunate enough to find a team of osteopathic medical doctors and a physical therapist who specialized in the swimmer's shoulder. Live X-rays confirmed that my shoulders dislocated at every stroke, causing severe impingement and multiple tendon tears. They said the same thing the surgeons said: Surgical repairs would tighten my shoulders so much that I wouldn't be able to rotate my arms quickly. They had an alternative solution: stop stroking. But how do you swim without using your arms? For months, I only kicked. Gradually, I worked my way up to stroking two hundred yards a day, and eventually one thousand yards a day. As I was used to swimming ten thousand yards in a day, this was a drastic change. I had to switch to sprinting because I wasn't capable of stroking the yardage that was required of my original events.

But I didn't take the easy route. While my teammates stroked, I either kicked or "stroked" along with them with therapy bands on land. I went to physical therapy every day, and iced and heated before and after every practice. I went to the pool by myself for extra practice to improve my core and fast-twitch muscle responses. I perfected the fine details of every start and turn that I knew would make or break a race that's won by hundredths of a second. Ultimately, I did everything I possibly could to make up for the yardage I was lacking.

I ended up becoming part of an experimental training program that attempted to prove that a less-is-more approach to training can be successful. The result? I didn't make state during my freshman year; there was too much ground to make up. But I got close, and my ability to race without training the traditional way motivated me. I persisted, and I ended up making state during my sophomore year and continued to advance at the competitive USA level. My physical therapist told me that I had a limited number of strokes in my life, and that even though he had faith that he could make me successful for as long as my shoulders held up, he thought my strokes would run out before college. This was another devastating blow to me, but I worked with him consistently for four years, and by the end of that time, I had not only finaled at state multiple times but also been recruited by a number of Division I college teams. I went on to swim at the Division I collegiate level and was even able to increase my stroke yardage to four thousand yards a day (far beyond what my treatment team ever expected).

We all learned many valuable lessons. The treatment team confirmed that there is something to the less-is-more approach, at least when it came to battling the "garbage yardage" mind-set of traditional coaches. It's not about putting in less effort, just about recovering better and being smarter with your resources (Kellmann, 2010). We also realized that there is always an alternative solution. You might not like your options, and success certainly won't come without difficult decisions and lots of persistence, but options exist; you just have to be willing to look for them. Finally, I learned that there are many people who are going to doubt you, including yourself. You might doubt that the work you're doing is going to lead to success, or wonder if the alternatives you're using are just attempts to hide a low work ethic. It is not easy to take an unconventional route. I had to be prepared to deal with judgment, whether it was from coaches, other swimmers, or other medical personnel. But I learned that if I trusted the process and worked as hard as I could with the resources I had, I could let the performance do the talking.

Take-Home Points

1. Don't give up. If something doesn't feel right to you, look for another option. Be creative and have fun with it. If you're passionate enough, then the difficulty that comes with the search for an alternative solution will be worth it.
2. When in doubt, remember your clichés: "less is more" and "work smarter, not harder."

References

Kellmann, M. (2010). Preventing overtraining in athletes in high-intensity sports and stress/recovery monitoring. *Scandinavian Journal of Medicine & Science in Sports, 20*, 95–102. doi: 10.1111/j.1600-0838.2010.01192.x

Orlick, T. (2008). *In pursuit of excellence: How to win in sport and life through mental training* (4th ed.). Champaign, IL: Leisure Press.

Thompson, R. A., & Sherman, R. T. (1999). "Good athlete" traits and characteristics of anorexia nervosa: Are they similar? *Eating Disorders, 7*(3), 181–90. doi: 10.1080/10640269908249284

RESILIENCE AND RECOVERY AFTER BIKE COLLISION
Anna Weltman

It was just a regular training ride, a cycling workout in the early hours of the morning to get the miles in before it was time to go to work. The route was a usual one, nothing fancy, and the sun was already coming up: same gear, lights, helmet, reflectors, and a bike in perfect working order. Benny was ready for his ride and was accustomed to being alert on the road, aware of the cars (not many at this time of the day), and familiar with his overall surroundings.

Benny rode four mornings a week before going to work. At lunch, twice a week, he pulled off a thirty-minute run at a fast pace, and on weekends he completed a long, slow, three-hour run. Swimming took up two of his weeknights at the pool and two evenings a week in open water to get used to ocean waves, currents, chop, salt, buoyancy, and variable water temperatures. Sometimes he even had energy left over for a yoga class (usually hot yoga), and at least eight months of the year he interspersed his workouts with races, following the taper techniques and periodization training that was recommended for racing triathlons.

Benny liked to compete and entered multiple races throughout the year. Sometimes they were long distances away, and often they were only a few weeks apart. If a race was a qualifier for a spot at a more prominent race, he prioritized that one, adding to the already intense pressure upon himself. He sometimes got frustrated when he could not complete all of his workouts in the week, feeling like he was falling behind in fitness and progressions. He was very serious about his training but also maintained a hectic work schedule and—lucky for him—he was single without dependents or else he would have had to let something slip.

With so many commitments and such a heavy training load, it was a wonder that he could keep on top of it all. Partly responsible was his "type A" personality: always organized, always prepared, and always positive. Any interruption in training resulted in a need to reorganize his goals, race schedules, and workouts. He was constantly aware of that and, so far, everything was running smoothly like a well-oiled machine.

Until he was hit by a car that morning—a car coming up a hill from the opposite direction, in the slight fog that hovered at the mark of the incline, which clouded the driver's view. The vehicle's left-turn at the top of that hill struck Benny; it was obvious that the driver did not even see him coming. Benny went flying into a ditch. Fortunately, the driver felt the hit and stopped the car to help. Benny was conscious but covered in blood, clothes torn from road rash, hands mangled and scraped, and unable to move.

"How do I get through this?" he thought as he was wheeled back to his hospital room after thirteen hours of surgery to repair broken bones and treat a variety of contusions, sprains, lacerations, and a concussion.

Recovery was a long, slow process. For weeks Benny had no movement in his bruised, swollen hands and fingers. His head, shoulder, collarbone, and ribs hurt. His back muscles still spasmed in agony. But he knew that—little by little—he would heal physically and be able to do more and more. He had to work on the mental recovery to keep up with his healing and not lose hope or feel discouraged and give up. The best way he knew to do that was to emulate the goal-orientation behavior that he adopted for racing throughout the year. He knew he had to come up with a "training" plan to harmonize with his healing and create attainable goals.

His ultimate long-term goal was to ride and race again. Working backward, his second-to-last goal was to ride the bike in the streets; the goal before that one was to simply sit on the bike in a safe position without pain. He inscribed these progressions in his calendar. He agonizingly exercised patience as a virtue, and each day something improved, allowing him to incorporate a new drill into his routine and reach one of his milestones. In all, it took about three months before he could get back on a stationary bike, remain on it comfortably, and ride for forty minutes. During those months, he continued to meet with his triathlon group whenever possible, attended club talks and meetings, met with a sport psychology consultant, and voraciously read books about accidents and recovery.

His first foray into the streets set him back a little. He became nervous and shook, even wobbled, and eventually had to get off the bike and walk. The sport psychology discussions had prepared him for this possibility, but this undesirable outcome still surprised Benny. He felt defeated although he knew a road setting would simulate the accident and trigger some physiological reactions. He was aware of this possibility during his recovery period, yet there wasn't any way to mentally train for it while on a stationary bike at home. He now needed to tackle this aspect head-on.

Realizing this new block, he broke down his riding into smaller, cautious segments, remaining on back streets and quiet residential roads for a month. Every day, he rode a little longer and ventured closer and closer to traffic. What kept him going on this painstakingly slow return to street riding was his desire to keep racing and his continual contact with his triathlon buddies, attending their races and cheering, and generally feeling the overall excitement of the sport he loved so much (Vallerand, 2004). He also had a strong belief in himself as a success—to ride well, to overcome obstacles, and to fully recover.

Research on amateur recreational cyclists indicates that along with physical coping and rehabilitation motives, there are psychological factors that influence decision making about whether an athlete will return to sport (Weltman, 2016): resilience, self-efficacy, and goal orientation. Resilience and self-efficacy are tied together when overcoming adversity or defeat. Athletes need to tune into their true motivation and inner belief as to whether they have an attainable goal (Anderson, 2014; Bandura, 1997; Faure, 2011); Benny saw himself as competent. He witnessed his prior races and successes. He remembered his constant progress and development and knew he was a contender. He accepted that it was an outside element, not his own inability to ride well, that caused his bike accident. Factors outside of the athlete can cause obstacles and an athlete aware of this will possess greater self-efficacy when interpreting an adverse situation. In other words, the athletes will not blame themselves for an adverse event (Milne, Hall, & Forwell, 2005).

It is important to recognize obstacles that directly result from one's own performance and those that result from exterior circumstances. There are things that we can change (our own performance) and things we cannot (exterior factors such as road conditions, cars not seeing where they are going, street closures, bike malfunctions, and the like). Having also witnessed other cyclists' crashes, Benny was keenly aware of the dangers and risks of the sport and knew that it came with the territory. This sense of "stuff happens in triathlon" allowed him to move through the incident and continue toward his goals.

Having those strong goals also proved beneficial, as they are what oriented Benny to move forward once his body was able to move again (Weltman,

2016). Having a goal, a plan, and a strong motivation to engage in the sport (loving the sport and being aware of why one loves what one does) contributes to greater persistence and to greater resilience in the face of adversity (Podlog & Eklund, 2005). Making short- and long-term goals with specific milestones along the way strengthens one's adherence to one's sport. The feeling we get from reaching each milestone should be pleasant so that we are continually drawn to pursuing goals. When obstacles arise, alter your goals to adapt to the new challenges. Use the feeling of success reached at each milestone to attract you back to your plan (Galli & Gonzalez, 2015). Goal orientation is an effective skill for planning one's sport involvement, yet it also plays an important role for easing through healing and recovery after an adverse incident such as a bike collision, crash, or accident. In the same manner that athletes strive for their goal, remember to break down recovery, rehabilitation, and retraining into smaller parts that can be gradually added back into a training plan (Podlog & Eklund, 2006, 2007).

Benny's story is but one of many incidents of cyclists who crash and return to ride again after physically recovering. In more than six hundred cyclists surveyed, most indicated that they had, in fact, returned to cycle again after surviving a crash (Weltman, 2016). Likely there are many who do not return to cycling for various reasons, but it's extremely difficult to reach people who are no longer participating in the sport. For those athletes continuing to ride, even after "stuff happens," it is useful to note that a very small percentage of them experience fear and anxiety while riding to the point of downgrading their riding intensity (Wadey et al., 2014). For the majority, continuing to pursue goals—and especially creating new ones—helps them move past the unpleasant bump in their cycling careers and not be affected by the unfortunate incident. Resilience is built from within and without. Benny sailed through the school of hard knocks and barely lost a year from his racing schedule. He continues to attend races and even succeeded in qualifying for one of the most notable triathlons in the world: Kona Ironman, which he completed two years after his crash.

Take-Home Points

1. Factors outside of the athlete can cause obstacles, and an athlete aware of this will possess greater self-efficacy when interpreting an adverse situation. Recognize obstacles that directly result from your own performance and those that result from exterior circumstances
2. Having a goal, a plan, and a strong motivation to engage in the sport (loving the sport and being aware of why one loves what one does) contributes to greater persistence and to greater resilience in the face of adversity.

Making long- and short-term goals with specific milestones along the way strengthens your adherence to your sport.
3. Goal orientation is an effective skill for planning one's sport involvement, yet it also plays an important role for easing through healing and recovery after an adverse incident such as a bike collision, crash, or accident. In the same manner that athletes strive for their goal, remember to break down recovery, rehabilitation, and retraining into smaller parts that can be gradually added back into a training plan (Podlog & Eklund, 2007).

References

Anderson, E. (2015). Five different types of motivation. E-How. Retrieved from http://www.ehow.com/info_12153839_5-different-types-motivation.html

Bandura, A. (1997). *Self-efficacy: The exercise of control.* New York, NY: Freeman.

Faure, M. (2011, October). The motivations of amateur cyclists. Retrieved from https://alpinecols.com/wp-content/uploads/2019/03/The-Motivations-of-Amateur-Cyclists.pdf

Galli, N., & Gonzalez, S. (2015). Psychological resilience in sport: A review of the literature and implications for research and practice. *International Journal of Sport and Exercise Psychology, 13*(3), 243–257.

Milne, M., Hall, C., & Forwell, L. (2005). Self-efficacy, imagery use, and adherence to rehabilitation by injured athletes. *Journal of Sport Rehabilitation, 14,* 150–67.

Podlog, L., & Eklund, R. (2005). Return to sport after serious injury: A retrospective examination of motivation and psychological outcomes. *Journal of Sport Rehabilitation, 14,* 20–34.

Podlog, L., & Eklund, R. (2006). A longitudinal investigation of competitive athletes' return to sport following serious injury. *Journal of Applied Sport Psychology, 18,* 44–68.

Podlog, L., & Eklund, R. C. (2007). The psychosocial aspects of a return to sport following serious injury: A review of the literature from a self-determination perspective. *Psychology of Sport and Exercise, 8,* 535–66.

Vallerand, R. (2004). Intrinsic and extrinsic motivation in sport. In R. Vallerand & C. Spielberger (Ed.), *Encyclopedia of applied psychology* (Vol. 2, pp. 427–35). Tampa, FL: Academic Press.

Wadey, R., Hamson-Utley, J., Podlog, L., Hall, M., Hicks-Little, C., & Hammer, C. (2014). Reinjury, anxiety, coping, and return-to-sport Outcomes: A multiple mediation analysis. *Rehabilitation Psychology, 59*(3), 256–66.

Weltman, A. (2016). *Back in the saddle: Factors indicative of cycling resumption in post-crash cyclists* (Master's thesis). San Diego University for Integrative Studies. San Diego, CA.

THE DORMOUSE: RECOLLECTIONS OF A LIGHTWEIGHT ROWER WITH OVERTRAINING SYNDROME
Lindsay Woodford

I am a sport psychologist, academic, and athlete who is currently conducting empirical research in the field of overtraining syndrome. My passion for furthering our knowledge of overtraining syndrome has been inspired by my personal experience of the condition when I was competing as a lightweight rower. My story is a raw, emotive account of my experience of the condition within the context of contemporary research. I hope it will provide a wider awareness of the symptoms, etiology, and risk factors of overtraining syndrome among the athletic and sport science community and allow a greater level of care for athletes.

Successful high-performance lightweight rowers require exceptional physical attributes, along with high levels of dedication and resilience. However, when faced with frustrating setbacks such as injury and illness, like many athletes, the qualities that elevated me to the top of my sport became my own worst enemy. It is well documented that vigorous, specifically targeted training, followed by a sufficient period of recovery, is essential for improving athletic performance. This is a difficult balance to strike in many sports, but when you layer on the added constraints associated with a weight-contingent sport such as lightweight rowing, training becomes more complex. Lightweight rowing places an upper limit on the body weight of competitors—

57kg for women and 70kg for men. Making weight was a real challenge for me at 5'7", so I maximized every opportunity to burn calories, and that often meant choosing an active recovery session over a rest day in my already challenging training schedule. The extreme and absurd weight loss strategies I employed in the days leading up to major competitions seem incomprehensible now; for example, it was not uncommon for me to frequently severely restrict my food and drink intake to the point of dehydration.

These strategies proved effective, as I won a bronze medal at nationals, and later a coveted place on the England lightweight women's rowing squad for the 2002 Commonwealth Games. Everything was going to plan when one morning at 5:30 a.m., as I reached over to turn my alarm off, I felt my head begin to spin, my heart was pounding, and I felt violently sick. I threw up to ease the nausea, sipped some water, put on my kit, and drove to the rowing club. I managed to complete the training session, but my legs felt like lead and my heart was racing. This was the start of a progressive decline in performance. One of the most debilitating symptoms I experienced was the need to sleep. I became affectionally known as "The Dormouse" because I slept more than ten hours a night and during the day. When I stood up, my heart rate would go through the roof and my blood pressure would drop; I felt constantly dizzy and sick. I caught cold after cold and I felt like I had a pair of golf balls permanently lodged in my throat. Despite these debilitating physiological symptoms, I was more motivated than ever to represent my country.

At this time in my career, I was not a lottery-funded athlete and I didn't have access to the sport science team at British Rowing. I therefore had to rely on my general physician for support. All tests came back negative: no glandular fever, no anemia, normal thyroid function. There was no other explanation, so I was diagnosed with depression and prescribed antidepressants. In hindsight, I wasn't depressed; I was in a state of helplessness and hopelessness because I couldn't find an answer to my problem. I was underperforming at an unprecedented level and I did not know why. As time went on, my symptoms didn't improve. I was struggling to hold down my part-time job. I had withdrawn from my rowing friends. I felt utterly alone. As I reached my lowest point, my coach found the details of a doctor who specialized in sports medicine and I paid for a private consultation. It confirmed I was experiencing persistent fatigue, elevated resting heart rate, recurrent infections, and mood disturbances, and he diagnosed me with overtraining syndrome (Budgett, 1998). I was advised to continue resting, and when my heart rate had returned to a normal rate when I first woke up in the morning and remained stable throughout the day, I could begin a phased return to training. This, however, was like a form of torture to me.

My recovery from overtraining syndrome was a challenging process, and I had various relapses along the way, but none as severe as the first one. I had gone from training three to four hours a day, six days a week, to five minutes a day, three days a week at best. I felt totally lost and alone—I missed the structure my training gave to my life, the camaraderie of my teammates, the buzz of racing, and my identity as a rower. The rehabilitation process was a gradual one, but after two years I was able to do a full training session in my boat with the rest of the squad.

By the time I was fit enough to trial for the national team again I was completely burned out. I had gone full circle; my mind-set had changed from balancing my continued drive to train with my physical inability to do so, to losing all motivation for rowing despite my body's readiness to return to training. The sport that I loved more than anything else in the world became something I absolutely despised. I quit rowing soon after I had made a full recovery and I never got in a boat again.

Overtraining syndrome can be a devastating condition, as the root cause of the characteristic fatigue is often not recognized until months of poor performance have passed. Accurate diagnosis is difficult as there are often numerous other medical and psychological conditions that present with similar symptoms. Overtraining syndrome can be diagnosed only after all other causes have been excluded. Until a definitive diagnostic tool for overtraining syndrome is developed, regular monitoring of a combination of performance, physiological, biochemical, immunological, and psychological variables seems to be the best strategy to help identify athletes who are failing to cope with the stress of training (Schwellnus et al., 2016a, b).

There are various warning signs that an athlete may be susceptible to overtraining syndrome, such as a decrease in performance that lasts weeks or months, persistent fatigue, muscle fatigue, increased sense of effort in training, loss of competitive drive, sleep disturbances, elevated resting heart rate, mood disturbances, loss of appetite, weight loss, loss of libido, excessive sweating, recurrent infections, sore throat, and increased fall in blood pressure and increased heart rate on standing. If an athlete is diagnosed with overtraining syndrome, the recommended treatment is rest. In some cases, relative rest is advised, with the athletes building up their training volume prior to intensity, starting from five to ten minutes daily until they reach one hour (Budgett, 1998). Given the psychological implications of overtraining syndrome, athletes should consider seeking support from a sport psychologist. This might help ameliorate some of the mental health concerns that are often associated with overtraining syndrome. Due to the complexities surrounding the diagnosis and treatment of overtraining syndrome, early identification and prevention is of the utmost importance.

Take-Home Points

1. Learn to listen to your body—treat the early signs of overtraining with rest and a phased return to training.
2. Individualize training programs—not all athletes are the same.
3. Seek support from a sport psychologist during the rehabilitation period.

References

Budgett, R. (1998). Fatigue and underperformance in athletes: The overtraining syndrome. *British Journal of Sports Medicine, 32*, 107–10.

Soligard, T., Schwellnus, M., Alonso, J.-M., Bahr, R., Clarsen, B., Dijkstra, H. P., . . . Engebretsen, L. (2016a). How much is too much? (Part 1) International Olympic Committee consensus statement on load in sport and risk of injury. *British Journal of Sports Medicine, 50*, 1030–41.

Schwellnus, M., Soligard, T., Alonso, J.-M., Bahr, R., Clarsen, B., Dijkstra, H. P., . . . Engebretsen, L. (2016b). How much is too much? (Part 2) International Olympic Committee consensus statement on load in sport and risk of illness. *British Journal of Sports Medicine, 50*, 1043–52.

Conclusion

We hope you have found the stories in this book enlightening, entertaining, thought provoking, and useful. We have enjoyed putting this book together, encouraged by the amazing variety of stories and experiences our contributors have shared, both their own and those of individuals and teams with whom they have worked.

These stories can be helpful in work with individuals and teams, often making a point more poignantly than a general lecture on some theory or model. They can also be useful in class settings and workshops to make points that personalize experiences more fully than theory and research can only hint at. Ultimately, they can be helpful to you, the reader, in your learning and continued professional development.

We encourage you to collect and share more stories to use in these various settings. We are sure you will find them to be useful and compelling narratives of the human experience and the application of sport and exercise psychology in the real world.

Appendix: Recommendations for Utilizing This Book in the Classroom

German children's book author Cornelia Funke once asked, "What are stories for if we don't learn from them?" Stories are powerful forms of learning because they create an opportunity for us to engage not only our thinking but also our emotions, imaginations, memories, experiences, and associations. In the classroom, there are many benefits to utilizing stories. First, they facilitate the ability to target higher-order learning objectives such as synthesis, analysis, evaluation, and application (Krathwohl, 2002). As Loehr (2007) stated, "Facts are meaningless until you create a story around them" (p. 5). Second, they enable learners to actively engage in the learning process, which has been shown to lead to more effective and enduring learning outcomes (Bonwell & Eison, 1991). Additionally, they make knowledge and learning less rote, inert, and disconnected by situating it in the context in which it can or will be utilized in the real world (Brown, Collins, & Duguid, 1989). Further, they facilitate the creation and continued expansion of mental representations in memory, which enables students to engage in deliberate practice in order to develop their knowledge and expertise (e.g., Ericsson, Krampe, & Tesch-Römer, 1993; Ericsson & Staszewski, 1989). Lastly, and specific to the field of sport and exercise psychology, they provide cases to be discussed that fill a gap in our training between learning in the classroom and real-world practice (Tashman & Tenenbaum, 2013). Below are several ideas for ways to incorporate the stories in this book into undergraduate and graduate classrooms.

EXAMPLE APPROACHES FOR FACILITATING HIGHER-ORDER LEARNING OBJECTIVES

1. The stories throughout the book utilize varying degrees of references to support them. Further, the references included in each story come from the perspective of the author(s) in terms of what they see as connected to the story (i.e., their mental representations). Thus, in order to facilitate synthesis of information and students' development of their own mental representations, students can be asked to connect more/different references to the story (i.e., theories, concepts, research).
2. Some stories include more or fewer details; thus, in order to target application and analysis, students can be tasked with filling in or providing alternative details and discussing their potential implications.
3. For classes focused on applied practice, students can develop their knowledge and skills by conceptualizing the case, discussing how they would approach a needs assessment and developing and explaining an intervention strategy they would take if they were the practitioner. For the stories in the book that discuss specific examples of applied practice, students can also evaluate the approaches taken by the practitioners and discuss alternatives.
4. The stories can also be used to help students synthesize and apply their knowledge in order to create their own stories.

EXAMPLE ACTIVE LEARNING APPROACHES INCORPORATING STORIES

1. One-Minute Prompt: After reading the story, have students write for one minute before discussing as a class. This can be a freewrite utilizing a very general prompt (e.g., What stands out to you?), or a more targeted question can be utilized specific to the story or applied practice.
2. Four Corners: Develop four prompts or questions related to the story, concept(s) it includes, and/or applied practice. Write each prompt/question on a poster sheet and place the sheets in the four corners of the room. Separate the students into four groups and have each start at one of the four corners. Give students a few minutes to respond to the prompt/question, writing their answers on the poster sheet. Then have the groups rotate to the next prompt/question following the same procedure. Rotate the groups around until each has had a chance to review all four prompts/questions. Then engage in a larger discussion.

3. Jigsaw: Separate students into small groups and assign each to be an expert on a facet of the story or part of an assignment utilizing the story. For example, for an assignment, students can be put into groups of three and assigned the following areas of expertise: related sport and exercise psychology concepts, related theory and research, questions for class discussion.
4. Role-Play/Rotating Roles: Students can be immersed into the story and asked to play (i.e., consider and analyze) the various roles of people in a story (e.g., what might they have been thinking/feeling/experiencing, why might they have done what they did, what else could they have done, etc.). They can also be asked to rotate their roles in order to facilitate perspective taking and considering multiple vantage points.
5. Pro and Con Grid: Students can be asked to discuss the pros and cons of the approaches taken in the stories.
6. What/How/Why Outlines: To assist students in analyzing and discussing the stories, they can create outlines that include the what (e.g., what are the key details of the story), how (e.g., how does the story relate to research/theory), and why (e.g., why did the practitioner approach it in this way, why did the outcome of the story potentially come about).

EXAMPLE PROMPTS/QUESTIONS FACILITATING A CASE-BASED APPROACH FOR APPLIED PRACTICE

1. Describe the characters in the story.
2. Describe the presenting problem.
3. What factors may be contributing to the presenting problem?
4. If you were conducting an initial consultation in this case, what questions would you ask?
5. Describe how you would design and conduct a needs assessment.
6. Identify and discuss theory, research, and course material that relates to the case.
7. What are some potential courses of action a mental coach could take? What are the potential outcomes of each course of action?
8. What ethical issues or guidelines are applicable to the case?

As instructors you have other stories available to you in addition to those in this book: ones you have experienced personally (e.g., you as an individual or as a result of your work with athletes/teams) and ones you have read in newspapers, magazines, and books. Students can also be encouraged to bring in stories of their own, from their own experiences or ones they have read.

The power of stories is unlimited, as is the manner in which they can be used to facilitate engaging, effective, and enduring learning! As the famous philosopher Buzz Lightyear has said: "To infinity and beyond!"

REFERENCES

Bonwell, C. C., & Eison, J. A. (1991). *Active learning: Creating excitement in the classroom.* ASH#-ERIC Higher Education Report No. 1, Washington, DC: George Washington University, School of Education and Human Development.

Brown, J. S., Collins, A., & Duguid, P. (1989). Situated cognition and the culture of learning. *Educational Researcher, 18*, 32–41.

Ericsson, K. A., & Krampe, R. T., & Tesch-Römer, C. (1993). The role of deliberate practice in the acquisition of expert performance. *Psychological Review, 100*(3), 363–406.

Ericsson, K. A., & Staszewski, J. J. (1989). Skilled memory and expertise: Mechanisms of exceptional performance. In D. Klahr & K. Kotovsky (Eds.), *Complex information processing: The impact of Herbert A. Simon* (pp. 235–67). Hillsdale, NJ: Lawrence Erlbaum Associates.

Krathwohl, D. R. (2002). A revision of Bloom's taxonomy: An overview. *Theory into Practice, 41*(4), 212–18.

Loehr, J. (2007). *The power of story: Rewrite your destiny in business and in life.* New York, NY: Free Press.

Tashman, L. S., & Tenenbaum, G. (2013). Sport psychology service delivery training: The value of an interactive, case-based approach to practitioner development. *Journal of Sport Psychology in Action, 4*, 71–85.

Bibliography

Looking for some additional resources for background material and/or stories? The list of references below is by no means exhaustive but provides a good place to start. Some of the books listed are more academic (e.g., Anshel, 2014; Hanrahan & Andersen, 2010; Razon & Sachs, 2018); others are trade paperbacks designed for athletes, coaches, and other educated laypeople (e.g., Baltzell, 2011; Danish & Forneris, 2018; Kamphoff, 2018; Orlick, 2016) but are also extremely helpful for students and professionals in our field. Many of these come from within the field of sport and exercise psychology or focus on the context of sport, while others come from other contexts but are nonetheless valuable resources.

Additionally, consider autobiographies, biographies, and memoirs of athletes, coaches, teams, and exercisers (famous and not so famous)—they often have compelling stories to tell (e.g., Corbett & England, 2018; Jornet, 2013). A recent fascinating story provides an account of John Urschel's football experiences and concussions (Urschel & Thomas, 2019). Dan Gable, one of the all-time greats in wrestling, has written a compelling book about his life (Gable & Schulte, 2015). Other books address lessons athletes learned from their experiences in sport and life, such Billie Jean King's eloquent account of lessons related to life, performing under pressure, and gender issues in sport (King & Brennan, 2008).

Books in this category also cover significant sporting events with considerable psychological overtones, such as, *Iron War: Dave Scott, Mark Allen & the Greatest Race Ever Run* (Fitzgerald, 2011). *Iron War* eloquently addresses the psychology of suffering within an elite athletic context. Richard Benyo (1991) talks about the challenges of running across Death Valley in California. There are also books that cover groups of individuals with fascinating stories, such as the famous Marathon Monks of Mount Hiei (Stevens,

2013) or the amazing Milan Miracle, for those of you who are basketball fans (Guffey, 1993).

Magazine and internet articles from sources such as *Sports Illustrated* and *Runner's World* can provide wonderful starting points for discussion about areas within exercise and sport psychology and their connection to performance excellence. The *Player's Tribune* provides a fascinating collection of stories written by athletes. Additionally, sources outside the realm of sport (e.g., *Harvard Business Review*) provide useful information, particularly when working with teams or leaders, while sources such as *Science Daily* provide summaries of the latest research in a vast number of areas. Lastly, there are a plethora of podcasts from members of the sport and exercise psychology field (e.g., *Finding Mastery*) as well as those outside the field (e.g., *WorkLife*) that are excellent resources and provide access to other fascinating stories (e.g., *Our Athletes*).

ACADEMIC BOOKS

Anshel, M. H. (2014). *Applied health fitness psychology*. Champaign, IL: Human Kinetics.

Anshel, M. H., Petrie, T. A., & Steinfeldt, J. A. (Eds.). (2019). *APA handbook of sport and exercise psychology* (vol. 1). Washington, DC: American Psychological Association.

Anshel, M. H., Petruzzello, S. J., & Labbe, E. E. (Eds.). (2019). *APA handbook of sport and exercise psychology* (vol. 2). Washington, DC: American Psychological Association.

Cremades, J. G., & Tashman, L. S. (Eds.). (2014). *Becoming a sport, exercise, and performance psychology professional: A global perspective*. New York, NY: Routledge.

Cremades, J. G., & Tashman, L. S. (Eds.). (2016). *Global practices and training in applied sport, exercise, and performance psychology: A case study approach*. New York, NY: Routledge.

Dosil, J. (Ed.). (2006). *The sport psychologist's handbook: A guide for sport-specific performance enhancement*. London, UK: Wiley.

Eklund, R. C., & Tenenbaum, G. (Eds.). (2014a). *Encyclopedia of sport and exercise psychology* (vol. 1). Los Angeles, CA: Sage Reference.

Eklund, R. C., & Tenenbaum, G. (Eds.). (2014b). *Encyclopedia of sport and exercise psychology* (vol. 2). Los Angeles, CA: Sage Reference.

Gardner, F. L., & Moore, Z. (2007). *The psychology of enhancing human performance: The mindfulness-acceptance-commitment (MAC) approach*. New York, NY: Springer.

Hanin, Y. L. (2000). *Emotions in sport*. Champaign, IL: Human Kinetics.

Hanrahan, S. J., & Andersen, M. B. (Eds.). (2010). *Routledge handbook of applied sport psychology: A comprehensive guide for students and practitioners.* New York, NY: Routledge.

Haslam, S. A., Reicher, S. D., & Platow, M. J. (2011). *The new psychology of leadership: Identity, influence, and power.* New York, NY: Psychology Press.

Hays, K. F. (1999). *Working it out: Using exercise in psychotherapy.* Washington, DC: American Psychological Association.

Hays, K. F. (Ed.). (2009). *Performance psychology in action: A casebook for working with athletes, performing artists, business leaders, and professionals in high-risk occupations.* Washington, DC: American Psychological Association.

Hemmings, B., & Holder, T. (2009). *Applied sport psychology: A case-based approach.* London, UK: Wiley.

Henriksen, K., Hansen, J., & Larsen, C. V. (2019). *Mindfulness and acceptance in sport: How to help athletes perform and thrive under pressure.* New York, NY: Routledge.

Kaufman, K. A., Glass, C. R., & Pineau, T. R. (2018). *Mindful sport performance enhancement: Mental training for athletes and coaches.* Washington, DC: American Psychological Association.

Lidor, R., & Henschen, K. P. (2003). *The psychology of team sports.* Morgantown, WV: Fitness Information Technology.

Meijen, C. (Eds.). (2019). *Endurance performance in sport: Psychological theory and interventions.* London, UK: Routledge.

Moran, A. P. (1996). *The psychology of concentration in sports performers.* New York, NY: Psychology Press.

Mugford, A., & Cremades, J. G. (2019). *Sport, exercise, and performance psychology: Theories and applications.* New York, NY: Routledge.

Razon, S., & Sachs, M. L. (Eds.). (2018). *Applied exercise psychology: The challenging journey from motivation to adherence.* New York, NY: Routledge.

Staurowsky, E. (Ed.). (2016). *Women and sport: Continuing a journey of liberation and celebration.* Champaign, IL: Human Kinetics.

Taylor, J. (Ed.). (2017). *Assessment in applied sport psychology.* Champaign, IL: Human Kinetics.

Van Raalte, J. L., & Brewer, B. W. (Eds.). (2014). *Exploring sport and exercise psychology* (3rd ed.). Washington, DC: American Psychological Association.

Weinberg, R. S., & Gould, D. (2019). *Foundations of sport and exercise psychology* (7th ed.). Champaign, IL: Human Kinetics.

Zizzi, S. J., & Andersen, M. B. (2017). *Being mindful in sport and exercise psychology: Pathways for practitioners and students.* Morgantown, WV: Fitness Information Tcehnology.

TRADE PAPERBACKS

Anshel, M. (2016). *Good to great: Coaching athletes through sport psychology.* San Diego, CA: Cognella Press.

Baltzell, A. (2011). *Living in the sweet spot: Preparing for performance in sport and life.* Morgantown, WV: Fitness Information Technology.

Beilock, S. (2010). *Choke: What the secrets of the brain reveal about getting it right when you have to.* New York, NY: Free Press.

Bronson, P., & Merryman, A. (2013). *Top dog: The science of winning and losing.* New York, NY: Twelve.

Cheadle, C. (2013). *On top of your game: Mental skills to maximize your athletic performance.* Petaluma, CA: Feed the Athlete Press.

Coyle, D. (2018). *The culture code: The secrets of highly successful groups.* New York, NY: Bantam.

Danish, S. J., & Forneris, T. (2018). *Enhancing performance and quality of life.* Morgantown, WV: Fitness Information Technology.

David, S. (2016). *Emotional agility: Get unstuck, embrace change, and thrive in work and life.* New York, NY: Avery.

Duckworth, A. (2016). *Grit: The power of passion and perseverance.* New York, NY: Simon and Schuster.

Ericsson, A., & Pool, R. (2016). *Peak: Secrets from the new science of expertise.* New York, NY: Houghton Mifflin Harcourt.

Galloway, J. (2011). *Mental training for runners: How to stay motivated.* London, UK: Meyer and Meyer Sport.

Goleman, D. (2013). *Focus: The hidden driver of excellence.* New York, NY: Harper.

Halvorson, H. G. (2011). *Succeed: How we can reach our goals.* New York, NY: Plume.

Hays, K. F. (2002). *Move your body, tone your mood.* Oakland, CA: New Harbinger Press.

Kamphoff, C. (2018). *Beyond grit: Ten powerful practices to gain the high-performance edge.* Minneapolis, MN: Wise Ink Creative.

Kahneman, D. (2013). *Thinking fast and slow.* New York, NY: Farrar, Strauss and Giroux.

Kuzma, C., & Cheadle, C. (2019). *Rebound: Train your mind to bounce back stronger from sports injuries.* London, UK: Bloomsbury Sport.

McGinn, D. (2017). *Psyched up: How the science of mental preparation can help you succeed.* New York, NY: Penguin Random House.

McRaney, D. (2013). *You are now less dumb: How to conquer mob mentality, how to buy happiness, and other ways to outsmart yourself.* New York, NY: Gotham Books.

Mumford, G. (2015). *The mindful athlete: Secrets to pure performance.* Berkeley, CA: Parallax Press.

Orlick, T. (2016). *In pursuit of excellence: How to win in sport and life through mental training* (5th ed.). Champaign, IL: Human Kinetics.

Pink, D. H. (2009). *Drive: The surprising truth about what motivates us.* New York, NY: Penguin.

Syed, M. (2015). *Black box thinking: Why most people never learn from their mistakes—but some do.* New York, NY: Penguin.

Thaler, H., & Sunstein, C. S. (2009). *Nudge: Improving decisions about health, wealth, and happiness.* New York, NY: Penguin.

Walker, S. (2018). *Captain class: A new theory of leadership.* New York, NY: Random House.

Weisinger, H., & Pawliw-Fry, J. P. (2015). *Performing under pressure: The science of doing your best when it matters most.* New York, NY: Crown.

Wooden, J., & Jamison, S. (1997). *A lifetime of observations and reflections on and off the court.* New York, NY: McGraw-Hill.

Yaeger, D. (2016). *Great teams: 16 things high-performing organizations do differently.* Nashville, TN: W Publishing.

Zak, P. (2017). *Trust factor: The science of creating high-performance companies.* New York. NY: American Management Association.

AUTOBIOGRAPHIES/BIOGRAPHIES/MEMOIRS

Agassi, A. (2009). *Open: An autobiography.* New York, NY: Vintage Books.

Babcock, M., & Larsen, R. (2012). *Leave no doubt: A credo for chasing your dreams.* Montreal, QC: McGill–Queen's University Press.

Benyo, R. (1991). *The Death Valley 300: Near-death and resurrection on the world's toughest endurance course.* Forestville, CA: Specific Publications.

Corbett, C., & England, D. (2018). *Reborn on the run: My journey from addictions to ultramarathons.* New York, NY: Skyhorse.

Feinstein, J. (2015). *Where nobody knows your name: Life in the minor leagues of baseball.* New York: Random House.

Fitzgerald, M. (2011). *Iron war: Dave Scott, Mark Allen & the greatest race ever run.* Boulder, CO: Velo Press.

Gable, D., & Schulte, S. (2015). *A wrestling life: The inspiring stories of Dan Gable.* Iowa City, IA; University of Iowa Press.

Guffey, G. (1993). *The greatest basketball story ever told: The Milan Miracle, then and now.* Bloomington, IN: Indiana University Press.

Jornet, K. (2013). *Run or die.* Boulder, CO: Velo Press.

Kapsalis, P. W., & Gregory, T. (2014). *To chase a dream: A soccer championship, an unlikely hero and a journey that redefined winning.* London, UK: Maidenhead.

King, B. J., & Brennan, C. (2008). *Pressure is a privilege: Lessons I've learned from life and the battle of the sexes.* New York, NY: LifeTime Media.

Knight, P. (2016). *Shoe dog: A memoir by the creator of Nike.* New York, NY: Scribner.

Nyad, D. (2015). *Find a way: The inspiring story of one woman's pursuit of a lifelong dream.* New York, NY: Vintage Books.

Savage, R. (2009). *Rowing the Atlantic: Lessons learned on the open ocean.* New York, NY: Simon and Schuster.

Stevens, J. (2013). *The marathon monks of Mount Hiei.* Brattleboro, VT: Echo Point Books and Media.

Strayed, C. (2013). *Wild: From lost to found on the Pacific Crest Trail.* New York, NY: Vintage Books.
Urschel, J., & Thomas, L. (2019). *Mind and matter: A life in math and football.* New York, NY: Penguin.
Verducci, T. (2017). *The Cubs way: The zen of building the best team in baseball and breaking the curse.* New York, NY: Penguin Random House.
Wambach, A. (2019). *Wolfpack: How to come together, unleash our power, and change the game.* New York, NY: Celadon.

MAGAZINE/INTERNET SOURCES

ESPN The Magazine
Harvard Business Review
Inc.com
Outside Online
Psychology Today
Runner's World
Science Daily
Sports Illustrated
Strategy-Business
The Player's Tribune
Thrive Global

PODCASTS

The Fenom Effect
Finding Mastery
High Performance Mindset
NPR Hidden Brain
Our Athletes
The Sport Psych Show
Wee Chats with Brilliant People
WorkLife with Adam Grant

Index

acceptance of pain, 162
adaptability, 60
adversity, 171, 191, 194–196
anxiety, 68, 72, 79, 81–83, 85, 95, 112–113, 115–120, 123–124, 126–127, 129–130, 145, 150–151, 181, 187–188, 198, 202, 205, 212, 217, 226; cognitive state, 112, 126–127; competitive state, 126–127, 220; performance, 81–82, 129, 150; somatic state, 112, 126–127
arousal, 79–80, 101, 107, 109–110, 126–127, 129, 141; inducing techniques, 109; level, 101, 109–110; reduction techniques, 109–110; regulation, 79
athlete activism, 14
athletic identity, 51–53, 55–57, 59–61, 63, 65, 68, 72, 74, 194, 214
athletic trainer, 93, 166–167, 187, 198
attentional, 79–80, 89–90, 106, 113, 123–124, 132, 162; control, 79–80, 124, 162; focus, 89–90, 106; techniques, 113
autonomy, 208–209

breathing strategy, 106
burnout, 37, 123–124, 181

cadre, 198–199; expectations, 199; member, 198
career retirement, 63
certified mental performance consultant, 127
Charging Bull, 13–14
client-specific coping strategies, 188. *See also* rehabilitation
clinical psychology, 156
coach-athlete relationship, 19, 154
coaching identity, 19
cognitive behavioral theory, 214
cognitive structure, 55–56
cohesion, 1, 17–20, 30; group, 30; social, 1, 17; task, 1, 17–18
common life skills, 60
competitive athlete, 59, 68, 155, 165
concentration, 82, 85, 89–90, 101, 122–123, 132–133
confidence, 24, 37, 59, 60–62, 83, 85–86, 90, 93, 95–96, 98, 101, 107, 113, 127, 134, 138, 145, 150–151, 159, 171, 173–174–175, 185, 188, 191, 196–197, 203, 205–206, 208, 212–215
coping, 57, 63, 65–67, 72–73, 137–138, 151, 155, 159, 166, 181, 188, 194, 205–206, 225; emotion focused, 137–138; problem focused, 137–138

CrossFit, 51, 53–54, 67
cues, 39, 79, 86, 95, 113, 119–120, 178–179; refocus, 119–120; verbal, 79
culture, 1, 6–9, 11–12, 14–15, 18–20, 161–162, 165; championship, 7–8; team, 1, 7–9, 11–12, 18–19

deep breathing, 93, 113, 151, 181, 187–188
deliberate breathing, 82
depression, 56, 72, 124, 145, 165–167, 201–203, 229
Dipeba, Coach J. D., 217–219
disconnected values model, 48
did not finish (DNF), 159, 161

ebbs and flows, 48, 79, 158
emotional state, 142
emotion regulation, 80, 137, 142
Enneagram, 11
environmental factors, 19
exercise, 1, 23, 25–26, 30, 38–39, 47, 49, 51–54, 63, 67, 120, 135, 142, 145, 159, 166, 174, 195, 205–207, 233
exercise addiction, 205, 207
exercisers, 51, 79, 181

Fearless, 1, 13–14–15; Female, 1, 14; Girl, 13–15
foundational movement, 38
functional equivalence theory, 101
FUN MAPS, 147–148
fundamental movement skills, 38

goals, 6–8, 18, 23, 25, 27, 29, 41–45, 48–49, 59, 63–64, 69–70, 76, 83, 93, 98, 100–101, 103, 119, 126, 129–130, 135, 137, 142, 154, 159, 162, 166, 170, 174, 178, 181, 184, 185, 188, 192–193, 196, 202–203, 208, 212, 214–215, 219, 220, 224–227; behavioral, 25; intermediate-term, 41–42; long-term, 42–43, 48, 70, 214, 226; orientation, 224–227;
outcome, 27, 44, 45; performance, 44–45; setting, 23, 41–43, 45, 83, 162, 181, 202; short-term, 41–42, 227; smart, 214–215
GOTE framework, 178
graduate, 17, 20, 41, 57, 60, 62–64, 66, 117, 141, 166, 195–196, 235; education, 20, 166; student, 20, 63–64, 195
grief, 63, 139, 166
grit, 178, 181, 190–193, 215, 220
gruppo ciclistico, 29–30

heart rate, 107, 123, 229–230

identity, 7, 11, 19, 26–27, 51–57, 59–65, 68–70, 72, 74, 76–77, 194–196, 201, 214, 230; discussion, 7; exercise, 51, 53–54; loss, 60, 63; self, 11, 27
imagery, 69, 79–80, 83, 85–86, 92–94, 98–99, 101–103, 109, 113, 115, 123–124, 126–127, 132, 134–135, 206; cognitive functions of, 126–127; external, 134; internal, 134; motivational functions of, 126; script, 102–103
inclusive excellence, 7–9
injury, 24, 52, 53, 56–57, 65, 69, 75–77, 79, 92–93, 119, 159–160, 162, 181–182, 184–185, 187–188, 195, 201–203, 214–215, 228; recovery, 31, 69, 93, 166, 188, 202–203, 214–216, 219, 224–230; rehabilitation, 75–76, 93, 181, 184, 188, 201, 214–215, 225–227, 230–231; spinal cord, 52, 75–76
internally focused, 123. *See also* mindfulness
internal distracters, 90
Inverted U Theory, 109

journaling, 98

Kasdorf, Tiffany M., 183
Kondos, Valorie, 10–12

leadership, 1–4, 6–9, 14–15, 18–20, 141, 195; athlete, 2, 4, 20; role, 2–3; shared athlete, 4; style, 3; transformational, 8
less-is-more approach, 221
Lutzow, Carley, 119

Mackrides, Matt, 68–70
maintenance, 49
Major League Lacrosse (MLL), 68–70
mantra, 8, 96, 132–133, 139, 161–162, 175, 193, 202
Makwala, Isaac, 217–219
mental, 7, 14–15, 17, 57, 67, 68, 79, 81–84, 86, 92–96, 98–99, 101, 105, 107, 113, 115, 118–119, 123–124, 126–127, 129–130, 134–135, 145, 147, 150, 158–159, 161–162, 165–167, 174–175, 177, 179–181, 190, 193–194–196, 201–203, 205–207, 212–215, 224, 230; coaches, 17, 82; health professional, 195, 214; performance, 79, 81, 127, 196; plan, 86, 95; skills, 94, 98–99, 107, 113, 115, 123, 162, 175, 179–180, 194–195; strategies, 57, 95; toughness, 119, 158–159, 161–162, 165, 167, 175, 181, 190, 193, 212–213; training, 82, 96, 98–99; training techniques, 83, 98
microculture, 159–160, 163
Millican, Clay, 190–193
Mills, Billy, 79, 98–99
mind-set, 4, 7, 70, 81, 145, 154, 160, 171, 173–175, 177–180, 185, 201, 217, 221, 230
mindfulness, 83, 123, 129, 130, 133; training, 123
Misner, Ken, 45
motivation, 23, 25, 37, 41–42, 49, 63, 67, 72, 98, 116, 123, 126–127, 134, 139, 145, 148, 150, 161, 188, 191, 203, 205–206, 209, 213, 225–226, 230; autonomous, 205–206; controlled, 205; extrinsic, 205; intrinsic, 161, 205, 209

movement mastery, 38
muscle, 105–107, 112, 115, 151, 221, 224, 230; relaxation techniques, 106, 151; tension, 105–107

Naber, John, 23, 41–42
National Athletic Trainers' Association (NATA), 167
National Basketball Association (NBA), 2–3, 14, 167, 202
National Collegiate Athletic Association (NCAA), 12, 41, 56, 59, 120, 154, 167, 194
National Hockey League (NHL), 1, 4
National Hot Rod Association (NHRA), 190–191
Nideffer's Model of Attentional Style, 132
noncompetitive athlete, 203

Olympics, 42, 56, 79, 99, 195
Oregonian, 26
overtraining syndrome, 182, 228–230

passion, 23, 32, 34–35, 62, 66–67, 190, 192–195, 201, 203, 228
peak performance, 72, 95, 102–103, 123
performance pressure, 105–106
performing arts, 79
personality traits, 73
perfectionism, 72, 178
perseverance, 60, 73, 94, 161, 190, 220
physical activity, 23, 29–30, 37, 47–49, 64, 67, 208–209
physiological changes, 105–107, 126
positive, 3, 26, 39, 47, 57, 66–67, 70, 86, 92, 98–99, 117, 120, 123–124, 137, 139, 147, 151, 153–154, 163, 173, 187–188, 192, 202–203, 206–207, 224; affirmations, 98–99; attitude, 57, 70, 86, 192; self-talk, 98, 117, 120, 123, 139, 151, 202
positive youth development, 39
prayer, 181, 187–188
preparation, 10, 15, 39, 79, 86, 93, 99, 113, 134–135, 174–175

progressive muscle relaxation, 151
progressive task practice, 113
psychologist, 33–35, 43, 54, 60–61, 122, 127, 167, 181, 198–199, 203, 228, 230–231; sport, 33, 43, 54, 60–61, 122, 127, 167, 181, 109–199, 203, 228, 230–231
psychological distress, 53, 57
Puski, Lenard, 101–103

Ranger Physical Fitness Test, 141
relatedness, 208–209
relaxation responses, 113
resilience, 14–15, 70, 73, 181, 190, 192–196, 213, 225–226, 228
respiration rate, 107
ritual, 32, 101–103, 129, 151
routines, 83, 101, 103, 108, 113, 151, 175, 179; competitive, 20, 31, 33, 39, 53, 54, 59, 65–68, 72, 75–77, 79, 95, 115–116, 118, 120, 123, 126–127, 129, 151, 155, 165, 192, 206, 220–221, 230; pre-performance, 101; pre-shot, 101

self: concept, 53, 55, 57, 70; confidence, 62, 205, 212–213, 215; determination theory, 208; efficacy, 173, 194, 225–226; harm behaviors, 72; instructional training, 113; worth, 11, 75–76, 201–202
semistructured play, 36, 39
social ecological model, 19
social media, 13–14, 218–219
social politics, 34
social support, 65, 76–77
sport psychology, 7, 51–52, 62, 66, 76, 82–83, 107, 112, 117, 154, 162–163, 166, 190, 224–225, 240
sports performance consultant, 81
soldiers, 141–142
stigma, 82, 165
stress, 11, 29, 37–38, 47, 73, 79, 82, 96, 105–107, 112–113, 123–124, 126, 130, 137–138, 145, 150–151, 154–156, 165, 167, 181, 187–188, 194, 198, 205, 212, 219, 230; response, 112–113, 154, 156
student-athlete, 18, 53, 62–64, 69, 72, 92, 98, 138, 150, 165–167, 195
stumbling block, 85
sympathetic nervous system, 105
synchronized skating, 80, 129

team goals, 18
team mission statement, 18
team-building, 18, 20
tenacity, 14–15, 61, 190, 192–193
The Mental Game of Baseball, 82
time management, 60
Toronto Raptors, 2
training, 17, 30, 37, 41, 48, 56–57, 63, 67, 70, 73, 79–80, 82–83, 86, 95–96, 98–99, 106, 113, 115–116, 118, 122–123, 126–127, 130, 138–139, 155, 169–171, 177, 187, 202, 206, 209, 217, 220–221, 223–224, 226–231; logs, 98; mental, 82–83, 96, 98–99; physical, 83, 155
transferrable skills, 60
transition, 18, 51, 53–54, 57, 60, 62–63, 65–67, 70, 72–74, 76–77, 165, 177–178, 203
Transtheoretical Model of Behavior Change, 48
traumatic stress response, 154, 156

UCLA women's gymnastics, 1, 12
ultradistance running, 159
ultramarathon, 158–159, 162
United States Army Ranger School, 141
United States Tennis Association (USTA), 37
unstructured play, 39
US Olympic Alumni Association, 41

values, 8–9, 11–12, 19, 23, 26, 29–30, 34–35, 47–49, 73–74, 174–175, 177–178, 187
Vegas Golden Knights, 4
video analysis, 102
visualization, 102, 162

About the Editors and Contributors

Michael Sachs is a professor in the Department of Kinesiology, College of Public Health, at Temple University in Philadelphia, Pennsylvania. He is coeditor of *Applied Exercise Psychology: The Challenging Journey from Motivation to Adherence* and is associate editor of *Psychology of Running* and coeditor of *Running as Therapy: An Integrated Approach*. He also cowrote *The Total Sports Experience for Kids: A Parents' Guide to Success in Youth Sports*. He is a coeditor of the twelfth edition of the *Directory of Graduate Programs in Applied Sport Psychology*. Sachs is a past president of both the Association for Applied Sport Psychology (AASP) and Division 47, the Society for Sport, Exercise and Performance Psychology of the American Psychological Association (APA). He is a certified mental performance consultant with AASP.

Lauren S. Tashman, PhD, CMPC, is a certified mental performance consultant with the Association for Applied Sport Psychology (AASP), providing mental performance coaching, leadership advising, and team/organization consulting in sport, exercise, and nonsport performance settings in New York City and worldwide. She has consulted with a variety of sports, such as golf, softball, baseball, gymnastics, soccer, rowing, swimming and diving, tennis, basketball, and volleyball at a variety of levels including youth, collegiate, professional, and national/Olympic. Tashman was previously an associate professor in sport, exercise, and performance psychology (SEPP) as well as coordinator of the master's program in SEPP at Barry University in Miami Shores, Florida. She also served as the coordinator of sport psychology services, providing mental performance coaching to Barry athletes, coaches, and teams as well as supervising the master's students with their practicum experiences. She is the coeditor of two books: *Becoming a Sport, Exercise,* *and Performance Psychology Professional: A Global Perspective* (2014) and *Global Practices and Training in Sport, Exercise, and Performance Psychology* (2016).

Selen Razon is an assistant professor in the Department of Kinesiology, College of Health Sciences at West Chester University. She is coeditor of the recently published *Applied Exercise Psychology: The Challenging Journey from Motivation to Adherence*. Razon's research interests focus on exercise promotion in underserved populations and the effects of exercise on cognitions and affects.

PERFORMANCE EXCELLENCE CONTRIBUTORS

Bassey Akpan is in her final year of the counseling psychology doctorate program at Springfield College, with a focus in athletic counseling.

Monna Arvinen-Barrow, PhD; CPsychol, AFBPsS (United Kingdom); UPV sert. (Finland) is an associate professor in the Department of Kinesiology, Integrative Health Care and Performance at the University of Wisconsin–Milwaukee.

Amie Barrow is a sophomore at Shorewood High School and a NCSA Junior National–level swimmer.

Matthieu Boisvert is a PhD student in the Department of Kinesiology at the University of Windsor, researching leadership and team culture. Matthieu is also a goaltending coach for his local minor hockey association.

Will Brown is a sports consultant in Atlanta, Georgia. He works with individuals and teams in order to optimize their performance.

Megan Matthews Buning is an associate professor of research in the College of Education at Augusta University, researching the intersection of sport psychology and strategies and education. She enjoys working as a talent analyst for the SECNetwork+ during softball season and loves working with game officials on their mental performance.

Kevin L. Burke is a sport psychology professor in the Kinesiology Department at Queens University of Charlotte. Since 2005 he has performed in more than forty stage productions in the states of Tennessee, Illinois, Maryland,

and North Carolina. He has also acted in commercials, television, web series, and in films and has twice won the Best Actor award for his stage work.

A former collegiate athlete in football, **Bradley J. Cardinal** is a professor in the Kinesiology Program at Oregon State University, where he holds an affiliate appointment in the School of Psychological Science. During 2018–2019, he served as president of the National Academy of Kinesiology.

Mark Cheney, CMPC, is the director of mental performance at Faith Lutheran Middle School & High School in Las Vegas. He teaches performance and sport psychology and coaches golf.

Jeff Cherubini is the department chair of Kinesiology at Manhattan College. His area of expertise within kinesiology is exercise and sport psychology, emphasizing an eco-developmental perspective to his work in physical activity, exercise, and sport environments.

Dr. Dolores Christensen is a licensed psychologist in the University of Oklahoma Athletics Department. She enjoys running for extended periods of time on mountain trails.

Michael Clark is a doctoral student in the counseling psychology program at the University of Wisconsin–Milwaukee. He owns a private practice specializing in sport and performance psychology and is an avid outdoorsman.

Damien Clement is the acting dean of the Honors College and an associate professor of sport and exercise psychology and athletic training in the Department of Sport Sciences at West Virginia University.

Bernadette Compton is a doctoral student in leadership studies at Bowling Green State University. She loves hanging out with her dog and learning from her athletes.

Tami Eggleston is the associate provost and professor of psychology at McKendree University in Lebanon, Illinois. She and her husband have competed in the National Hot Rod Association (NHRA) for more than thirty years, currently with their 1200 horsepower rear-engine dragster.

Arna Erega is a licensed professional counselor, specializing in sport and performance enhancement counseling. She is a former Division I and professional hurdler for Croatia.

Emily Galvin is a certified mental performance consultant who works in private practice in Philadelphia. She enjoys running and staying active outdoors.

Kerry Guest is a PhD student in counseling psychology at Indiana University Bloomington, specializing in sport and performance psychology. In his spare time, Kerry is a natural bodybuilder and fanatic of all things St. Louis sports.

Associate Professor **Stephanie Hanrahan** holds a joint appointment with the School of Human Movement and Nutrition Sciences and the School of Psychology at the University of Queensland, Australia. In addition to dancing and kayaking, her passion is delivering LifeMatters, a program combining mental skills and physically active games that promote trust, communication, and problem solving.

John Heil is a clinical and sport psychologist, a partner at Psychological Health Roanoke, and a consultant to sports, medical, and public safety organizations.

Rick Howard is an assistant professor in applied sport science at West Chester University, specializing in the application of physical literacy through a long-term athletic development framework. He is a master's strongman competitor.

Anna-Marie Jaeschke is a cognitive performance coach for US Army Special Operations Command. She enjoys reading, cooking, trail running, and kayaking.

Karin Jeffery teaches in the Kinesiology Department at San José State University. She currently leads study-abroad trips to Rwanda and Vietnam; Botswana is next on her list.

Tiffany Kasdorf is a wife, mother, and softball coach who resides in Tallahassee, Florida, with her family. When she is not helping run the family construction company, she is homeschooling her boys and teaching pitching to young aspiring female athletes. Go Noles!

Lindsey Keenan is an assistant professor and athletic trainer at West Chester University, teaching in the Department of Sports Medicine and working clinically with the university's NCAA women's rugby team. Her research focuses on student-athlete mental health, which led to the development of her mental health screening application and company, PROmotion Health.

Alan Kornspan is a professor in the School of Sport Science and Wellness Education at the University of Akron, where he teaches courses related to sport psychology and coaching education.

Dora Kurimay is certified mental performance consultant (CMPC) based in New York City helping young and professional athletes maximize their performance through stress management and confidence maintenance. She is a table tennis champion and enjoys running, yoga, and skiing.

William Land is an associate professor of sport psychology in the Department of Kinesiology at the University of Texas at San Antonio.

Karen Lo is the first certified mental performance consultant (CMPC) in the greater China area of the Association for Applied Sport Psychology and runs her own sport and performance psychology consulting company, Inner Edge. She was a former Hong Kong national swimmer, holds an MEd in counseling/sport psychology from Boston University, and is a part-time lecturer at the Education University of Hong Kong.

Dr. Todd Loughead is a professor in the Department of Kinesiology at the University of Windsor, where his research interests are in the area of leadership and group dynamics. In his spare time, he enjoys coaching hockey and soccer and recently has taken up the sport of golf.

Michelle McAlarnen is an assistant professor of sport and exercise psychology at Minnesota State University, Mankato. She is a certified mental performance consultant (CMPC), and her professional curiosities lie in the areas of supervision, mindfulness, mental health, and socioecological models.

Laura Miele is a sport, fitness, and recreation expert who specializes in working with injured athletes and athletes who suffer from anxiety and depression.

Nikola Milinkovic is a director of sport psychology at Intensity Tennis Academy, specializing in youth sport performance. He does stage theater as a hobby and enjoys playing basketball.

Deborah Munch is a mental skills consultant and owner of Munch Mental Training in Concord, California. She also teaches sport psychology at Dominican University in San Rafael, California, and supervises sport psychology graduate student interns with John F. Kennedy University in Pleasant Hill, California.

Dr. Kate Nolt is assistant professor of public health and practicum coordinator in the Master of Public Health Program at Creighton University. Dr. Nolt has been a practicing health behavior therapist for nearly twenty years and focuses on health behavior modification and addiction prevention and intervention.

Maximilian Pollack is a cognitive performance specialist with Marines Special Operations Command at Camp Lejeune, North Carolina. His previous experience includes the R2 Performance Program with the United States Army.

Meghan Ramick is an assistant professor in the Kinesiology Department at West Chester University, specializing in cardiovascular and exercise physiology.

Shaya Schaedler is a former swimmer for Washington State University and currently a behavioral health therapist in Philadelphia, specializing in antioppressive frameworks and working with LGBTQI+ populations and athletes. Go Cougs!

Jen Schumacher, MS, CMPC, is a performance psychology instructor at the Center for Enhanced Performance at West Point, working with several Division 1 teams and military training groups, and directs the Virtual Reality and Internship Programs. She is pursuing her PhD and is a marathon swimmer.

Paul Soter is a fencing master in San Francisco. He has been US National Champion in team and individual events and was the first US National Coach for Women's Epee. As US National Coach for Men's Epee, he was a coach of the 2004 US Olympic Team.

Ellen J. Staurowsky is a professor in the Department of Sport Management in the LeBow College of Business at Drexel University, specializing in social justice issues in sport including (but not limited to) college athletes' rights, Title IX and gender equity, equal pay, and equal treatment in sport workplaces, and the misappropriation of American Indian images in sport. In recent years, she has traded long runs in for long, long walks.

Alexandra Szarabajko is a doctoral student in the Kinesiology Program at Oregon State University.

Tshepang Tshube is a senior lecturer in the Department of Physical Education, Health and Recreation at the University of Botswana. His research interests include elite athletes' career path, dual-career, and elite athletes' retirement transition.

Amanda J. Visek, PhD, CMPC is an associate professor in the Department of Exercise and Nutrition Sciences in the Milken Institute School of Public Health at the George Washington University.

Joann Wakefield is an athletic academic advisor at Georgia Southern University, working with the men's golf, men's tennis, women's rifle, and women's soccer teams. She is a former Division I swimmer.

Anna Weltman is a warm-hearted ocean therapist, and enthusiastic yoga instructor who specializes in mental skills training for athletes. She loves to surf, plays competitive golf, and races triathlons in her spare time.

Diana Wildermuth is an associate professor and Counseling Psychology Program coordinator in the Psychological Studies in Education Department at Temple University, specializing in school counseling and multicultural issues. She is a mom of two young athletes and can be found on the sidelines when not in the classroom.

Taylor Wise is a clinical psychology doctoral student at the University of Denver, specializing in sport, health, and military psychology. She is a passionate runner and outdoor adventure seeker.

Lindsay Woodford is a chartered sport psychologist and senior lecturer at the University of the West of England, Bristol, UK. She loves the great outdoors and lives on a farm with her husband, Charlie, and daughter, Amélie.

Derek Zike is a doctoral student of health sciences in the Department of Kinesiology at the University of Wisconsin–Milwaukee, specializing in sport and performance psychology.

www.ingramcontent.com/pod-product-compliance
Lightning Source LLC
Chambersburg PA
CBHW032035300426
44117CB00009B/1071